Champagne Charlie
and
Pretty Jemima

Champagne Charlie *and* Pretty Jemima

Variety Theater in the Nineteenth Century

GILLIAN M. RODGER

UNIVERSITY OF ILLINOIS PRESS

Urbana, Chicago, and Springfield

Library of Congress Cataloging-in-Publication Data
Rodger, Gillian M.
Champagne Charlie and pretty Jemima : variety
theater in the nineteenth century / Gillian M. Rodger.
p.   cm. — (Music in American life)
Includes bibliographical references and index.
ISBN 978-0-252-03539-5 (cloth : alk. paper)
ISBN 978-0-252-07734-0 (pbk. : alk. paper)
1. Vaudeville—United States—History—19th century.
I. Title.
PN1968.U5R63   2010
792.70973'09034—dc22   2010016575

For Geri Laudati and Adrienne Fried Block—
you are both greatly missed.

Contents

Illustrations

Acknowledgments

This book could not have been completed without a great deal of assistance and moral support from a great many people. While the core of the research was conducted while completing my dissertation, considerably more has been completed in the decade since then. A University of Wisconsin–Milwaukee Graduate School Research Fellowship underwrote the expense of research trips to the University of Iowa, the Harry Ransom Research Center at the University of Texas, and public libraries in Cincinnati, Boston, and New York City, as well as the Museum of the City of New York and a return trip to the New York City Municipal Archives. I am also extremely grateful for the help of librarians at all of the libraries named, as well as at the Hoyt Main Library in Saginaw, Michigan, the Carnegie Public Library in Pittsburgh, and the Main Library in New Orleans, and the library staff of the University of Wisconsin–Milwaukee. Special thanks are due to Rebecca Littman, the music librarian, who was always willing to help me figure out how to get my hands on what I needed.

The first draft of the book was completed as a fellow at the Center for 21st Century Studies at the University of Wisconsin–Milwaukee, which provided me with a quiet space to write and a lively intellectual climate that shaped my thinking on this topic. The year at the Center was made possible with the generosity of the former dean of the Peck School of the Arts, Robert Bucker, who gave me teaching release to take this residency. My colleagues at the University of Wisconsin–Milwaukee have also been incredibly supportive of my research. I am grateful to Sharon Hansen for programming a concert of nineteenth-century songs from my research files and allowing me to work with members of Milwaukee Choral Artists to bring this repertoire back to life. This experience allowed me to think closely about what variety performers actually did while they were on the stage. I am also extremely grateful for the lively and challenging conversations with my senior colleague, Mitchell Brauner, who was always ready to bat ideas around with me and to challenge me to rethink and rethink and rethink.

Part of my research on variety in East Saginaw, Michigan, was supplemented by a graduate research seminar I taught at the University of Michigan during 2002. Two students in that seminar, Eric Saylor and Tim McAllister, completed a comprehensive summary of the records of the Opera House in that city, and this has proved to be extremely useful. I also need to acknowledge the encouragement of Joseph Lam, who was the chair of the Musicology and Ethnomusicology Department, and thank him for allowing me to teach this seminar. It was one of the most pleasurable teaching experiences I have had in my career. Thanks, too, to my colleagues at the University of Michigan, particularly Mark Clague, Amy Stillman, Richard Crawford, Judith Becker, Albin Zak, Hugh De Ferranti, Travis Jackson, and Naomi Andre, whose friendship made my two years there so rewarding.

My colleagues in the wider field of American music studies have been instrumental in encouraging this work. It has been so gratifying to take my mass of archival material to conferences and to compare notes with scholars who are both more knowledgeable and more experienced than I. I am grateful to Dale Cockrell, Deane Root, Tom Riis, Kitty Preston, Paul Charosh, Sandy Graham, and many others for their support, enthusiasm, and every issue they have raised that challenged me to refine my thinking. My colleagues in ethnomusicology have always encouraged me to transgress disciplinary boundaries, and thanks go to the small but growing Historical Ethnomusicology Section of SEM; both Revell Carr and Sandy Graham have provided me with much to think about. I also need to thank Judy McCollough at the University of Illinois Press, who has encouraged me to pursue this topic for more than a decade, and Laurie Matheson, who has been so encouraging and positive through the last two years.

I am also extremely grateful to my friends who have put up with my often boring diatribes on things theatrical for many years now. Particular thanks go to Nancy Guy and Mary Lewis, always the voices of reason; Liz Wood, who has periodically reassured me that I am right when I needed to hear it; Jane Orgel, for keeping me in the country; and Anna Reidy, my sharp-witted and precocious "daughter" who scrambled to help tie up a few loose ends in New

York when I couldn't get there. Last, but by no means least, I apologize to Jean for my obsessive preoccupation with the nineteenth century and thank her for her patience and for periodically reminding me that not everyone can tell what century I am talking about. Thanks for keeping me real, dearest, and thanks for your humor and support during the last year.

As always, I am entirely responsible for all of the mistakes.

Introduction

The crowds in the street gathered in the twilight of early evening, flocking outside the new Opera House and spilling out onto Broadway. All over lower Manhattan the word spread that a riot would break out in Astor Place, and the news drew more people to the area around the theater. Two days earlier William Macready had left the stage after being booed by men in the gallery, who also threw seats onto the stage, and the performance ended early. Macready's supporters had encouraged him to perform one more time, and the word on the street was that he should be punished for his insults against the great American favorite, Edwin Forrest. The personal argument between the tragedians paled in comparison to the offense it represented against national pride, and when another performance was announced, men gathered outside the theater to watch the ensuing conflict.

The crowd watched as upper-class men and their wives and daughters entered the hall. The word went through the crowd—someone had been turned away from the box office, apparently because he was dressed too shabbily—and muttering broke out complaining about the snobbery of the wealthy and the unfairness of the prices of the new hall. How dare they turn hard-working men away? A placard announcing that the house was full and no more tickets were for sale was placed at the box office, but the rumor that the doors had been shut to keep regular men out of the hall persisted. A few young men picked up stones from the street and threw the missiles as hard as they could, hitting the walls and windows of the theater, but not breaking them. Another rumor flew through the crowd—the National Guard had been turned out to protect the theater. The men on the street yelled their disgust to each other and vowed to fight for their rights.

Inside the theater, every seat was filled and two hundred policemen patrolled the auditorium to keep order. When the curtain finally rose, men in the gallery and parquet seating booed and hissed but calls of encouragement and cheers came from the box seats. As the performance began, four young men in the parquet yelled loudly at the stage for Macready to go home, and the police descended on them as people in the boxes encouraged them to eject the protesters. Cheering was heard around the house as the young men were dragged out by the police. The audience continued to be restless throughout the first two acts, and it was difficult to hear the actors over the noise in the auditorium and the sounds of rocks pelting the theater from outside. The windows of the theater shattered as street paving stones hit them, several women in the boxes screamed in fear, and their husbands and a police captain gathered to arrange for them to be escorted out of the house to avoid danger. The women and the men who had accompanied them left from the back of the theater with police, who then returned to the battle in front of the building once their charges were safely out of harm's way.

As the National Guard arrived to quell the riot, sounds of gunfire were also heard from inside the theater, and the performance finally came to a halt. Rumors that the theater was going to be set on fire were whispered, increasing the sense of panic in the house. William Macready was escorted from the back of the theater in disguise, and he left the city in the early hours of the morning to avoid causing further outbreaks of violence. Members of the audience, afraid for their lives, rushed out of the theater, adding to the chaos on the street outside. The National Guard tried in vain to quell the crowd, shooting over the heads of the rioters, who continued to pick up rocks and loose paving stones and hurl them toward the theater. The bullets passed over the crowd, hitting bystanders who were trying to escape the chaotic scene. In front of the theater the police and the National Guard finally managed to gain some control, but all around the theater members of these forces lay injured and bleeding. Out in the crowd, there were also dozens of injured among the rioting men and the crowd that had gathered to watch the disturbance, and young boys were sent running to summon horse carts and other vehicles to carry them to the hospital. As the fighting ended and the crowd began to disperse, the police were able to regroup and collect the bodies of the dead and injured outside the theater.[1]

The Astor Place riot, which occurred on May 10, 1849, was a major turning point in American theatrical history. It marked a change in the way theater riots and public disturbances were viewed by the general populace, as well as the end of the period in which public disturbances were viewed as a legitimate protest to a perceived slight. It was also the first time in American history that the National Guard was called out against citizens, although subsequent inquests agreed that the additional force had been necessary. The riot came to be blamed on agitators and troublemakers who incited the city's workingmen, on the bystanders who gave aid to the rioters and hindered the efforts of the police to quell the disturbance, and on the upper-class supporters of the English actor, who recklessly encouraged him to return to the stage for a final performance. The deep social division that caused the riot was evident even in the placement of blame. The very existence of the Astor Place Opera House was symbolic of the growing divide between the social elite, whose money was crucial to theater managers, and the mass of workingmen, who were ardent patrons of the theater and whose tastes also needed to be accommodated. These disparate portions of the American audience had attended the theater together in the past and had also engaged together in similar protests over theatrical performances and programming choices, but by the 1840s, this was no longer the case.

In its reporting of the riot, the *New York Herald* noted the popular opinion that the riot was caused by "a collision between those who have been styled 'exclusives,' or 'upper ten,' and the great popular masses."[2] The divide between the elite members of the theater audience, who bought the most expensive seats in the auditorium, and the workingmen, who occupied the seats in the pit and gallery of the theater, had emerged during the 1840s, and by the time of the riot the elite had lost patience with the rowdy behavior that interrupted performances in theaters. While they had financial resources, the wealthy could not win against the sheer numbers of people in the cheaper seats, so they withdrew from the older theaters, including the Park and the Bowery, leaving them to the masses. This would appear to be the beginning of what the historian Lawrence Levine notes as the highbrow/lowbrow divide,[3] but the conflict was not nearly so simple as a binary split. Even in the 1840s, the range of theatrical entertainments available to audiences went well beyond high and low, indicating the degree to which the audience of the mid-nineteenth century was fracturing into smaller constituencies based on class and later ethnicity.

The theater had already come to be a venue in which urban Americans debated what it meant to be American, not only in terms of what was presented on the stage, but also as a kind of interactive sport in the auditorium. The withdrawal of the elite audience offended and angered those who could not afford the price of admission to the new theater, because it changed the rules of the game as it had been played since before the Revolution. These men had, over the years, won concessions from theater managers in terms of what was staged, but they also attended performances by leading actors and actresses and shared a common culture with the social elite. This was part of the strength of an egalitarian American tradition, and the withdrawal of the elite audience to separate theaters opened fault lines within that common culture. The men who battled with the National Guard on the streets saw themselves as defending the democratic and independent traditions of their new nation. Flyers that appeared in the wake of the riot protesting both its suppression by the city authorities and the conditions that had led to the riot cited American traditions of freedom of expression and the defense of national pride: "Americans! Arise! The great crisis has come!! Decide now whether English Aristocrats!!! and Foreign Rule! shall triumph in this American metropolis."[4]

These sentiments also fueled members of the audience inside the Astor Place Opera House. The *Herald* reported that about one third of the men seated in the parquet and almost all of those in the gallery had jeered loudly through Macready's first New York performance, while his supporters yelled encouragement at the beleaguered actors on the stage, who were pelted with rotten fruit and other missiles, including chairs, from the gallery. It also reported that a number of the rioters complained that they had been denied admission to the theater because they were dressed inappropriately. Clearly the riot outside the Astor Place Theater was fueled not only by the rivalry between two actors, but also by the distrust by the masses of anything that sought to be exclusive and sought to narrowly define American culture. The forcible suppression of this riot only confirmed the sharp social divide along class lines that had been steadily emerging in the course of the previous decades.

The class divide was also reflected in the growing range of entertainment available to the city's residents during the 1840s. Minstrelsy had emerged as an independent form in the years preceding the riot, and troupes competed for audience share with the Park and the Bowery Theaters. And, while the announcements of "Amusements" in the daily newspaper did not include them, the advertising section carried small notices of singing and glees accompanied by a pianist at a number of saloons in the city, as well as enticingly entitled displays of "living statuary" and novelty and singing acts at "museums." An emerging middle-class audience, including those who eschewed theater on moral grounds, was catered to by circuses, exhibitions of curiosities, and novelty acts, which proliferated in this period. Barnum's and other museums staged "moral" dramas in their auditoriums, and by the mid-1840s concert rooms presented "drawing room" entertainments consisting of music and singing, or lectures, or demonstrations of science or other wonders. Theaters offering serious drama and opera increasingly vied for the elite audience, who valued the acting skills of the actors and actresses, good singing, literary value in the plays performed, and an auditorium free of behavior that would offend respectable women. Theatrical advertising in New York City newspapers reflects the number and range of amusement options available to the city's residents each evening, but the reviews of performances also reflect the degree to which the older theaters continued to present bills that sought to please all of the portions of their audience, from the boxes to the upper gallery. Each evening a drama was staged, followed by a farce or comedic piece. Between the pieces, or even between the acts, dancers and singers performed in front of the drop curtain on the apron of the stage. Urban and topical dramas featuring local and familiar characters were popular, as were spectacular pieces that united the audience with wonder at the daring of the performers. Parody and fun were a feature of many of the works, and for much of the audience theater was sport that demanded a reaction.

Theater and opera history relates the narrative of elite theatrical forms from this period, noting star performers and illustrious imported players and repertoire through the rest of the century. Theatrical genres that offered respectable fare for a middle-class audience are also acknowledged, although to a lesser degree. But what of the entertainments that targeted the masses? What kinds of entertainment were available to those who did not qualify as the "upper ten" or aspire to join them? This book will focus on entertainment that for the majority of its history was aimed almost exclusively at a working-class population. These miscellaneous amusements known as variety, which are the forebears of what developed into vaudeville by the 1880s and 1890s, featured singing, dancing, and novelty acts in sequence with no overarching theme or narrative structure and no claim to artistic or educational value, and they often drew the ire of civic authorities and middle-class reformers. I am particularly interested in how these small venues developed into a large, well-organized entertainment business, especially in the face of this opposition, but I am also interested in the ways that the performances themselves represented the interests, aspirations, and desires of their audiences.

The primary audience for variety was drawn from the same masses of workingmen who had rioted at the Astor Place Theater or bought seats in the pit and gallery of the Bowery or Park Theaters during the 1840s; this was the portion of the audience that the social elite actively sought to exclude from their theaters. These men did not represent a united group, however. While the elite withdrew from the debate about what it meant to be an American, the debate continued in venues that catered to these working-class men. Variety was one of a small number of forms that unabashedly catered to a working-class audience, and it reflected and aided in the process of class formation as well as the renegotiation of class boundaries from generation to generation. The earliest forms of variety that emerged in the 1840s and 1850s offer insight into American working-class culture at a time when this population had its own meaningful identity separate from ethnic affiliation. Later in the nineteenth century, variety also reflects the gradual incorporation of ethnic populations into the working class and, at the end of the century, the process by which white, native-born Americans sought to distance themselves from the working class through the adoption of middle-class identity. This period was marked by the emergence of vaudeville, which, as scholars such as Robert Snyder and David Nasaw note,[5] reflects an expansion of the middle class in the first decades of the twentieth century, along with a growing range of public commercial amusements that catered to this class. As part of this study, I want to suggest that this apparently sudden flowering of nightlife was not sudden at all, but rather a result of a slow and steady growth of entertainment that had occurred over the preceding two or three generations. And variety entertainment was, in many ways, central to this process.

The acts presented on the variety stage reflected the changing composition of its audience, as well as the shared concerns and sympathies of the disparate groups that patronized variety halls. During the period under consideration, audiences included both the American-born and immigrants, those who aspired to rise socially and those content with their working-class status, and, over time, audiences in these small venues also came to include women. Variety introduced working-class Americans to newly arrived immigrants, but it also introduced immigrants to America, and the depictions of each of these groups changed as immigrant performers entered variety. Within a single generation, Irish immigrants found roles within this form and brought a sympathetic view to the depiction of their countrymen. The same was true for Jewish and Italian performers later in the century. By the 1880s variety was less and less engaged in the debate over class identity and increasingly focused on whiteness—through song and comedy, variety entertainers humanized the foreign, inscribing a racial hierarchy through its acts. This new debate was no less fraught than older debates about class, and in the twentieth century newer forms of entertainment continued to build on the stereotypes that had emerged in variety in the previous half century.

Variety also contributed to an increasing range of musical theater that catered to middlebrow tastes and fell between elite highbrow forms and the lowest forms of theater. By the 1880s variety performers increasingly moved into the new musical comedies and topical dramas that were often glorified variety shows with the flimsiest of narrative structures. These were designed to please the grandchildren or great-grandchildren of the rioters at Astor Place,

6

who increasingly identified as middle class. Following this whole range of middlebrow entertainments falls well beyond the scope of this work, but they are very much part of a larger story to which this contributes. While my focus will be on entertainment that catered to a working-class audience, I have no illusion that the audience was a stable entity, and class and geographic mobility were very much part of the nineteenth-century American landscape.

Variety was marked not only by the social mobility of its audiences, but also by ever-expanding geographic coverage. Between the 1840s and 1880s, the number of venues offering variety proliferated and spread outward from New York to other East Coast cities and to cities in the Midwest and the South, and areas that did not host a variety theater were visited periodically by touring variety troupes that traversed the entire nation. By the 1880s variety was making serious inroads into the Western states, and in each city it adapted to meet the needs of its audience and engaged in local debates over not only identity and class, but also over community standards and rational leisure. As was the case in New York City in the 1840s, variety came to represent chaos and riotous release for many communities, and it was seen as an unwelcome and corrupting outside influence. Variety managers adjusted their business practices to accommodate local hostilities and complaints, while still pleasing their audience. These accommodations highlighted the differences between two different strands of variety—sexualized and respectable—and by the 1880s variety had also fractured along these lines. This was part of the larger process that had occurred earlier in the century in New York in which a gap formed between high and low, respectable and obscene, only to be filled by new forms that catered to narrower segments of the population based on class and ethnic identification. In variety entertainment, the divide came to be between sexualized forms that catered to an audience of working-class men and respectable forms that were appropriate for a family audience.

My narrative is broken into three roughly chronological parts: the first decade in which variety existed as an independent form, roughly 1850–60; the period of expansion in which variety performers came to the fore, from about 1860 to 1873; and the consolidation of the form in a period of great economic instability, roughly 1873–85. In each of these sections there is discussion of the business models employed by managers, the development of support infrastructure, and the kinds of acts that appeared on the stage. I have not attempted to discuss the emergence of vaudeville in the 1880s, nor have I attempted to document all of the performers and managers active in this genre. This would be a Herculean task and well beyond the scope of a single researcher or book. Instead, I focus on individual managers and performers who exemplify trends within variety and on case studies of individual cities that show the forces that shaped variety in the second half of the nineteenth century.

8

The prevailing picture that emerges in this narrative is one of class conflict and the strategies employed to head off opposition and accommodate middle-class values. But it is equally clear that this is not a narrative in which hegemonic forces bear down and impose new standards on a working-class population, but rather one in which working-class performers and managers and audiences selectively adopt some aspects of middle-class culture, reinterpreting them to suit their own needs. And, as some working-class families moved up into the middle class, they also had the effect of transforming middle-class values, reimagining them in ways that made some working-class behavior acceptable. This complex dialogic process based in public debate is, at its heart, a uniquely American one and was both reflected in and shaped by the entertainments chosen by these people—variety.

The First Decade

The Singing Saloonkeeper

CARE TO OUR COFFIN ADDS A NAIL, NO DOUBT, While every grin so
merrily draws one out. Spend an hour at HITCHCOCK's free concert
... [this] evening, those unrivalled comic singers, Hitchcock and
Fraser.

—Advertisement in the "Amusements" section of the *New York
Herald*, August 26, 1856: 7

Young men in search of entertainment in New York during
the spring of 1849, the season in which the Astor Place riot
took place, had numerous choices available to them. The
Park and the Bowery Theaters offered melodramas and farces for just twenty-
five cents for a seat in the gallery. Christy's minstrels charged twenty-five
cents for an evening of song and revelry. A quarter also paid for admission to
Barnum's, although the museum curtailed opportunities for fun, and the show
there cost an additional twenty-five cents. Up and down Broadway, miscellaneous concert rooms offered musical performances by singers and musicians
performing operatic and light classical repertory. But, while these rooms were
free of charge, their clientele did not welcome young working-class men, and
the quiet atmosphere was no fun at all. For men lacking the money or desire
to see a theatrical performance, the saloon was where they were most likely
to seek companionship and leisure. Each evening, thousands of working-class
men gathered in saloons to bond through drinking, storytelling, and singing,
and the growing numbers of these venues during the 1850s speak to their
importance in urban culture.[1]

During the previous three decades leisure had come to play a greater role
in the lives of men as their workplace conditions changed. By the 1840s a slow
but steady shift had begun from the artisanal workplace in which craftsmen

trained apprentices, who in time became mechanics and finally saved enough money to open their own workshop and to marry and start a family, to the large industrial factory in which men could not hope to learn all aspects of the manufacturing process and advancement was less certain. This process transformed the workday, imposing a more regular work schedule with more defined work hours on workingmen. It also eliminated alcohol and socializing from the workplace. In the first decades of the nineteenth century alcohol had been consumed during the workday as the master-craftsman and his apprentices ate meals or took breaks from their work together. Apprentices and master also often socialized together, singing and telling stories as they worked and attending the theater in the evening when work was done, sitting together on benches in the pit.

Larger factories broke the bonds between employer and employee, and their owners were opposed to anything that detracted from their workers' productivity. Factory owners tended to support temperance crusades, blaming saloons and other commercial leisure for corrupting and distracting their workers.[2] During this period changes to liquor licensing laws were passed in response to agitation by temperance reformers in East Coast cities, and while these were intended to limit and control the availability of alcohol, they also had the ironic effect of moving drinking from relatively informal, home-based businesses into public spaces such as barrooms that were licensed and regulated by law. The more structured and defined workday of the factory and the introduction of shorter working days allowed men more time to enjoy leisure and to patronize these barrooms.[3] For workingmen, leisure provided not only a relief from the exhaustion of physical labor, but also the context to which much of the socializing that had once occurred in the workshop moved; partaking in leisure became a kind of protest against a more restrictive and impersonal workplace.[4]

It was not hard to find a saloon in lower Manhattan in this period; indeed, for the saloonkeeper, the challenge was to distinguish his venue from those around it. Uptown saloons, close to the fashionable new theaters and the houses of the city's wealthy, were opulent, with gleaming brass, lavish draperies, and paintings hung on the walls. These catered to wealthy men and to visitors who stayed in the city's expensive hotels. In lower Manhattan, near the homes of poorer residents and the older theaters that had been abandoned by fashionable audiences, saloons were more modest, although they were certainly more lavish than the homes of their customers.[5] Saloonkeepers in lower Manhattan fostered repeat customers by providing men the small comforts of home, including food, a warm and comfortable gathering place, and the comradeship of men with similar expectations and experiences. The singing and storytelling that had once been found in the workplace now moved into the saloon, along with gambling, boxing, and other kinds of sport. The saloon became the venue in which men could now prove their stature as men—it became the locus of an alternate economy that had earlier been bound to the workplace and acquiring the skills of a trade.

13

Singing was a tradition that had long been associated with drinking—as men drank and their inhibitions dropped, group singing might follow storytelling or one-upmanship. The barroom was a safe space for men to express the frustrations of urban living, and songs played a part in this. Familiar English ballad tunes and melodies borrowed from opera or theatrical productions were paired with new lyrics that commented on topical events or made fun of the original using puns and wordplay.[6] Songs could protest social and working conditions, but many were unabashedly sentimental, focusing on love and loss.[7] Given that men sang together in saloons, it is not surprising that at some time during the 1840s, or perhaps even earlier, saloonkeepers began to schedule sing-alongs one or two nights each week at their bars. The saloonkeeper led the men in singing and acted as a host and master of ceremonies. He also hired other singers to entertain the men at his saloon and to reinforce group singing, as well as a pianist to accompany them. But, as the advertising copy in the epigraph suggests, the personality of the saloonkeeper was central to these gatherings, and it fell primarily to him to create the kind of atmosphere in his saloon that would bring men back week after week.

As these gatherings that were known as "free and easies" became an established part of the saloon's business, they were allotted space inside the saloon so that they would not be interrupted by the noise of the bar. Saloons often maintained concert rooms or large rooms with a capacity of two hundred or three hundred people adjacent to the main barroom that could be rented out for community gatherings or for meetings or other events. These stood empty unless they were rented, and free and easies offered the saloonkeeper a way of making additional income from his premises. Performances most likely took place at floor level, with no raised stage, scenery, or accompanying ensemble. Given the informal nature of the gathering, singers were probably dressed in street clothing rather than stage costumes.

There are no records of these earliest organized entertainments presented in saloons because newspapers did not review these performances and saloonkeepers relied on word of mouth to publicize their gatherings. It is also not clear why the saloonkeeper so often took the role of master of ceremonies at these events. Perhaps he had been called upon to lead singing because of his good voice, sure pitch, and his engaging personality, or perhaps he had worked on the stage before acquiring a liquor license. In either case, free and easies were common enough by the mid-1840s that saloonkeepers began to place advertising in city newspapers, and particularly the *New York Herald*, to attract new customers to their venues. Advertisements for free and easies share some common features: they all stressed the personality of the saloonkeeper, sometimes noting that he would be "hosting" a gathering or that he would be "at home"; they all indicated that a pianist was employed to accompany singing; and all note the presence of professional singers who were featured as part of the evening.[8]

From the perspective of the customers, the most attractive feature of the free and easy was that it was free of charge. From the perspective of the saloonkeeper, the gathering was successful if it led to greater sales. Singing encouraged men to remain in the bar, and this increased the chance that they would continue to drink. The conviviality fostered by these gatherings was also intended to bring repeat customers and to guarantee ongoing sales. If the saloonkeeper did not make money from these musical evenings he discontinued them, but the growing numbers of advertisements for venues such as Hitchcock's gatherings at the Fountain Chop House at 179 Canal Street, or T. F. Shell's Free Concerts at 401 Broadway, or any number of other saloons on Broadway, Bowery, Grand, and Canal Streets, indicate the popularity of these gatherings with their audiences. By the mid-1850s there were dozens of free and easies operating in the city, and the most prominent of them—those that placed advertising to increase their audience—ran shows daily.

William Hitchcock was not the first saloonkeeper to advertise his free and easy; he did not begin placing advertisements until 1856, a boom year for these venues. His advertisements stand out from those of other free and easies, mostly because of their flowery and overblown language. The phrase used most frequently in his advertising was "Pro bono publico," or free to the public. Hitchcock's saloon, the Fountain Chop House, was not centrally placed. Located on Canal Street between Elizabeth and Mott Streets, Hitchcock's saloon was just a little over a block from Bowery, but it was north of both the Park and Bowery Theaters. It was also a long way from the thriving thoroughfare of Broadway, which is where many of the other free and easies were located. While Hitchcock had little immediate competition, customers were also less likely to find his place unless they were specifically looking for it, and his advertising was designed to pique the curiosity and to entice young men to seek out his saloon.

Hitchcock's advertising, and the appeal of his gathering, won him a loyal following, and by the middle of the 1856/57 theatrical season he was offering performances every day of the week. His bills featured a small number of seasoned performers, including Jerry Merrifield, who came to New York from the theaters in Philadelphia. When the weather grew warmer, Hitchcock moved his performances outside and advertised a "summer garden." While his competitors offered larger and more elaborate bills or the lure of female waitresses, Hitchcock maintained a more conservative approach and relied on a small number of performers and his own formidable personality to attract his audience. Hitchcock was regularly featured as a singer at his free and easy, and he also occasionally sang in New York theaters at benefit performances for theatrical performers. By volunteering his services at benefits, Hitchcock found a way to forge relationships with other performers, who might later appear at his venue. By 1856 the fierce competition between different venues meant saloonkeepers needed to find ways to foster personal relationships with the best and most skilled performers if they wanted to hire them.

The sheer number of these concerts during the early 1850s increased the demand for performers, and advertising also began to include requests for singers and pianists in their copy. Young women with suitable skills were particularly sought after. One hall advertised for "two young ladies wanted to sing plain English ballads also one to play the piano," while another requested "a young lady to sing in a saloon; one who can play the piano preferred."[9] The presence of women in saloons also increased their appeal for young men, and these advertisements suggest that saloonkeepers had more difficulty recruiting women to perform than men.

There are a number of reasons for the relative shortage of female singers in this period. The men who sang professionally at free and easies were very often not novice performers, but had already gained experience singing in theaters in New York or in other cities or with minstrel companies or circuses. Theater was an overwhelmingly male profession in the 1840s—there were many more roles for men than women, even in serious dramatic pieces, and in genres such as circus women were vastly outnumbered and sometimes entirely absent from the ring. Both circus and minstrelsy included comic singing, and singers active in these genres could also find employment in theaters, performing olio acts. These were acts performed in front of the oiled drop cloth on the apron of the stage, and they functioned primarily to divert portions of the audience, who might otherwise have grown restless or even disruptive during changes in scenery—or at moments when stage machinery failed or jammed—and between acts. The audience seated in the pit and gallery of the theater treated the event as a form of spectator sport, and "pittites" were not shy about interjecting themselves into the drama with yelled commentary or volleys of fruit, nuts, and other missiles thrown at the stage.[10] Managers presented variety acts in order to keep the men in the pit amused so that they did not turn their attention to fighting or causing other kinds of trouble in the theater auditorium.[11]

Male singers had, in many ways, followed their audience as theater fractured along class lines. The newer venues such as the Astor Place Theater did not need olio performers, but the older style theaters continued to hire them, as did newer forms such as minstrelsy. Most of the theaters in the United States retained the old-style performance until the 1860s, and men could also find ample employment outside of New York. Performers such as Jerry Merrifield, Ben Stevens, Dick Berthelon, and Martin Flavin all worked at different saloons during the mid-1850s, and all had links to entertainments in other cities or to minstrelsy. Their acts were such that they could be adapted to a number of different genres and audiences, and free and easy performances provided an additional source of potential employment.

While men had ample opportunity to learn the skills necessary to work as ballad singers, women did not, and this is reflected in the small number of women mentioned and the regular calls for experienced female performers in early advertising. Women were also vastly outnumbered in theatrical stock companies, but actresses were greatly loved by their audiences, and the most valuable actresses had rudimentary singing skills. Billing for melodramas made careful note when the actresses were called on to sing.[12] It is possible that some of these actresses, especially those who lacked the skills to perform more serious drama, were among the early singers in free and easies. But by the mid-1850s billing for these women also began to indicate foreign origins; both Mrs. Muller "the Swiss Warbler" and Jennie Reynolds "the Scottish nightingale" performed in free and easies during 1856. By the end of the 1850s an increasing number of English-born singers, who had begun their careers in music halls in that country, were singing in New York.

It seems likely that few of the singers active in free and easies had formal training. These were people with strong voices and sure pitch, and they may well have grown up in theatrical circles, learning performing skills by watching more seasoned performers work. The olio performers with the most formal training were female dancers, most of whom had training in ballet. Ballet was one of the few theatrical contexts in which women outnumbered men on the stage, and it was extraordinarily popular in nineteenth-century theater. While the leading prima ballerinas of the period were imported from Europe, American-born dancers—often the daughters and students of imported French and Italian ballet masters—formed the ballet corps.

The relative lack of mobility for American ballet dancers had driven a small number of women to appear as olio performers during the 1830s and

1840s. These dancers were constrained by the small performance area, and they often danced popular dances—particularly polkas—to appeal to the men in the pit. Like male ballad singers, ballet dancers followed their audience into the saloons, which allowed them to take featured positions in which they were named on the playbill and to perform solo. This opportunity to take starring roles that were otherwise closed to them explains the growing numbers of dancers featured in free and easies.[13] But unlike male ballad singers, female dancers and singers ran a real risk performing in saloons, especially given the proximity of the audience to the performers. There was little to stop the men in the audience from molesting these women or treating them as prostitutes, who were not infrequent visitors to saloons. As a result, the earliest female performers appeared in saloons operated by close friends or relatives who could protect them.

By 1856 free and easies were well established in New York's entertainment scene, and saloonkeepers jockeyed to attract larger audiences to their saloons. They hired more performers, and some relocated to larger buildings that could accommodate a raised stage. The attention increasingly centered on the entertainment, although alcohol continued to underwrite the expenses of the shows. In order to increase sales, saloonkeepers employed young women as waitresses to serve alcohol to the men in the audience. The larger venues were called concert saloons, but they were related to the earlier free and easies; saloonkeepers like William Hitchcock, who had hosted a free and easy, were among the early managers of concert saloons, and they employed many of the same performers who had appeared in their saloons. The lines between a small convivial gathering of workingmen and other theatrical enterprises such as minstrelsy and museum shows began to blur as saloonkeepers moved into larger venues and presented daily shows on a raised stage. When a small admission charge of six cents was introduced to help underwrite the cost of these shows, this line became even less clear.

The escalating competition between free and easies and concert saloons was checked by a financial panic in August 1857. While this panic was short-lived and considerably less serious than the financial collapse of 1837, its effect on free and easies was profound. Advertising for many smaller free and easies and concert saloons disappeared from the pages of the *Herald* completely, and William Hitchcock abandoned his larger show and returned to offering a free and easy just twice a week. Hitchcock's most formidable competition, larger concert saloons such as the Melodeon and the Adelphi, weathered this downturn but only by raising their admission charge. By the end of 1857 twelve cents, which was still half the cost of admission to a minstrel show, had become the standard entrance charge for concert saloons.

While concert saloons foundered in shaky economic times, other forms of theater did not. During this same period legitimate drama at the newer theaters that catered to the wealthiest New Yorkers continued to flourish, and the advertising and reviews for theaters staging plays and other legitimate genres showed no signs of an economic downturn. Despite the financial panic, the number of advertisements placed by these theaters remained about the same, and the theater season began in September as usual. A major difference between concert saloons and legitimate theaters was the composition of the audience; the income of legitimate theaters relied more on box seats and seats in the parquet than the cheaper gallery seats. Concert saloons and free and easies, on the other hand, relied on a working-class and primarily male audience, and their patrons overwhelmingly came from a segment of the population with the most meager financial resources and those most likely to be laid off from their jobs in financially difficult times.

The saloonkeepers who survived this economic crisis were the ones with the strongest ties to performers and those who could adapt quickly to changing circumstances. William Hitchcock had not moved into a larger theater but had stayed in his old saloon on Canal Street. It was easy for him to scale back the performances to just two nights a week and to return to operating an older style free and easy. And, given that the financial panic hit all of his competition equally hard, Hitchcock's conservative business strategy gave him an advantage. The same can be said of most of the concert saloons that survived. The largest and most successful venues on Broadway raised their prices and sought to attract a broader audience of men of all classes. The smaller venues scaled back to rely on their traditional audience and offered less entertainment at lower prices or for free. Once they had found a strategy that worked, these men waited until they were certain that the financial climate had improved, and it was more than two years until the number of advertisements for these venues began to increase in the pages of the *New York Herald*. Ironically, the event that helped revive the fortunes of free and easies and concert saloons was the Civil War, and the anxiety caused by this conflict eventually brought about changes to the excise and theatrical licensing laws that largely curtailed the entertainment careers of William Hitchcock and other singing saloonkeepers.

2

Girls! Girls! Girls!
The Entrepreneurial Manager

FREE LOVE—FREE LOVE—FREE LOVE—GREAT sport every afternoon
and night at the TEMPLE OF THE MUSES, 316 BROADWAY, where the
VENUSES OF AMERICA consisting of a DOZEN OF THE FINEST WOMEN IN
THE WORLD, can be seen. N.B.—The above are not "daguerrotypes"
of unknown persons, but living beauties.
—"Amusements" [Advertising], *New York Herald*, December 7,
    1855: 7

In 1849 George Lea was an enterprising young man in his 20s,
not unlike many of the men who went to the Bowery or Park
Theater each evening for amusement or who gathered together
to drink and sing in saloons. Lea was an immigrant who had been born in
Paris and trained as a pharmacist in England, and he had come to New York
determined to seek his fortune. When he arrived he found a job at a pharmacy
on Crosby Street, in lower Manhattan. He worked and saved and bought
the shop from his employer, and, using the income from his first pharmacy
to underwrite him, he later acquired a number of other stores close to both
the Bowery and Broadway.[1] But, like the young men in the theater audience,
George Lea sought success and wealth and the exciting and lavish life that
went with it, and it may well have been these desires that drew him into theatrical management.

George Lea differed from saloonkeepers like William Hitchcock in two
ways. First, Lea was not a careful and conservative businessman. While Hitchcock had begun his career in the 1830s as a fruit-seller who expanded his business to sell alcohol and gradually moved into saloonkeeping and then variety

over a twenty-year period, Lea moved fast, acquiring interests in pharmacies and theaters within a single decade. He was impatient to make his fortune, and he was not afraid to jump into a business with which he had no connections. Lea was fueled by optimism and the stories of the quick fortune to be made in this new country that he had heard before arriving in the United States, and his quick success only reinforced those beliefs.

Second, unlike William Hitchcock, George Lea had no performing skills at all, and he never appeared on the stage at his theater. This was unusual in the world of theater. Most theatrical managers were men who had begun their careers as actors and whose connections to other actors allowed them to more easily make bookings. In a period when theatrical agents did not yet exist, personal connections and referrals from one friend to another was a common means of finding work. Actors wrote to managers outlining their skills and the salary they sought, and managers responded, offering employment or sometimes suggesting another manager who might help them.[2] This system of referrals made it difficult for anyone to break into the theatrical scene from outside, but, like the saloonkeepers with whom he would come to compete for an audience, Lea discovered it was possible and that his keen sense of ambition and his business skills gave him an advantage over more tradition-bound theatrical managers.

George Lea's first venture into theater was in partnership with the manager J. Pesch. Pesch had brought a troupe of female acrobats and tableaux vivant artists to the United States in 1848, and after touring around the country he settled into the city during the summer months. Pesch's troupe was featured at the Temple of Muses on Canal Street and was successful enough that he expanded the show to include singing and dancing as well as reenactments of statuary. When the fall theatrical season opened, Pesch went into partnership with the manager William Handcock, and they moved the show into the old Franklin Theater on Chatham Street.

The Franklin had been opened in 1835 to provide a safer and more moral alternative to its rivals, the Bowery and Park Theaters, by its first manager, W. Dinneford.[3] Like Barnum's Museum, the admission to this theater was reasonably priced, and the managers sought to appeal to a similar audience. In its first seasons the Franklin had consistent success, but by 1837 it had begun to falter and closed soon after the beginning of the new season. During the rest of that season and in subsequent seasons, the theater was opened by a succession of managers, but each failed to make a success of the house. It was also renovated at least once to increase its seating capacity, but even these improvements did not help. By 1839 the theater hosted miscellaneous performances that included short one-act plays, comic sketches, and olio acts, and it also briefly hosted German opera companies and minstrel troupes.

Handcock took over the Franklin at the end of the 1848 theatrical season and opened his show presenting a troupe of "Arab Girls" and female minstrels. This show, which was very similar to the one presented by Pesch, ran throughout the summer in opposition to Pesch's show. While these shows both drew good audiences in the summer months when other theaters were closed, Pesch and Handcock knew that they needed to provide a larger and more elaborate entertainment to survive in the regular theatrical season, and this drove the former rivals to combine their shows. In collaborating, the two managers brought together the elements that would become standard in shows offering sexualized variety in subsequent decades: women in near or total undress, singing and formation dancing, and comic or novelty acts. The first part of the show presented tableaux vivants, or living statues, in reenactments of classic statuary, while the third part consisted of singing and dancing and sometimes also acrobatic displays by an all-female troupe. Between these they presented an olio of novelties.

While none of the acts presented in these shows approached obscenity in their content, the combined effect offered a critical mass of sexuality that was designed specifically to appeal to young men. When Handcock withdrew from his partnership with Pesch, George Lea took his place and for the next several months he learned the basics of the business. At the end of 1848 the two managers parted ways, Lea remaining at the Franklin while Pesch moved to a new theater, the Walhalla, on Broadway. Despite the split, the two managers worked cooperatively and exchanged acts, presenting essentially the same show in two different venues.

The appeal of this potent combination of female sexuality and the wonder and horror of watching women do the apparently impossible is difficult to comprehend today. Shows by troupes of acrobats and contortionists such as Cirque du Soleil continue to be popular with today's audiences, and the admiration of the physical skills involved was certainly part of the appeal of these shows in the nineteenth century. But early-nineteenth-century audiences did not often have the opportunity to see large numbers of women on the stage, which gave these presentations a particular impact. In narrative drama, especially in the Bowery and other theaters in lower Manhattan that staged melodramas, plays called for just two or possibly three actresses, who were outnumbered on the stage at least two to one by actors. Most theatrical stock companies had more male than female members, and the few women in these companies appeared dressed in the respectable fashions of the period and enacted an ideal femininity. In tableaux vivant troupes women outnumbered men, and their costumes revealed the curves of their bodies and sometimes the full length of their legs.

Ballet was the other theatrical genre that allowed men to see more than was typical of women's bodies, and its popularity had increased during the 1840s with tours by European dancers such as Fanny Elssler. Elssler had taken precautions not to offend her conservative American audience in a period in which women's dresses covered their legs entirely and often also covered most of their upper body too. She lengthened her skirts by twelve inches, from above the knee to well below it, but this concession did not spare her from outraged reactions and protests. At the same time, her performances were spectacularly popular, and she drew crowded houses wherever she appeared and was reputed to have earned a small fortune during her tour.[4] Even though we now tend to think of ballet as a form more patronized by women than men, during the nineteenth century enthusiastic male fans of female ballet dancers were so common that they became a joke in newspapers. In 1877 the *Chicago Inter-Ocean* referred to the presence of "bald heads" in the seats near the stage at a performance by Emily Soldene's Troupe in the opera *Poulet and Poulette*, noting that "a greater proportion [of bald heads] is to be found where the female form divine in all its delicious and undulating grace is shown with more than usual generosity."[5] The shows staged by Pesch and Lea capitalized on the popularity of ballet dancers and other scantily clad female performers with male audiences. The contradictory emotions—those of sexual attraction and moral disgust—raised by women dancing on the stage, and the unfettered view of women's bodies came to be central in marketing their shows.

The idea of reenacting classic statuary is also unfamiliar to modern audiences, but these acts were incredibly popular during the 1830s and 1840s, and they shared features with ballet on one hand and with acrobatic acts on the other. Tableaux, or a staged scene in which actors and actresses stood motionless on the stage, were a standard part of operas and other dramatic pieces, often at the dramatic climax of the scene or at the end of an act.[6] In the early nineteenth century these frozen scenes began to be presented alone, out of the context of a dramatic narrative. Acrobatic displays and the presentation of tableaux vivants were often combined into a single show, and circus entertainments featured both kinds of acts—in many cases the same performers appeared in both the tableaux and in contortion or acrobatic acts.

The presentation of tableaux that imitated classical painting or statuary first came into vogue in Germany during the 1820s and soon after that in England, and these displays arrived in the United States during the 1830s. Initially, these exhibitions were aimed at a respectable audience, and in the case of America they can be seen as democratizing high culture—if one could not afford to travel to Europe to see classical art, one could see a reenactment of it at a respectable museum such as Barnum's. In his discussion of English entertainment, Richard Altick classes tableaux vivants with the exhibition of wax models of famous historical figures, such as those found at Madame Tussaud's in London, and they occupied a similar position within the New York theatrical scene. As was the case with Madame Tussaud's, a number of cheaper imitators existed, and to attract customers the displays at these venues tended toward the prurient.[7] Critics complained that they catered to low and unsophisticated taste at best, and even Tussaud's was not free of its detractors. One nineteenth-century author complained that Tussaud's museum was "the resort of the curious, a sham to please or alarm children" and "the most abominable abomination in the great city, and the very audience-hall of humbugs." Tussaud's primary appeal was to "the untravelled countryman and his rustic daughters."[8]

Tableaux vivants, and related exhibitions such as anatomical and disease museums,[9] had come to be thought of as disreputable amusements in the United States by the 1850s and were more often associated with small, seedy storefront museums far from the fashionable neighborhoods and respectable theaters and catering to a male audience. The decline from respectable to seedy did not happen overnight, and the 1840s was a decade in which the merits of tableaux vivants and similar exhibits were debated in the pages of newspapers. Supporters touted their cultural and educational value and the tasteful way in which statues were displayed, while detractors noted the numbers of women on the stage, the immodesty of their costumes, which were flesh colored body stockings and classical robes, as well as the rowdy and improper reaction of the men in the audience.

By the late 1840s troupes of tableaux vivant artists began to be met with opposition when they toured the United States, and sometimes their performing licenses were revoked. Pesch's troupe encountered opposition as he toured the United States in 1848, and he was banned from performing in Charleston, South Carolina, in late February.[10] While being banned caused an immediate loss of income for troupes, in the long term the publicity value of these actions increased their popularity, especially with young male audiences who wanted to see what the fuss had been about. One New Orleans newspaper ran regular reports during 1848 in anticipation of a tableaux vivant troupe directed by Dr. Collyer. When they opened in the respectable St. Charles Theatre, the newspaper reported that the house was crowded to overflowing with men—the reporter had seen only two women in the lower part of the house.[11] Collyer's Model Artists continued to attract crowded houses for close to three months in this city, performing at the St. Charles even after the end of the regular season. While Collyer's performances were described as "chaste" and there were no disturbances at the theater, another troupe appearing in New Orleans at the same time elicited much more vocal reactions from the crowd. The *Crescent* reported that "when the curtain had fallen upon the last scene of the first part, a most hideous yell was raised by a majority of the gentlemen present. Various screams and howlings, mingled with whistling and cries of the most equivocal character, were thrown in by way of *lagnappe*."[12] This was the reaction that made performances of tableaux vivant artists so unsuitable for a female audience, and therefore indecent, and it was this reaction that managers such as Lea sought from their audiences. Despite the fact that in the 1840s the members of these troupes were most often highly trained and experienced acrobats, contortionists, or dancers, they increasingly played to exclusively male audience in small theaters and museums because of the opposition they encountered when they were booked into larger and more respectable theaters where women might be present.

All of the acts presented by Pesch and Lea held a similar attraction to their audience, and all relied overwhelmingly on the sexual spectacle of large numbers of women—dressed and undressed—on the stage. While the tableaux vivant troupes included both male and female performers, the women were the real drawing card, and they were the main feature of many of the tableaux, as evidenced by suggestive titles. The "Arab Girls" presented by Handcock were similar to the tableaux vivant artists, in that they were trained as acrobats and performed balancing, contortionist, and other circus-style acts. These women were dressed in similarly revealing costumes and also excited contradictory emotions in their audiences, and contemporary reviews reflect this, seeking to reduce women to their appearance and attractiveness, while at the same time marveling at the apparently impossible feats they performed.[13] Troupes of women performing material more commonly associated with black-face minstrels must also have had a similar effect. Unfortunately there are no good surviving descriptions of the acts performed by Lea's troupe of "female minstrels," although there are some indications that they played traditionally male instruments such as banjos and fiddles and also appeared in songs and dances. Descriptions of the acts found in advertising reveal that the number of men in the troupe dwindled over time, and Lea's advertisements increasingly stressed the women on the stage—the numbers, their beauty, and the suggestive titles of the tableaux or other acts they presented.

Advertising was the realm in which Lea far surpassed his partner Pesch, and he understood the power of publicity and of keeping his venue in the public eye. Lea ran daily advertisements, and when he moved his museum to a new building at 127 Grand Street in 1856, he began running multiple advertisements in each issue of the *New York Herald*. These short items reminded his audience that the theater had moved, gave the name of the troupe of model artists appearing, stressed the number and beauty of the women on his stage, and encouraged the reader to attend the performance. At first he ran two or three advertisements in each issue, but within a year the number had increased to five or six, and on one occasion Lea ran nineteen advertisements in a single issue of the *New York Herald*.[14] Lea's approach to advertising surpassed the innovations of even P. T. Barnum. He understood that to be successful he had to establish the name of his theater firmly in the public imagination. At first he did this with numerous short advertisements, and his obituary later claimed that he was the first theatrical manager ever to place a full-page advertisement.[15]

Advertising placed by Lea also gives insight into his development as a theatrical speculator and entrepreneur. During the decade in which he operated the Franklin Theater in New York, Lea's competition and his view of that competition changed dramatically. In his early advertising, George Lea noted the proximity of his venue to other major theaters, including Niblo's—three doors below the Temple of the Muses—and the Bowery Theater—opposite the Melodeon. Lea targeted the men in the audience of those theaters, and his ticket prices reflect this. While free and easies and concert saloons offered shows at low or no cost, Lea's most expensive seats were generally around fifty cents for seats in private boxes. The cheapest seats in his theater were twelve-and-a-half cents—twice the cost of the concert saloons in that period, but comparable to the cheapest seats at a minstrel show. While saloonkeepers catered to a relatively homogeneous crowd of workingmen, Lea sought to attract men of all classes to his theater.

Lea never acknowledged the presence of free and easies or concert saloons in the vicinity of his theater, even after he relocated to Grand Street in 1856. In his new location, Lea was closer to Broadway and closer to fashionable theaters that had moved uptown, but he was also surrounded by concert saloons that represented his primary competition for an audience. As Lea's competition changed from large theaters to smaller concert saloons that catered primarily to working-class men, his business model also had to change. Lea had never offered the cozy conviviality and the opportunity for like-minded men to bond over common experiences that was the feature of free and easies. His theater was a place where men bonded by expressing their shared admiration for women and taking pleasure in watching women, with none of the consequences such behavior would elicit outside his theater. The men in Lea's theater did not have to worry about politeness or offending the people around them, as they did in more respectable theaters, because every man at Lea's was there for the same reason, regardless of their social class. Lea's success in running theaters during the 1850s shows the appeal of this approach, but it would soon come to be a business model that invited attack from moral reformers concerned that the potent combination of sex and alcohol represented a threat to public morality.

After his initial investment in the Franklin Theater in Chatham Street, Lea continued to acquire theatrical properties during the next decade. He placed advertising offering these theaters for rent or for sale, and if he could not find a tenant for the buildings, he opened shows modeled on the show at the Franklin Theater so that the buildings could generate income. During the 1850s, Lea was associated with the Walhalla at 36 Canal Street, which was the building Pesch moved into, the Melodeon Theater at 53 Bowery, the St. Charles Theatre at 17 and 19 Bowery, the Temple of the Muses at 316 Broadway, the Franklin Museum at 127 Grand Street, as well as a summer pleasure garden on the East River, called the Vauxhall Garden. He also operated a number of saloons in theater buildings, including Burton's Theatre, on Broadway, and he acted as an agent for novelty acts such as Monsieur Gregoire, the strong man. From the late 1840s until the late 1850s, Lea not only established himself as the leading manager exhibiting tableaux vivant troupes and other sexualized variety, but also expanded his business interests into more respectable entertainment venues. Probably more than anyone else active in this period, Lea brought business acumen into theater management.

That Lea often ran simultaneous shows at as many as four different venues raises serious questions about the quality of the performances he staged. Pesch had brought a highly trained troupe into the partnership in 1848, but it is unclear how many of those performers remained with Lea. By the early 1850s Lea had begun to place advertisements in the *Herald* seeking young women to perform at his theaters. Like the free and easies, managers offering sexualized variety suffered from a shortage of female performers. Even at the height of their popularity, there had been only a limited number of tableaux vivant troupes in the country, and the tableaux artists that performed with circuses were more often male acrobats who also appeared in other acts. Lea's advertisements stand out from those placed by saloonkeepers, who sought specific skills and previous theatrical experience, in that the language was less specific—he only requested young women interested in appearing on the stage to call at his office and promised steady year-round employment to "those who suit."[16]

In 1856, acting on complaints about the indecency of Lea's show, the police raided the Franklin Museum and arrested all of the performers. A report published in the *New York Times* confirms that none of the women appearing on his stage had previous theatrical experience. It gave the names, ages, and previous occupation of the six women arrested and held by the police. All of these young women were 18 or 19 years old, and most had worked at the theater for just two months. Two of them had previously been employed as model artists by Lea at other theaters, but the rest had all worked in other professions. The report of the raid noted that all of the women pleaded that they "had always led virtuous lives, and that they exhibited themselves merely to gain a livelihood." They claimed that "they would not be allowed to appear unless clad in a suit of flesh colored tights and a thin gauze skirt."[17] These women earned $4 or $5 a week on Lea's stage, which represented a good salary for a young woman in that period, although it was less than was paid to trained female performers such as experienced ballet dancers or actresses at the time.

Lea's business model differed from that of saloonkeepers in a number of important ways. Lea's approach to business was to attract as broad an audience of men as possible by promising a large spectacular show that he increasingly did not deliver. On the other hand, he provided what his repeat customers wanted—an unfettered view of women. Lea's lack of connection to the theatrical world meant that either he did not fully appreciate the traditions and skills of the performers who appeared with the best of the troupes of model artists or he did not feel bound by them. While he failed to live up to the most grandiose promises of his advertising, he did provide a show that satisfied his audience, whose delight in watching female acrobats may well have come as much or more from viewing scantily dressed women as from any skills or training they possessed. Lea's failure to employ trained performers also allowed him to undercut the prevailing salaries of the period, and this gave him a business advantage in an increasingly crowded entertainment field. Lea also suffered less from the shortage of female performers than did his competitors, although the low quality of his show and the rowdiness of his audience as well as his lack of connection to the profession most likely also made booking novelty acts for his olio difficult. And the sexual nature of the performance at Lea's theaters also made it more likely that his venues would be raided by the police or that he would be denied a license to operate theaters in the city.

Despite these risks and his lack of a deep connection to theater, Lea was active as a theatrical manager in New York City into the mid-1860s. As variety expanded and developed, Lea's lack of connection to performers increasingly placed him on the periphery of the genre, but ironically this was also the fate of William Hitchcock, who despite his singing skills remained a saloonkeeper at heart. Both Lea and Hitchcock were overtaken in the late 1850s by enterprising and ambitious performer-managers who had deep connections to the theatrical world, but also had the business acumen to succeed in management. And it was under the guidance of these men that variety entertainment reached its full maturity.

Performers Take Charge

American Concert Hall 444 Broadway. The best and cheapest place of amusement in the world. CROWDED HOUSES, HUNDREDS UNABLE TO GAIN ADMISSION, RIVALRY DEFIED. Our motto is emblazoned on our banner, that we are foremost in the field of novelty, which has been endorsed by the test of success and time against the attempt of early expiring competition. The admirers of WIT, HUMOR, DROLLERY, COMEDY, SONG, BURLESQUES, NEGRO FARCES, ACTS, BALLETS, VAUDE-VILLES, &c., will be gratified by the performance of the best artists in each of their particular departments the world ever produced, and the whole entertainment so interspersed with varied acts as must please any cast of mind. THE STAR COMPANY OF THE WORLD.

—Advertisement for the American Concert Hall, *New York Herald*, October 6, 1861: 7

In 1857 a financial panic gripped the United States, and businesses failed and protests ensued as workers were laid off. The economic downturn hit concert saloons and free and easies hard, and many of the venues that had opened in the previous several years closed. William Hitchcock scaled back his operation and returned to running a free and easy twice a week, relying on his core business of saloonkeeping to generate income and cutting the additional expenses for performers and waitresses. George Lea, on the other hand, took advantage of the downturn to cement his position in the entertainment world. He moved his show from its home in the distinctly unfashionable Bowery to an empty hall on Grand Street that was close to Broadway and its more respectable audience. To ensure success, he increased his advertising in the *New York Herald*, placing so many short advertisements in each issue that it was almost impossible not to see at least one of them. Both of these managers survived the downturn and were well positioned to take advantage of an improving economy in the last years of the 1850s, but as concert saloons reappeared in New York, Hitchcock and Lea faced competition from a new and formidable foe: variety performers.

Variety had become a permanent part of the theatrical landscape during the 1850s, and even the national trade newspaper, the *Clipper*, began carrying news and advertising for these venues during 1857, albeit somewhat reluctantly. Coverage in the *Clipper* became more regular during 1858 as its proprietor, Frank Queen, realized the benefit of expanding to include more of the theatrical world. Queen had no particular interest in theater—his newspaper carried all kinds of sporting news that was of interest to men, including men from the working class. The *Clipper* fell between the two other major sporting newspapers of the nineteenth century in its sympathies; the *Spirit of the Times* was dedicated to elite pastimes, and the *National Police Gazette* was unabashedly popularist and dedicated to scandal and crime as well as sport and theater. The *Clipper* carried reporting on sailing, horse-racing, and cricket, but it also carried advertising for gambling equipment and reports on boxing and dogfights. The theatrical coverage was equally broad and included spoken drama and opera, but also variety, minstrelsy, and circus. It carried poetry and excerpts of literature as well as topical commentary in dialect. Queen, a skilled businessman, saw the economic advantage to this broad coverage—like variety and circus owners he did not want to exclude anyone, including the working class—although he understood that encouraging moral and decent performance also made good business sense in the long run.

Clipper coverage reflects the recovery of variety as the economic situation improved, and it also reflects the early expansion of the form into other parts of the northeastern United States. The *Clipper* noted the presence of variety halls in Wilmington, Philadelphia, Brooklyn, Albany, Boston, and as far west as Milwaukee. All of these cities had at least one venue offering variety, and many were home to more than one; Philadelphia had six variety halls operating at the end of 1858. The expansion of variety meant that performers were once again in great demand, and for the first time halls began to be operated by variety performers rather than by businessmen. During 1859 and 1860 three large concert saloons opened on Broadway, and two of them were managed by men who were also active as theatrical performers. The large concert saloons and the bills they offered dwarfed the offerings of the smaller concert saloons, and they quickly came to dominate the scene.

The first performer to enter variety management was Charley White, who was active in minstrelsy. White opened his theater called the Melodeon on Bowery in 1849. While he is not remembered as a pioneering variety manager, White's contributions to the form are important. Over the period of a decade he operated a number of different theaters on Bowery and Chatham Street, before finally moving the Melodeon onto Broadway in 1857. White was part of the first generation of minstrel performers, and he had worked as a singer and accordionist in circus and theatrical olios in the early 1840s. He was also associated with a number of different minstrel troupes and briefly operated his own minstrel quartet during the 1840s. But White also had ambitions to enter theatrical management, and he did so on a number of occasions. When White's theaters failed, as they always did, George Lea was waiting to buy the buildings. While Charley White lacked the business acumen and experience of Hitchcock and Lea, his personal connection to other performers gave him an advantage over his rivals, and his experience as a performer allowed him to imagine variety on a grander scale than his competitors.

White was important in providing a model for variety as it developed in the 1860s, and in many ways he was a man ahead of his times. He began by operating his venue in a very similar way to other concert saloons but with a much more substantial bill. As early as 1849 he also emphasized the chaste and respectable nature of the performances he offered in his advertising, stressing that women would not be admitted unless accompanied by a "gentleman."[1] White's advertising shows a real concern for the kind of act that was presented on his stage, as well as the recognition that venues offering miscellaneous amusements were coming to be associated with indecency and prostitution, at least in the minds of urban moral-reform forces. Early in his career, White had performed in temperance theaters, and while he was not dedicated to the temperance cause his early engagement with reformers gave him insight into their concerns.[2] White's desire to include women as part of his audience was important, and his insistence that no unaccompanied women would be admitted was not only an attempt to head off charges of indecency but also an indication of his desire to expand his audience beyond men—White sought to provide a venue that accommodated women as well as men. The question of whether it was possible for respectable women to be present in a variety audience was one that went unresolved into the early twentieth century.

Charley White ran the Melodeon at 53 Bowery for about three years, but by his second year at that address he had begun to rely more heavily on minstrel performers, and for at least one season the theater was home to his minstrel troupe. This indicates that, despite his best efforts, he had not managed to expand his audience. In 1852 he sold his theater to George Lea and moved to a larger theater near Chatham Street. This theater also failed, as did two others he managed briefly in subsequent years. In each case White began by presenting variety entertainment but quickly moved to minstrelsy before the theater failed. White's connections with performers allowed him to begin these ventures, but he had not found a business model that generated the income to support the larger-scale show. White discovered that income generated solely from alcohol sales was insufficient to sustain his business, and the presence of alcohol in the auditorium also created an atmosphere that was unsuitable for respectable women. The men in the variety audience were unwilling to pay admission to a concert saloon, even when it offered more substantial entertainment, but by the mid-1850s White had succeeded in introducing a nominal charge for admission to the Melodeon on Sundays, a day on which the New York law forbade alcohol sales; the men who attended his theater on Sundays came for the performance alone.

That White charged admission to underwrite the cost of his Sunday performances shows the degree to which alcohol sales underwrote the costs of staging entertainment in this period. White's show was free during the week, and his advertising promised the "best of Wines, Liquors and Segars" and "lager bier fresh every day from Philadelphia" as well as the "best behaved and prettiest female attendants" in the city.[3] These young women encouraged the patrons to drink and increased the concert saloon's sales. On weekdays the alcohol and the young women who served it were as important as the performers he offered. White's real innovation was an alcohol-free, performance-centered show on Sundays that brought the entertainment to the fore. The admission charge of six cents helped underwrite the costs of these performances, and it also proved to other managers that it was possible to charge admission for a show; within several months other venues had followed suit. By May 1856 a number of concert saloons charged six or six-and-a-half cents admission to all weekday performances.

The economic failure in 1857 brought a halt to White's experimentation with a more substantial variety bill, but as concert saloons were reestablished in the late 1850s performer-managers took a leading role in the form, and they built on the foundations laid by White in the earlier part of the decade. Three of the largest concert saloons were established between 1859 and 1861. While the theatrical entrepreneurs Curran and Fox ran the Canterbury, Charley White's Melodeon was taken over under the new management of Frank Rivers, and Robert W. Butler opened the American Concert Hall at 444 Broadway. The American came to be the preeminent variety hall in the city, but in its first seasons it was challenged by fierce competition from both the Canterbury and the Melodeon. Butler was a gymnast and pantomimist who had performed in theater and with circuses during the 1850s, and, like Charley White, he drew on his connections in the entertainment world to form bills for his theater. But while White's connections were primarily in the world of minstrelsy, Butler's previous career provided him connections not only to minstrelsy and circus but also to ballet, pantomime, and burlesque. The new manager of the Melodeon, Frank Rivers, had similar connections in the circus world, and these two influential managers exploited their connections to gymnasts, dancers, minstrels, and other performers to shape the variety bill in competition with each other. All of these elements came to be a crucial part of variety in the 1860s and 1870s.

The Canterbury, the Melodeon, and the American Concert Hall all featured a similar mix of entertainment and alcohol. These halls ran on a model very much like the one used by Charley White earlier in the 1850s, presenting a substantial bill on a raised stage and accompanied by an ensemble of musicians. While it is not certain how large the orchestras at these theaters were, advertising named a music director for each venue. The composer David Braham began his career at the Canterbury, leading the orchestra there and providing music and arrangements to accompany the acts. The more substantial musical accompaniment was necessary because these concert saloons were large. The Canterbury boasted that it could seat 1,500 people, and the seats were arranged theater style, with the most expensive seats in private boxes and the cheapest seats in the parquet.

The variety bill came to be arranged into three "acts," each introduced by an orchestral overture. There was no narrative to provide these acts with a shape. The first two acts presented a series of unconnected specialties in succession, while the third act consisted of a spectacular display, usually ballet or a comic burlesque or a reenactment of a topical event. The bills at the American and the Melodeon reflected the professional connections of their respective managers. Butler's connections in the pantomime world gave him access to dancers, and the American Concert Hall featured a number of highly skilled ballet dancers, some of whom had danced with the opera ballet and in legitimate theaters. Mlle. Ernestine de Faiber, who performed as the leader of the corps for Max Maretzek's company and also appeared at Barnum's Museum, frequently appeared at both the American and the Melodeon. Butler could also attract other pantomimists, such as Josh Hart, who also frequently performed in pantomimes in Boston, to perform on his bill. Other kinds of acts that were perennials on the American's bill included gymnasts, singers and dancers, and occasional minstrel performers, and especially Charley White, whose engagement with variety had not ended with his failure as a manager.

Rivers's connections with the circus world meant that under his direction the Melodeon featured gymnasts, aerialists, and equestrian acts. Rivers also operated a variety hall in Philadelphia, and he frequently moved acts between the two cities, which allowed him to continually present a novel bill. Rivers was responsible for bringing a number of circus and olio performers from

Philadelphia to New York. Like Butler, Rivers frequently employed ballet dancers because of their appeal for the largely male concert saloon audience. The bills of both of these theaters, and also the Canterbury, show the interconnected nature of a number of genres that presented miscellaneous acts with no linking narrative. These include minstrelsy, circus, and pantomime in particular and, to a lesser extent, ballet. Circuses often featured individual minstrel singers, quartets, or even larger troupes. Pantomime was also featured as part of circus performances, and young female performers in circus trained as dancers. Marietta Zanfretta, for example, was a tightrope artist and ballet dancer, and the equestriennes Rosaline and Eloise Stickney also danced. When performers such as Butler and Rivers moved into variety management, they were able to use their connections within other kinds of entertainment to recruit performers, and particularly women, to their stages.

The ability to attract a wide range of performers gave performer-managers an advantage over entrepreneurial managers such as George Lea. And performer-managers had a particular advantage in hiring female performers. All concert saloons relied on the display of women for success, and there were a number of different ways in which women were exhibited in these venues. Women were employed to serve alcohol to male patrons and to encourage them to drink. Given the importance of revenue generated by alcohol, these positions were crucial to the managers, and waitresses were expected to mingle in close proximity to customers. Physical attractiveness was the primary qualification for waitresses, although it was also important that they be able to withstand physical harassment by their customers. Waitresses who could not sell enough alcohol or who were upset by the attentions of men in the audience were dismissed and new ones were hired. The other position in which women appeared was on the stage in a wide range of acts, all of which required considerable training and skills. In sharp contrast to the women who traversed the auditorium, female performers on the stage expected to be treated with the respect commanded by male performers in the same specialties. Skilled performers would not mingle with the men in their audience, nor would they tolerate being mistaken for the unskilled waitresses by either the audience or the manager.

The ability to draw the distinction between unskilled waitresses and highly skilled performers was necessary for managers who wanted to continue to attract the best and most popular female performers to their theaters. When women appeared in the small venues operated by saloonkeeper-managers such as Hitchcock, it was often because they were related to that manager. So, for example, the saloonkeeper J. Schell began by hiring his relative—probably his daughter—Emma Schell and, through her, gained access to other dancers.

These managers had an interest in protecting the physical safety of their female relatives and their friends and colleagues. George Lea, on the other hand, had clearly not drawn this distinction when he hired untrained women to appear in tableaux vivants at his theater, and this not only made it more difficult for him to hire professional theater performers, it also helped to cement the bad reputation of an entire genre of performance and limited the employment opportunities for trained gymnasts who specialized in presenting tableaux vivants. None of the large concert saloons established in the early 1860s exhibited tableaux vivants—venues such as Lea's Franklin Museum had brought these exhibits into disrepute, and managers also understood that the exhibition of these tableaux brought them to the attention of the civic authorities and the police, who could close a show on the grounds of immorality.

Performing managers had no trouble making the distinction between skilled and unskilled women because they were part of the same theatrical world as the actresses, gymnasts, and dancers they hired. While the theater world was by no means closed, the majority of the people active in it were connected through family relationships—theater and circus people married within their profession and their children were born into it and often began performing early in life. This resulted in a sense of kinship between theater people, who were also generally not well regarded by the general population because of their geographic mobility and lack of community ties. This kinship was further cemented when performers volunteered their services for the benefit of others, either through participating in a benefit performance or by assisting in another performer's act. The care with which performer-managers detailed the skills of female performers stemmed from the respect they had for them as professionals, as well as their desire to be seen as honorable and chivalrous by other theater people.

While performer-managers were late to enter variety management, they may well have done so to provide a more favorable working environment for their colleagues. Men like Robert Butler and Frank Rivers introduced the theatrical concept of the "stock" company to variety, and their bills relied on a core group of performers who periodically left to take other short bookings, but always returned to their theater. This stock company allowed Butler, Rivers, and others to present comic sketches and comic pieces that relied on performers' intimacy with each other and their familiarity with shared conventions. Similarly, both Butler and Rivers hired small corps de ballet of six to eight ballet dancers, who performed as a group and sometimes also in solo or duo dances. The stock companies and ballet corps of variety differed from those found in legitimate theater, which were marked by a hierarchy in which some actors were paid more than others and the leading actors had the most power in the company. Ballet corps operated in a similar manner with a small number of leading dancers who commanded high salaries and a larger number of lower paid supporting dancers. In variety, the stock company was made up of seasoned and versatile performers, and the most experienced performers were paid more because of their versatility, and they also tended to perform most often on each bill. Similarly, the dancers in the ballet corps took it in turns to dance leading roles or appear in solos or duos, and all of them were named on each bill. Unlike legitimate drama, early variety was marked by an egalitarianism that was also found in circus and minstrelsy.

While performer-managers appear to have worked cooperatively with each other, there is some evidence that they resented the competition they faced from entrepreneurial managers such as George Lea, especially in the early 1860s when competition among concert saloons grew fierce. Acts moved easily between theaters, and managers whose theaters failed returned to their lives as performers and worked for managers who had once competed with them for business. Charley White frequently appeared at the American Concert Hall and during 1861 was part of the stock company that formed the core of the entertainment at that theater. Performer-managers did nothing to impede performers from working for their competition as long as they viewed the competition as fair. Friendly cooperation and informal agreements among managers on wages and other employment terms benefited all variety managers. Each of these men understood that if their business failed they would rely on each other for employment.

Saloonkeeper-managers like William Hitchcock who also performed participated in this reciprocal relationship mostly by contributing to benefit performances, but they tended to operate on the periphery of this world, not fully a performer-manager but also not entirely an entrepreneurial manager. George Lea, on the other hand, operated independently of his fellow managers. Earlier in his career he had not managed to sustain his relationship as co-manager with Pesch, and he had no performing skills to fall back on; his skills lay in business, and he used his primary profession as a druggist and his speculation in theater properties to underwrite his theatrical ventures. Lea was also quick to capitalize on the failure of other managers, acquiring, running, and leasing out theaters in Manhattan when managers found themselves in trouble. To variety managers and performers—and particularly to Charley White—Lea must have seemed like a vulture circling, waiting to swoop in and make the most of their failure. That he also operated theater in competition with them was a further insult.

A lawsuit brought by Robert Butler against the ballet dancer Annetta Galletti gives some insight into the contentious relationship between Lea and performing managers, but also it also provides insight into the relationship between performers and managers generally as well as the expectations of performers active in variety. Annetta Galletti was an Italian ballerina who had come to the United States with the Ronzani Troupe in May 1858 and performed with this company during the next several seasons. While the Ronzani Troupe did not find great success in New York, Galletti was quickly an audience favorite and appeared in a number of different contexts as an olio dancer as well as with the troupe. During the period between 1858 and 1861 Galletti danced on the same stage as opera singers Anna Bishop and Caroline Richings, but she and the Ronzani Troupe also took bookings in a number of different concert saloons.

Galletti first appeared at Robert Butler's American Concert Hall during its opening in the summer of 1861. Butler secured a six-month contract with Galletti, promising her $50 a week, and she had fulfilled more than half of the contract when Butler fired her due to a "misunderstanding." This might not have come to public notice except that George Lea, always the canny businessman, immediately offered Galletti a contract for $100 per week. Lea had taken over the management of the Melodeon from Frank Rivers, and Butler quickly filed for a legal injunction to prevent Galletti from performing for his rival. The *New York Times* reported the incident with great amusement and did not take the dispute seriously, but a number of important facts emerge from its coverage.[4] First, the dispute between Butler and Galletti was about how much she was required to perform each day—Galletti felt that Butler asked too much of her. As the leading dancer of a ballet company, Galletti expected to take a single role in a long performance, and her experience as an olio dancer taught her that two or possibly three dances were required in a single evening. Butler asked her to dance solo, but he also expected dancers to take roles in longer choreographed pieces, and dancers were sometimes pressed into service in afterpieces. These were typical working conditions for ballet dancers in variety but may well have seemed like arduous requirements for a prima ballerina who was used to being treated as a star.

The *New York Times* coverage also hints at a contentious relationship between Lea and Butler. Butler was offended that Lea had taken advantage of his contract dispute with Galletti. In hiring her at twice the wage Butler was paying, Lea not only rewarded the ballerina for her refusal to fulfill the terms of Butler's contract with her, he was also trying to poach Butler's audience. Butler filed a restraining order against Galletti and argued that she should not be allowed to perform anywhere until the six-month period had expired. The argument failed in court, and Galletti continued to work for Lea. Butler hoped the law would support the professional ethics and practices of variety and the cooperative relationship and goodwill between managers and performers. Instead it treated it as a business matter, supporting Lea's view of theatrical endeavors. While the *Times* was unaware of it, this dispute was based in the conflicting worldviews of the businessman and the theatrical professional, and it taught Butler and other performing managers that if they were to succeed they would have to adapt their practices and to figure out how to work more cooperatively with entrepreneurial managers.

Advertising placed by Lea in the *Herald* in the weeks after the suit was settled confirms the ill feeling between these men and between George Lea and Charley White, and Lea took delight in reminding his adversaries that he had won. Lea not only prominently advertised Annetta Galletti's performances and challenged two of the leading dancers to compete with Galletti and another dancer, Monsieur Valarde, for a prize of $500 in order to increase the public interest in his show, but he also placed personal notes in his advertising taunting Robert Butler and particularly Charley White, who was acting as manager at the American Concert Hall while Butler performed elsewhere. On October 6 his personal note read: "Notice for the information of a certain stage manager connected with what was once a respectable theatre. We give him notice that, the manager has not got CRAZY YET. Neither does he rope people in; neither will the authorities interfere with him as long as he pays his performers and minds his own business; but if talented artists will prefer to appreciate the MELODEON ABOVE ALL OTHER, they are sure to meet with the approbation of the public, and what they like best, they get a LARGER SALARY than at any other establishment. We shall still continue to engage all the talent that comes along. A word of advice:—The stage manager advises your manager to pay higher salaries, and he will get the talent, perhaps."[5]

These cryptic notes in Lea's advertising confirms the personal tension between him and White and Butler and also highlights their two quite different business models. Lea's reference to roping in performers confirms that performing managers used personal ties and obligations to obtain acts for their stage and that these ties enabled them to save money on payroll. Personal relationships and the desire to foster goodwill also drove performers to volunteer for benefits. Lea, on the other hand, had only money with which to tempt performers to his hall, but his financial security also allowed him to pay extra money when needed to acquire the services of star performers. Lea could not rely entirely on money to fill his bill, and his triumphant crowing in advertising after his legal win over Butler continued into the following month, which suggests that he resented the advantage that performing managers had over him when it came to procuring bookings.[6] These business models could not be reconciled, and the men on each side of this divide clearly saw each other as a threat.

Unlike Lea, the primary sympathies of performing managers were with the performers on the stage, rather than the men in their audience. From a performer's perspective, a quieter and more orderly audience provided a better performing context. But the economics of the concert saloon and importance of alcohol sales to underwrite the expenses of hiring performers for the bill worked against this. The pressure on performing managers was also increased by competition from entrepreneurial managers, who had fewer ties to performers and often had better financial resources on which to draw. Once George Lea moved into concert saloon management, he had to be more concerned with performers' concerns if he wanted to maintain a first-class bill, but his primary identification remained with the men in his audience. His first concern was to provide them with the leisure they sought. The acts on the bills of the Canterbury and the Melodeon under Lea's management reflect the managers' desire to construct a spectacular entertainment that did not interfere with the service of alcohol. Both Fox and Curran's and Lea's venues relied heavily on circus-style acts and ballet troupes, while Butler's theater relied more on his stock company and individual singers. The difference in the bills also reflects the greater economic power of the entrepreneurial managers.

By the end of 1861 the competition between these three large halls and a number of other secondary halls offering similar entertainment was fierce, and had it continued unabated, Butler would almost certainly have succumbed. He lacked the resources of his rivals, who continually presented larger and larger bills in order to outdo each other. The Canterbury and the Melodeon were so focused on each other that Butler was of little concern to them. But Robert Butler was not the only manager endangered in this war of giants. The popularity of concert saloons also threatened the livelihoods of the legitimate theaters nearby, both by robbing them of portions of their audience and because the crowds of men who flocked to their performances made the neighborhood seem unsafe and disreputable. The managers of the legitimate theaters found unlikely allies in moral-reform societies in New York and, beginning in the late 1850s, sought to gain support for a change to theater licensing laws. These efforts, which are reflected in commentary and protests published in the *New York Times*, gained little traction until the uncertain and anxious first years of the Civil War. But when the new licensing law passed, it changed the business model for variety completely.

4

Novelty Acts in Concert Saloons
Equestrians, Trapeze Artists, and Acrobats

Academy of Music—Last night there was another great turn out of the patrons of this popular place of amusement. M'lle Leah danced as prettily and charming as ever. Delehanty and Hengler in their great wooden shoe dance and "Southern Flirtations" were received with enthusiastic applause, and twice encored. The Miaco Brothers astonished the spectators by their terrific double trapeze act and their gymnastic feats on the horizontal bar. "The Black and Tan Convention" was again called to order in due form, and with due burlesque solemnity.

—Review of the performance at Spalding's Academy of Music,
New Orleans Commercial Bulletin, January 21, 1868: 1

The audience leaned forward in their seats, watching a slightly built woman dressed as a ballet dancer balancing above the stage on a taut wire, stretched between two braces and anchored at the back of the stage. In the theater's orchestra pit, the musicians played, occasionally glancing up nervously at the woman on the wire, as she danced and pirouetted above them. Then, as they continued to play, she danced along the wire and began her descent from the stage, across the orchestra pit and into the parquet seating, which is where the other end of the tightrope was tethered. Marietta Zanfretta, renowned for her beauty as well as her daring, had her audience entranced, and they collectively held their breath until she reached the floor. Then they exploded in applause, and Zanfretta acknowledged them briefly, before returning to the rope and ascending back up onto the stage. After a final pirouette, she descended from the rope to the thunderous applause of the men in the audience.[1]

40

Marietta Zanfretta, among the most successful tightrope performers of the 1850s and 1860s, was born into a family of acrobats in Venice. She and her brothers grew up performing in circus. The Zanfretta family arrived in the United States in 1855 or 1856 and were almost immediately hired as part of the Ravel Troupe. There are few records of Marietta's brothers, but she came to the attention of the public and the press almost immediately because of her beauty, charm, and performing skills. The Zanfrettas performed with the Ravel Troupe during their extended booking at Niblo's Garden in New York City, which lasted for three hundred performances during 1857–59.[2] Reviews of performances by the Ravels often noted the presence of Marietta Zanfretta, and they also reflect the range of skills she brought to that troupe. In addition to tightrope and acrobatic training, Marietta also received ballet training as a child, and reviews of the Ravel Troupe note that she performed solo and ensemble dances, as well as performing en-pointe on the tightrope; she was renowned for pirouetting while on the rope.

Marietta Zanfretta was booked to perform her famous tightrope descent in variety and as part of theatrical olios after her booking with the Ravels ended. George Odell's *Annals of the New York Stage* includes a lithograph of her performing this trick in Boston in 1861, and later newspaper reviews indicate that this became her signature feat.[3] In addition to her not inconsiderable skills, Zanfretta was also noted as one of the most beautiful dancers of her age, and she had the ability to charm her audience even when a performance of her famous trick went awry. One of a series of glowing reviews in a Kansas newspaper noted: "Even what at first appeared a contre temps, the fall of the beautiful Marietta Zanfretta from the rope into the parquet, was so gracefully and skillfully gotten over by the charming danseuse, that the sympathy and applause of the large audience was accorded her, so vociferously, indeed, that we have a lingering suspicion that the fall was only another French coup d'etat of this Napoleon of tightrope performers, to take the house by storm."[4] But Marietta Zanfretta's skills were considerably more varied than tightrope walking and ballet dancing. The Zanfretta Troupe also performed with a number of different circuses in the United States, and in this context Marietta performed in an equestrian act, balancing and dancing on the back of a horse as it circled the ring, and also with her brothers in high-wire and acrobatic acts.

This brief summary of a single performer's bookings describes forms of circus performance that are very different from modern circus performances, with their large roster of specialist performers, trained exotic animal acts, and attendant sideshow attractions. It also shows a world in which circus, pantomime, variety, ballet, and other theatrical genres were interconnected. In the mid-nineteenth century, circus acts appeared as olio acts in dramatic performances and on variety bills. Acrobats were often hired by pantomime companies to provide tableaux scenes and tumbling and comedy. Like Marietta Zanfretta, young female circus performers learned ballet as part of their training and could supplement ballet corps or dance solos. Just as circus performers could move into other forms of theater, circuses also frequently incorporated a range of theatrical genres, particularly minstrelsy, variety, and pantomime.

Circuses in the mid-nineteenth century were relatively small family-based troupes featuring as few as a dozen performers who had wide-ranging skills that allowed them to appear in a number of acts during the evening. If the circus traveled with trained animals, they were most likely to be horses or dogs, and the focus of the entertainment was on gymnastics, acrobatics, trapeze and tightrope acts, and clowns. Circus bills could also include songs, dances, the presentation of tableaux vivants, and minstrel performances. In many ways, the circus and variety were quite similar in terms of content, but while variety was the province of saloon, the circus was more likely to be staged under canvas, and while variety flourished during the winter months, circuses were most active during the summer. Most circuses disbanded during the coldest months of the winter, while a small number headed south to ride out the cold in a Southern state or to tour Cuba or elsewhere in the Caribbean.[5] Circus performers who remained in the northern part of the country were forced to find alternate employment, performing olio acts for minstrel and theater companies or by taking bookings in the concert saloons that staged variety exclusively.

The careers of acrobats, gymnasts, and other performers active in circus and theater in the mid-nineteenth century reflect the complex interrelationships between a number of different theatrical forms, as well as the futility of trying to draw hard dividing lines between them. There were certainly performers who worked primarily in a single genre, such as circus or pantomime or minstrelsy, but most performers moved between two or more forms, adapting their acts to new contexts in order to maintain employment throughout the year. And the longer performers managed to sustain their career, the more likely they were to form the contacts—with other performers, with managers, and with agents—to allow for this flexibility. In many ways, the flexible format of both circus and variety encouraged easy movement between these forms. The major difference was that, despite the presence of spectacular acrobatic, gymnastic, or other troupes, variety relied primarily on singing, dancing, and individual acts that spoke directly to their audience. And, while circus included singers, dancers, minstrels, and pantomimists, it was a form that was based, first and foremost, on largely silent and spectacular displays and feats of daring—speaking was the province of the ringmaster and to a lesser extent the clowns.

The lack of spoken dialog in most circus acts meant that circus was, on the whole, a much more international form than variety, which was much more rooted in English and Anglo-American song traditions. In circus, the clowns were most often American or English, and these men had skills that allowed them to work in pantomime, as well as in minstrelsy and variety as comic singers. The variety manager Tony Pastor, who entered variety as comic singer in the 1860s, began his career at the age of 6 as a minstrel performer and tambourine player before apprenticing with the circus owner John J. Nathan. Pastor's performing skills included comic singing, riding, acrobatics and tumbling, as well as dancing, and he also worked as a clown and ringmaster. This broad range of skills was typical in early performances and particularly in circus, minstrelsy, and variety.[6] Pastor lacked the skills to be a specialist rider or acrobat, but his versatility was an asset for circuses, allowing him to assist in a number of different kinds of acts, and it also gave him an advantage when he entered variety. Pastor's brothers Frank and William also apprenticed with Nathan, and both had greater success in equestrian and vaulting acts, touring to Europe and the Caribbean. William eventually made the move into variety, like his brother Tony, while Frank remained in the circus as an equestrian for his whole career.

While there were numerous American-born circus performers, many of the gymnasts, acrobats, aerial, and equestrian performers were European, and there were also a small number of troupes of Arabic and Japanese acrobats active in both circus and variety. European-born performers were more likely than American or English performers to stay in a single specialty and to return to Europe when they retired. The performers with the least career mobility were non-European; while some French, German, and Italian performers settled in the United States and married American women from circus families, there is little indication that this was the case for Japanese performers.[7] Even though these performers remained limited to a single specialty, such as acrobatics or gymnastics, they were able to find bookings in genres such as variety. There were a number of Japanese performers active in variety, including the contortionist Yamadiva, the juggler and gymnast Prince Satsuma, and the juggler King Sarbro, and troupes of Japanese acrobats and gymnasts had begun to be featured in a number of different genres of theater from the mid- to late 1860s along with troupes of Arab acrobats.[8] Exotic origins were central to the appeal of these troupes and also to the appeal of individual acts, such as the gymnast Ali Hassan.[9]

The presence of Japanese, Chinese, Arabic, and other "exotic" performers on the variety stage provides an early link to museum exhibits such as those presented by P. T. Barnum. A central part of the appeal of Barnum's show was that it challenged the audience to examine the item presented and determine its authenticity for themselves.[10] Audience members were complicit in Barnum's humbug, which enabled them to believe in the rational world of science and progress without fully renouncing older beliefs in magic and the supernatural. The intermingling of popular science and religion in this same period in the context of "wonder shows" presented in a theatrical context fulfilled much the same function.[11] In an age in which pseudoscientific language came to dominate the discourse on racial differences, it is not surprising that the "Oriental" Other found a role that relied on performing the apparently impossible in variety and other popular entertainments. These performers enacted the mystical powers that had long been associated in European culture with both the Middle East and Asia, but, like other ethnic acts in variety and later vaudeville, they also reassured members of the audience that they were essentially nonthreatening, and that none of these performers spoke reinforced the idea that they were distinctly separate from the audience.

43

The problem for Japanese and other exotic acrobats, however, was that they were limited to that role alone. European and American acrobats or gymnasts could move into related specialties such as knockabout comedy and dance routines, and from there to other theatrical forms such as variety and minstrelsy in comic singing and acting roles in which they related directly to the audience, but I have found no evidence of similar mobility by Japanese performers. King Sarbro worked as a juggler and acrobat for more than a decade before his death of tuberculosis in 1882, and another Japanese gymnast and juggler, Prince Satsuma, worked for forty years in the same specialty.[12] Both men appeared on the variety stage, but they were limited to their specialty and were not included in the comic and burlesque afterpieces that ended each show. This meant that as they aged, they were inevitably replaced by younger performers who were able to perform more spectacular feats of daring.[13]

While it is difficult now to imagine the kinds of equestrian or even trapeze or tightrope acts that could be staged, theaters hosted all sorts of circus-style acts, including acrobatics and animals, and circuses were often staged in theater buildings during the mid-nineteenth century. The equestrian S. P. Stickney ran a circus and equestrian theater in New Orleans during the 1840s and also briefly staged a circus at the Bowery Theater in New York. Stickney's New Orleans theater sacrificed parquet seating—more respectable theatrical seating that had replaced the bench seating of the old-style pit—to construct an amphitheater in which trick riding was presented, but he also presented equestrian dramas on his stage. Stickney's featured specialties were his trained horses, which often received equal billing with the other performers.[14] During the equestrian drama *Dick Turpin*, Stickney advertised that "the Trained Mare Black Bess will perform many wonderful Leaps" during the play.[15] Stickney also staged the equestrian drama *Mazeppa* during the same season, and this play featured high-speed riding and leaps by the horse.

There were few laws to protect the safety of the performers in the nineteenth century, but even with the risky feats performed I have found no reports of equestrian accidents on the stage, despite descriptions of these acts that often defy credibility. Reports of trapeze accidents in variety can occasionally be found in the *Clipper* and other newspapers, however, and these show that by the 1870s some minimal provisions had been mandated by law to protect the audience, and to a lesser extent the performers, from the dangers of performing in the confined space of a theater. In reporting an accident in 1875 at Robinson Hall in New York City, the *New York Times* noted that the performer who fell said "he had no net, and although he could have procured one, there was not room to spread it if he had wished to, as the ceiling is only twenty-four feet high and the trapeze swings eight feet below the ceiling, which leaves only room enough for the swinging feats he is accustomed to perform, without any space for the net. He says he does not know exactly what the provisions of the law are in relation to a net being spread in such cases, but he understands that it is framed for the protection for those underneath, and not of the performers. In Robinson Hall the trapeze was so placed that the swinging is over the centre aisle and toward the stage, so that none of the audience were beneath the performers."[16] The introduction of safety laws during the mid-nineteenth century may well have reinforced the divide between circus and variety that began in the 1860s after legal changes in New York forced variety managers to pare down their bills considerably.

Circus, like most forms of theater, was an overwhelmingly male world, and female performers were just as popular and in demand with circus audiences as with variety audiences. The demand for female performers in both variety and circus was so great that in a number of cases young boys were dressed as girls and billed as young women in advertising. The equestrian and circus manager Spencer Q. Stokes was known to dress young boys as girls to appear in acts at his New Orleans circus in the 1840s and 1850s. The equestrienne Ella Zoyara, whose real name was Omar Kingsley, was the most famous of these performers who appeared first in circus and later in variety; Kingsley performed in female attire into his 20s before assuming male garb and continuing his equestrian career.[17] As Omar Kingsley, he married Eloise Stickney, who was famous for dancing and skipping rope on horseback, and while their marriage did not last long, they did have a daughter who was later active as a high-wire performer. The circus trapeze artist Farini also presented his adopted son as a girl, under the name of Mlle. Lulu, and written references to male acrobats dressed as women date back to the eighteenth century.[18] These incidents, and particularly the case of Omar Kingsley, suggest that circus and variety managers recognized that these subterfuges occurred within the circus world, although they could not publicly acknowledge or condone that performers deceived their audiences in this way, and when the subterfuge was discovered managers always expressed the appropriate shock at the revelation and claimed to have been as deceived as their audience.

45

The popularity of female performers was due in great part to their costumes, which revealed the curves of their bodies and often exposed the full length of their legs, as was the case with ballet dancers. Female circus performers seem to have received at least rudimentary training in ballet as part of their training, and I have found many references to them performing solo dances or songs and dances as part of the circus bill. But the appeal of women performing in specialties that required strength and training was also due to the mix of horror and fascination elicited by women transgressing the boundaries of female gender roles. Female acrobats performed feats of strength and skill that popular imagination held to be impossible for women to master. This explains the popularity of strong women who lifted weights and other heavy objects on the stage, or trapeze artists like Madame Sanyeah, who held the weight of her male partner with her mouth. Contemporary reviews of female acrobats reflect ambivalence about these acts, at once reducing women to their appearance and attractiveness, while at the same time marveling at the apparently impossible feats they performed.[19] In many ways, female acrobats represented the perfect kind of act for variety managers who sought to attract an audience without incurring the wrath of civic authorities. Like dancers, women in acrobatic acts could be billed as professionals with remarkable and unique skills, while their brief costumes—deemed necessary by the nature of the act—allowed men a full view of the actresses' bodies. B. F. Keith later employed this tactic in vaudeville when he presented the champion swimmer Annette Kellerman in an aquatic act. A review of one of her performances noted that the audience was largely indifferent to the staged musical portions of Kellerman's act, but their interest was piqued by the aquatic sections in which Kellerman was presented in a "union suit" that clung to her body when wet.[20]

A number of hugely successful female circus performers were also active in variety and other theatrical genres during the mid-nineteenth century, and as was the case with Marietta Zanfretta, these women began their careers performing as part of a family troupe. Circus, like theater, was a profession that was passed from parents to children, who began training from very early in life and whose professional careers started in childhood. One of the most famous performing families in the mid-nineteenth century was the Ravels, a troupe of acrobats and pantomimists who came from France to the United States in 1832 and continued to perform in American theater for more than three decades. The core of the troupe was drawn from the Ravel family, but it was supplemented with additional circus performers and ballet dancers, most of whom were French or Italian like the Zanfrettas, who had links to both French and Italian circuses. While the Ravels were not active performing under canvas, they staged what was essentially a circus in miniature. Their show consisted of high-wire and acrobatic acts, supplemented with singing and ballet dancing as well as pantomime. Their performances combined acrobatics and ballet in what they billed as pantomimic ballet. The entertainment they staged relied as much on comedy and acting as it did on choreography, and it drew on European dance and Harlequinade traditions, as well as on circus specialties.

Marietta was the best known of the Zanfrettas, and when she wasn't performing solo, she frequently appeared with her family troupe. The Zanfretta Troupe was comprised of Marietta and her brother Alex, along with her husband, François Siegrist, and his brother Auguste. François Siegrist was a French clown, gymnast, and acrobat, and Auguste Siegrist was a tightrope performer. The Siegrist brothers were born in Germany and apprenticed to famous French Equestrian, Mons. François Tourniaire. The brothers performed at the Paris Hippodrome before moving to the United States. It is likely that François and Marietta had met and possibly married before emigrating. The Zanfretta Troupe performed a similar act to the Ravels that included pantomime and acrobatics, but unlike the Ravels they also took booking with circuses. While Marietta continued to take theatrical booking through the 1870s, she also regularly worked with circuses, even after the family troupe had disbanded. François Siegrist, who was eight years older than Marietta, performed for several years in partnership with her brother Alex and then dedicated himself to training his children; at the end of his career he appeared with Marietta and their children, as well as a troupe of performing dogs he had trained. After François died suddenly of a heart attack in 1878, Marietta married the French clown and pantomimist François Kennebel.[21] She continued to perform until 1880 and then lived in retirement with her husband in the United States; she died in 1898, at the age of 66.

Marietta Zanfretta had as wide a range of skills as any of her male contemporaries, albeit in different areas, and she had the added advantage of being an attractive young woman whose beauty held great charms for her audience and

46

made her a firm audience favorite. While her beauty and charm were exceptional, her wide range of skills was not. Many young women active in circus acts also developed skills that allowed them to appear in solo acts within the context of circus, but also to move into variety or other theatrical work during the winter season. Male acrobats and equestrians were more likely to have skills in comedy and perhaps acting that could take them into minstrelsy or into variety as a comic or character singer, while female circus performers tended to be dancers and only very occasionally ballad singers. The result of this was that most women had more limited careers than men. At the same time, women were also more likely to periodically withdraw from performance for marriage and pregnancy, and they were also more likely to take positions behind the scenes after retirement, teaching younger performers or making and maintaining costumes and performing other support duties while their male counterparts moved into management and other public positions. In this way, the circus and other parts of the theatrical world echoed the prevailing gender construction of the broader world, even though they clearly subscribed to models of gender in which women could be both active and public as well as respectable.

Despite her popularity in variety, Marietta Zanfretta did not make a permanent move into the genre, and it is likely that the reason for this was based in family ties and connections with other circus performers. It is telling that as Marietta aged, she worked exclusively in circuses, where her ties to her own family troupe and to managers were more likely to find her bookings. This was equally true for male performers, and while large numbers of circus performers occasionally took bookings in concert saloons, few moved permanently into the form. It is also likely that when one member of a family chose to move into variety, it increased the chances that other members would follow him—this was certainly the case with Tony Pastor and his brother William.

In New York City, the 1862 change in theater licensing laws curtailed the presentation of large, spectacular circus displays in concert saloons. Without income from the sale of alcohol, concert saloon managers could not afford to hire troupes of acrobats and trapeze artists. But individual circus performers continued to work in variety and later vaudeville, and occasionally a variety manager hired a troupe when they represented a novelty that would draw an audience to the theater—this was certainly the case with the touring Japanese acrobatic troupes who represented the twin inducement of a spectacular display of physical skill performed by people with the appeal of the exotic. But these large-scale acts were rare in the later nineteenth century, and circus and variety grew further apart after 1870 as variety came to rely even more on singers and dancers.

Tripping the
Light Fantastic

Dancers

Melodeon, 539 Broadway, between Spring and Broome streets,
Greatest Talent in America, . . . All Our All Favorites Returned. J.
H. Odgen, Sam Sharpley, Annetta Galletti, Miss Eva Brent, Miss
Fanny Forrest, Mr. James Dunn, Miss Kate Pennoyer, Miss Adele
Calla, Miss Augusta Walby, Mr. James La Mont, . . . The great Ballet
Troupe, Under the control of Ronzani, Who produces all the Ballets
after the French school, with the entire company of the Melodeon,
numbering over One Hundred Performers, the Largest, Best and
most Talented in America. Great attraction for Christmas Day, A
grand new ballet pantomime, by Ronzani, entitled the Brigands
of the West, in which Annetta Galletti will sustain the principal
character.

—"Amusements," *New York Herald*, December 23, 1861: 7

If acrobatic performances provided the spectacle of physical
daring for concert saloon audiences, then ballet provided the
thrill inherent in the mass display of women's bodies. As a result,
many of the descriptions of dance in early variety carry the suggestion that
these women were badly trained and performed the mid-nineteenth-century
equivalent of bump-and-grind for a largely male audience.[1] That some of
the leading foreign dancers of the period, such as Annetta Galletti and Rita
Sangalli, also appeared in concert saloons complicates this assumption, and
the work histories of ballet dancers born and trained in the United States who

frequently appeared on variety stages dispels the notion that the dancers in concert saloon ballet corps were unskilled. Indeed, a number of these women were highly trained and highly skilled dancers who worked in a broad range of theaters, including the ballet corps for Max Maretzek's opera, the ballet corps at Laura Keene's theater, and in P. T. Barnum's theater.

Men also presented dance on the variety stage, but male dancers primarily appeared in folk and popular styles, such as jig and clog dancing, that were associated with minstrel performance. These dance styles were also part of circus, performed either as a solo act or as part of a minstrel performance. Dick Sands, a jig and clog dancer, was active in both variety and minstrelsy in the 1860s and was billed as a "champion" clog dancer in both contexts. Even though Sands regularly performed with minstrel troupes, including the George Christy's Minstrels in 1862, the San Francisco Minstrels in 1865, and Leon and Kelly's Troupe during 1866, it is likely that he did not appear in blackface, but rather as an Irish character. During the 1870s and 1880s Sands also performed as a "song and dance artist" with touring variety shows and circuses.[2] Some male dancers had ballet training, and this allowed them to work in pantomime as well in classical ballet. Pantomime performance also called for a degree for acting skill, so these men were extremely useful on the variety stage, where their flexibility allowed them to be featured in popular dances as a solo act, to partner with the one of the female members of the corps de ballet, and also to take supporting roles in the dramatic afterpiece that finished the bill. The dancer Henry Leslie appeared at Frank Rivers's Melodeon in Philadelphia during May 1860, billed as a "celebrated pantomimist and dancer." On this occasion he appeared as a solo dance act, in the role of Colin in the comic burlesque of Shakespeare entitled *Hamlet Indisposed*, and with Sallie Bishop, Mlle. Marie, and the ballet corps in *La Polka de Boheme*; Sallie Bishop had also taken a leading role in the burlesque.

While male dancers most often entered variety performance from minstrelsy and circus performance and gained their first theatrical training and performance experience in those genres, women tended to come to variety from classical ballet. In order to understand why highly skilled dancers might be drawn to perform on the popular stage in the rough-and-ready context of the concert saloon, it is necessary to understand the working conditions these women faced, as well as the options available to them in their career paths. As Maureen Needham notes, American-trained dancers were largely relegated to working in the ballet corps during the nineteenth century.[3] Imported French and later Italian ballet masters preferred to hire dancers from their home countries to dance the leading roles. Given the large number of theaters that employed ballet corps, there was ample employment for American-trained dancers, but they were relegated to the lowest paying positions in the theatrical world and worked largely anonymously for their entire careers.[4]

Variety not only offered young American ballet dancers an additional source of employment, it also allowed them to take featured positions. Variety bills of the late 1850s and early 1860s gave the names of the members of the ballet corps on the playbill, and these women were also frequently given the opportunity to perform in solo or duo dances, where they were featured—and presumably paid—as leading ballerinas. Variety ballet corps were relatively small and consisted of only around a dozen women in the 1860s. Because variety demanded versatility of its performers, ballet dancers were encouraged to develop other skills such as singing or acting and were pressed into service in other areas of the bill. This allowed dancers who desired to remain on the stage to develop and display their singing and acting skills in a way that would have been more difficult in legitimate drama. While most women in variety, even featured singers, had relatively short careers of less than a decade, variety enabled dancers and other women who wanted to extend their careers into their 20s and 30s an opportunity to learn additional skills that would enable them to do so.

When following the careers of dancers in early variety, it quickly becomes evident from surviving records that dancing was a family profession that was passed from one generation of women to the next. During the 1860s and into the early 1870s, the Walby Sisters—Augusta, Harriet, Julia, Lizzie, and Louise—were active as dancers in and around New York City and worked in a broad range of theatrical genres, including variety, burlesque, and dramatic performances. Harriet worked primarily for P. T. Barnum's theatrical company both as a dancer and as an actress and on at least two occasions found employment for one or another of her sisters with that theater. The other sisters, Augusta, Lizzie, and Louise, were active primarily in variety, but also occasionally in burlesque, and they danced together as part of the same corps on numerous occasions and also frequently appeared in a dance act on the bill. Of the three women, Augusta had the longest career. She first appears in George Odell's chronicle of the New York stage in 1859 and was still active as late as January 1878.[5] She also appeared in variety in other cities, including Washington, D.C., and was part of a production of the *Black Crook* that toured the Midwest in 1868.[6] Augusta's sisters had considerably shorter careers of a decade or less and also worked primarily in New York and occasionally in other East Coast cities. It is likely that they left the stage to marry and raise families as they reached their late teens or early 20s. Later, a dancer named Josephine Walby worked in variety as a skipping rope and jig dancer from 1872 until around 1882, which suggests that a younger generation of Walby women had found employment on the stage.

This pattern of employment was not peculiar to the Walby Sisters. Augusta, Louise, and Cora Lamoureaux worked in New York in the same period: Augusta danced in ballet and variety, Louise had a brief ballet career with the Ronzani Troupe and in corps for spectacular drama staged by Laura Keene, and Cora was also active in variety as a dancer and actress.[7] As with the Walby sisters, both Louise and Cora left the stage, while Augusta continued to perform, changing specialties twice before her death in 1875; after leaving dance, Augusta was billed first as a cantatrice and soon afterward as a protean performer, or male character singer.[8] The sisters Minnie and Ernestine de Faiber also worked in ballet corps attached to variety theaters, but also for burlesque, Barnum's Theater, and even as part of Max Maretzek's corps at the Academy of Music. The largely anonymous labor of dancing in a ballet corps makes it difficult to know exactly how long the careers of these women lasted and also makes following the careers of the many hundreds of young women who performed in ballet during the late nineteenth century all but impossible.

51

Very occasionally it is possible to construct a more complete history for a dancing family, largely because one or more of its members achieve a level of fame that brought them to wider public notice. The Wesner family of Philadelphia is one such family. There were six women in the Wesner family: Emma or Emmeline, the mother, and her daughters Mary, Ella, Sally, Lizzie, and Maggie.[9] Emmeline's husband was Charles Wesner, and there was just one son in the Wesner family, Charles Jr. Like his father, he was never active on the stage, working as a laborer and assisting his mother in running a saloon during the 1870s and 1880s; the 1900 census gives his profession as a painter. Charles and Emmeline Wesner had met and married in New Jersey, and all of their children except the youngest, Charles Jr., were born in that state. When Charles and Emmeline moved to Pennsylvania during the late 1840s, they brought only two of their daughters, Ella and Sarah, with them; the two girls were 9 and 7 respectively.

The Wesner women danced as part of ballet corps in Philadelphia theaters, including both variety and legitimate theater, and it is likely that Emmeline had brought her daughters to that city with her to find employment for them in a juvenile ballet corps.[10] Life for the family was extremely difficult, and Charles turned to petty crime for extra income. In 1851 a short report in the newspaper noted that Charles and Emmeline had been arrested in New York City, along with five women and one man, on the charge of passing counterfeit money.[11] I have found no other records of Emmeline, or Emma as she was most often known in theatrical billing, running afoul of the law, but Charles was arrested on a number of occasions during the 1870s and 1880s, and during this time he served at least one prison sentence of three years.[12] Charles's various run-ins with the law only increased the financial strain on the family, and by 1860 all five of the Wesner girls were living in Philadelphia and working in ballets there. The oldest daughter, Mary, had two daughters of her own, Sarah and Williminia Yeager, who also lived with the Wesners, and at least one of these girls also performed as a dancer.[13]

During the 1860s Mary and Ella performed as dancers in variety, primarily in Philadelphia but also occasionally in New York, and sometimes their mother joined them on the stage. Emma worked as the lead dancer of a ballet corps of fifty dancers for performances of the pantomime of the *Seven Dwarfs*, which was staged for the Easter holiday at the Bowery Theater in 1869.[14] At the time Emma was 48, and she continued to perform into her 50s; she paired with Ella in variety in the early 1870s. But Emma had also begun to make plans for her retirement from the stage, and as early as 1868 the Philadelphia City Directory listed her as the proprietor of a tavern on St. John Street. It is likely that Emma obtained a liquor license and opened a tavern to support herself in old age and during the periods in which her husband was in prison and to help support her children in periods in which they were not working. In 1875 the City Directory listed Emma as the widow of Charles Wesner, but when Charles was arrested again in 1877, the address given was the same as Emma's.[15] Because the Wesner's son was also named Charles, it is unclear whether Emma lived with her husband after 1881.[16] When Emma left the city to perform in New York it is likely that she left her business in the hands of her husband and then later her son, who was 17 years old in 1870.

Ella was by far the most successful of the Wesner sisters. She worked in ballet from 1850 to around 1870 and appeared in both legitimate theater and variety. Ella's first appearance in variety was in the late 1850s—she was part of a troupe that traveled from Philadelphia's Melodeon concert saloon to perform in the New York Melodeon, which was also managed by Frank Rivers.[17] She returned to New York to perform at the American Music Hall in November 1862, and in 1864 she was part of the large ballet company attached to the production of *Bel Demonio* that was staged at Niblo's Garden from mid-May to early July and starred the singer and actress Felicita Vestvali.[18] In 1869 Ella appeared in variety as a dancer on the same bill as America's first male impersonator, Annie Hindle, and it may have been this meeting that prompted her to change specialties in the early 1870s. In 1870, at the age of 28, Ella was recruited as an olio performer and utility player for the theater at Galveston, Texas, and in that context she began to appear in small speaking roles and gained the experience necessary to emerge as one of the leading variety performers in the 1870s.

While the other Wesner women were also dancers, considerably less is known about their careers because they danced primarily as members of ballet corps. Lizzie Wesner, who was four years younger than Ella, worked as a dancer until her death in 1881, at age 36.[19] Ella's youngest sister Maggie, who was also a dancer, followed in her sister's footsteps and worked as a male impersonator with mixed success between 1875 and the early 1880s, a period in which Ella was working in English music halls. Ella's obituary noted that she had spent much of her substantial earnings supporting her extended family, and Maggie stepped into her sister's role as the family's major money-earner during Ella's prolonged absence. When Ella returned to the United States, Maggie either retired from the stage or returned to dance. Despite a career of substantial earnings, Ella and her older sister Mary were supported by the Actors' Charitable Fund at the end of their lives; both sisters are buried together in the same charity grave.[20] Ella had helped support her extended family for most of her career and had not been able to save for her retirement; she most likely worked into her 70s due to financial need.

53

In the early 1870s a third generation of the Wesner family began dancing on the stage when Mary Wesner's daughter Minnie Wesner (Williminia Yeager) appeared as a dancer in Philadelphia variety. She later moved to Cincinnati, where she was part of the ballet corps at the Vine Street Opera-House from the late 1870s into the early 1880s. This theater was notorious in that city for staging the cancan, and Minnie Wesner was part of the corps of cancan dancers that Thomas Snelbaker, the theater's manager, sent to a theater in New Orleans in an effort to quiet the protests from some Cincinnati residents about the entertainment he staged. In 1880 Minnie was also part of a cancan presented at the Apollo Theater in Chicago; the report protesting this dance described the performance as "lewd" and "vulgar." This show was shut down when police raided the theater and arrested the dancers.[21]

This brief account of the working lives of the Wesner women provides insight into the kinds of families that produced American ballet dancers as well as the options available to dancers as they aged. It is clear that this family was not wealthy. Training was, mostly likely, undertaken within the family, and the children began work extremely early. When Emma and Charles first moved to Philadelphia they left the oldest girl, Mary, in New Jersey along with her two younger sisters. I am presuming that the children were left with Emma's family, which is where they received dance training. Mary had her first child at the age of 15, and a second, two years later, after moving to Philadelphia to live with her family—she may have been married briefly during this time.

The evidence suggests that Emma had made the necessary connections in the city to find work for herself and her daughters before sending for her remaining children. Philadelphia was a city in which corps of juvenile ballet dancers were extremely popular, and Ella began her dancing career at the age of 9. In the Wesner family, the children contributed to the family economy as soon as they were able. Even if their wages were relatively low—contemporary sources agree that the least experienced corps dancers earned about $3 per week—the five girls could contribute a minimum of $15 a week dancing in ballet corps in the city.

The case of Charles Wesner confirms that this family lived on the edge of poverty, barely making ends meet. A shoemaker by trade, Charles was also a small-time counterfeiter for most of his life. He may well have seen passing counterfeit bills and checks as a victimless crime—the victim was most likely to be the bank on which the check was drawn.[22] Commentaries printed in popularist men's newspapers such as the *National Police Gazette* in the mid-nineteenth century reflect a similar view that businessmen and the wealthy gained their wealth at the expense of the working classes. Song texts from this period express the same view, also charging the upper-middle class as being uncaring and hypocritical. It is easy to imagine Charles seeing his exploits as an effort to even the score with the wealthy.

The brief histories of ballet dancers active in variety during the 1850s and 1860s show that there were opportunities available for those American dancers who chose to extend their careers, and the more detailed history of the Wesner family also confirms this. While some dancers were able to move into acting in theatrical stock companies, the hierarchical nature of legitimate theater tended to work against this mobility. Variety was a context that not only allowed but encouraged flexibility from its performers. Because variety pressed performers into service wherever possible, young dancers were able to appear as an act on the bill, dancing solo or duo, and were also often included in the dramatic afterpiece, where they learned to deliver lines and even improvise comedy. In a number of cases dancers gradually began to take on speaking roles in the afterpiece or to develop singing skills as part of a song-and-dance act. In all cases, however, the majority of roles for women on the variety stage exploited their youth and their looks—women in variety were overwhelmingly young and pretty.

The Wesner family history includes information about dancers of three generations active over a period of more than thirty years and also shows the changing—and shrinking—employment opportunities for American dancers between the 1850s and the 1870s. While Emma Wesner and her daughters were able to find work in a wide range of theatrical genres, this was less true of Emma's granddaughters, who entered the profession after the Civil War. In 1873 the United States suffered a financial crisis that resulted in a severe economic downturn. In the face of this financial panic, theaters across the country failed or consolidated their activities, laying off their stock companies and ballet corps and relying more and more on touring shows. This shift in theatrical employment patterns was devastating for local and regional performers, who either left the profession or were forced to go to larger cities to look for work in an increasingly competitive marketplace. In this period, the sexualized strand of variety that had been fostered by managers such as George Lea continued to hire dancers, and it became almost inevitable that young American dancers who wanted to continue to work ended up in a touring female minstrel troupe dancing the cancan and presenting tableaux vivants; this was what happened to Minnie Wesner. But, this career trajectory also left dancers open to exploitation by managers and, more critically, to arrest by police. It also made it more difficult for young classically trained dancers who were able to find positions in legitimate corps to learn another specialty and to be able to extend their stage careers once they were too old to continue to dance.

Another question that emerges from the Wesner family history is why only one member of the family chose to extend her career by moving from dance to performing as a comic singer. At the height of her career, in the early 1870s, Ella could claim a wage of between $150 and $200 per week; for most of the period in which she worked, she was a leading performer who would have demanded at least $100 per week, and only in the last ten or fifteen years of her career did this amount decline.[23] Given the difference between the incomes of solo acts in variety and ballet corps dancers, one might wonder why more of the Wesners did not pursue solo careers. These women were well-trained dancers, and some were able to work their way up to the position of leading dancers in ballet corps in East Coast cities. While some of these women may have lacked the skills of their older sister, my suspicion is that most of Ella's sisters preferred the stability of a settled life in Philadelphia, where they had the support of an extended family network and could marry and raise families and when necessary find work dancing in theaters in that city, to the uncertain and solitary life on the road. On the few occasions that Ella's career foundered she inevitably headed back to Philadelphia for the comfort of her family. It is entirely possible that Ella Wesner's long career was due to family need as much as personal ambition, and this further suggests that even though biographies and autobiographies of leading players in nineteenth-century American theater are shaped by the prevailing ideology of that period—that of the "self-made" man—older patterns of kinship ties and family obligations were also an important force in shaping the careers of individual performers.[24]

La Nuit—Amazon Chorus, four anonymous dancers in burlesque costume for Amazon Chorus, with spears and shell shields. Unknown photographer, ca. 1880. Author's collection.

Marietta Zanfretta, tight-rope dancer. Lithograph, unbound page from *Ballou's Pictorial*, Boston, March 20, 1858. Author's collection.

Leona Dare, trapeze artist. Photograph by Gurney & Son, New York, ca. 1870. Author's collection.

Little Sallie Marks, child equestrian and circus performer. Photograph by Glass, Janesville, Wisconsin, ca. 1875. Author's collection.

El Niño Eddie, acrobat active in variety during the 1870s. Photograph by C. D. Fredericks, New York, ca. 1870. Author's collection.

Marietta Ravel, ballet dancer and member of the Ravel Family Troupe. Unknown photographer, ca. 1868. Author's collection.

Betty Rigl, ballet dancer active in variety and pantomime, dressed in costume worn in *The Black Crook*. Photograph by J. Gurney & Son, New York, ca. 1868.

Louise Whelply and Julia Melville, two ballet dancers active in variety. Photograph by J. Gurney & Son, ca. 1862.

Jennie Hughes, dressed to perform in variety in fringed short pants with feather in hair. Mounted on blank cardstock, photographer not named but probably Napoleon Sarony, New York, ca. 1875. Author's collection.

Jennie Hughes in respectable dress or stage costume, hair up in elaborate style with pearl headdress and long curl over shoulder. Photograph by Napoleon Sarony, New York, ca. 1880. Author's collection.

FRENCH TWIN SISTERS

French Twin Sisters, "sister act" active in variety during the 1870s. Mounted on blank cardstock, photographer not named but probably Napoleon Sarony, New York, ca. 1875. Author's collection.

Clinetopp [*sic*] Sisters, dancers and pantomimists active in variety. Unknown photographer, ca. 1870. Author's collection.

Clinetopp Sisters.   (Over.)

Entertainment Comes to the Fore

Legal Intervention
The Anti–Concert Saloon Bill
and Its Aftermath

One may well ask in alarm what has come over us, that Broadway should thus of a sudden break out in these pestiferous eruptions. It has been said that these establishments have been introduced in New York in imitation of similar establishments in London, Paris, and other European cities. We do the European cities wrong—never in any European city has there been, nor would there be tolerated, such a combination of vilenesses.

—"A Nuisance to Be Squelched," *New York Times*, December 21, 1861: 4

On the evening of Thursday, April 24, 1862, lower Broadway was abuzz with rumors and anticipation. Just a week earlier the state legislature had passed a bill aimed at stemming the rise of the concert saloons that had begun to proliferate in this once-fashionable neighborhood. During the week, concert saloons offering an enticing combination of variety entertainment and alcohol served by "pretty waiter girls" had continued to operate in defiance of the law, but the police were under pressure to act, and local patrolmen had warned proprietors that action was imminent. The locals had come out in force to watch, and crowds of patrons, sympathizers, and friends of the proprietors and employees had begun gathering at these halls in the early afternoon to see what the authorities would do. Other locals came, drawn by the crowds and rumors, to watch the arrests. Inside a number of Broadway concert saloons audiences gathered in the doorways in anticipation of raids, while others sat and watched the shows, which were comprised of the usual assortment of circus-style novelty acts and singers and dancers. The waitresses, who were young and good looking and a major attraction of these establishments, continued to ply their customers with beer and other beverages. The proprietors of these saloons looked on, happy for the business but concerned about the imminent raids and worried about their ability to make a living under the new law.

At 8 P.M. the police mobilized in the lower Manhattan precincts in which concert saloons abounded. Every policeman knew that the crowds in and around the theaters sympathized with the saloon owners, and a good number of the police were also sympathetic to their cause. But the law was clear in compelling the police to enforce it, and editorials in the *New York Times* had raised the stakes even higher by accusing the police force of being corrupt. Despite the protests from saloon owners and the growing crowds on the streets, the police moved through the streets of lower Manhattan. To the delight of the crowd, they did not discriminate between high- and low-class establishments. The new law targeted the concert saloons, but it also forbade alcohol in theaters frequented by middle-class patrons. As a result both Wallack's Theatre and the Winter Garden were raided and their bars shut.

At the American Concert Hall at 444 Broadway, Captain Williamson of the Fourteenth Ward and his men were met by the proprietor who assured them that his bar was closed and the waitresses dismissed. The police, not trusting his word, spent some time moving through the densely crowded hall hoping to catch some infraction of the law, but they saw nothing. The manager had mounted a grand show of compliance for the benefit of the police. Young boys had been pressed into service and carried trays of temperance drinks through the audience. On the stage the performance continued as usual. The police saw a number of young women who had worked in these halls as waitresses sitting in the audience, but as they were dressed in street clothing and were perfectly well behaved they did not arrest them. At about 9 P.M. a single waitress entered the auditorium. Dressed in a short skirt, a white shirt, apron, and pom-pommed socks, the young woman carried a single glass of what appeared to be liquor. Slowly and seriously she crossed to a customer and handed him the glass and he, equally seriously, paid her for it. She was immediately arrested. In the Eighth Ward, a single waitress was also arrested at the Canterbury. The managers of both of these halls had decided to test the constitutionality of the law in court.[1]

The passing of the law popularly known as the Anti–Concert Saloon Bill in the New York State Legislature in April 1862 proved to be a watershed moment in the history of variety entertainment. This bill forbade any theater manager or proprietor from holding both a liquor license and a theatrical license, and it directly attacked the business practices of the concert saloons that had begun to proliferate in lower Manhattan as the economy recovered from its brief downturn during 1857. By 1860 concert saloons were found on almost every block of lower Broadway south of Houston Street, and there were more than a dozen of these venues in the four blocks between Broome and Bleeker Streets. Smaller concert saloons and museum shows were also found in the cross streets in the blocks closest to Broadway. The appearance of these venues on Broadway not only alarmed members of New York's elite society, but also threatened the livelihood of many of the theaters that catered to this population. This was especially true for Wallack's Theater, at the corner of Broome and Broadway; Niblo's Garden, at the corner of Broadway and Prince; and Laura Keene's, in the block between Houston and Bleeker. The men who visited the concert saloons that surrounded these theaters thronged on the sidewalks, representing a level of chaos that potentially deterred the patrons of the more respectable venues. For this reason, legitimate theater owners joined moral-reform forces in petitioning the state legislature to change theatrical licensing laws. The theater owners resented the huge appeal of the concert saloons and the ease with which they attracted audiences with alcohol and variety, while the moral reformers saw these venues as having no value and as endangering the morals of the men in their audiences.[2]

Examining the passage of this law and the tensions between moral-reform forces and variety managers that emerged beginning in the 1850s shows that reformers did not share a single motivation or even a single goal. Reform movements represented uneasy alliances between often disparate social groups that crossed class and ethnic lines and religious beliefs; they also represented tensions within local communities between those who aspired to upward mobility and those who did not and efforts by both groups to defend themselves from outside forces and to determine their own values. Both the reform forces and the defenders of variety worked within an increasingly complex legal system, and, despite strong convictions about the rightness of their respective causes, neither could be sure that the law would defend their position. Moral reformers agitated to pass state statutes and local ordinances that specifically targeted variety theaters, and in turn variety managers subtly shifted their business practices to comply only with the letter of the law, while continuing to meet the needs of their audience.

Rather than presenting legal reform as simply a process by which the hegemonic forces of middle-class order imposed their will on the working class and the institutions that catered to this population, it is more productive to view this legal struggle as a complex dance between multiple forces, including the civil authority of government and police, competing reform movements, and theater managers who were in fierce competition with each other for audiences. While government was a force that had traditionally been associated with the social elite, by the mid-nineteenth century, those seeking office were coming to realize that in politics sheer numbers mattered more than social standing. Political machines mobilized votes in support of their candidates, who in return needed to please constituents through support of their local institutions, and these included saloons and other forms of commercial leisure. Roy Rosenzweig describes this process of struggle and negotiation in his study of saloons as a center for ethnic and working-class culture in Worcester, Massachusetts.[3] Like saloons, variety halls across the country provide insight into local community tensions, which, if anything, were heightened by the presence of female performers on the stage and competing views of appropriate female behavior. The potent combination of sexualized performance and alcohol on offer in many variety halls represented a double threat to nineteenth-century moral reformers; similarly, the performances staged in these theaters also reflect hostility to moral reformers and ambivalence about class mobility.

The passage of increasingly restrictive laws during the 1860s through the 1880s in the East and Midwest was instrumental in creating an environment in which B. F. Keith, the prominent vaudeville manager of the early twentieth century, could prosper with his "clean" vaudeville theaters. Keith was not the first manager to offer a politer form of variety entertainment; he inherited a legacy from at least two generations of earlier managers active on the East Coast of the United States. Reform in variety was a slow process that began in the 1860s and 1870s on the East Coast and continued through the end of the nineteenth century in other regions of the country; the transition from variety entertainment to the polite form offered by Keith was just as gradual and was shaped to a great extent by the need for managers to adapt to changes to theatrical licensing laws in order to remain in business. But the development of politer forms of variety did not mean that the older-style entertainments disappeared. The presence of multiple strands of variety, and an increasingly competitive marketplace, eventually resulted in rifts within the world of variety and the breakdown of the cooperative traditions of early variety entertainment.

The older and more developed cities on the East Coast were, not surprisingly, the first to pass laws regulating theatrical entertainment. The earliest laws required those offering commercial entertainment of all kinds, including juggling, tightrope and circus acts, singing and dancing, and spoken drama, to procure a license from the city. Licenses were issued annually, but could also be issued for shorter periods of time for a reduced fee. The latter case was particularly necessary for traveling shows such as circuses. These laws also included the proviso that those holding a license should ensure that no acts appearing on their stage offend public decency, but none specifically defined decency or indecency. Managers were also often required to maintain good order in their theaters, and some ordinances explicitly required managers to pay for the services of the local police.[4] Even when managers were not required to hire local police to maintain order, many did, and the records of the New York City police force held in the city's Municipal Archives note receipts from the local precinct for services rendered by individual policemen.[5]

By the mid-nineteenth century, these general laws were coming to be seen as inadequate on the East Coast, and legislatures and councils began to amend laws to make them more restrictive and, in some cases, to target particular kinds of theatrical entertainment. New York City began to tie theatrical licensing law, excise laws regulating the sale of alcohol, and laws supporting the moral reform of juvenile delinquents together from as early as the 1830s. In the view of moral reformers, institutions and habits that contributed to the delinquency and degradation of the city should be forced to pay for the rehabilitation of their victims. At the same time, the Society for the Reform of Juvenile Delinquents, the moral-reform society that benefited from both licensing fees and fines paid for infractions of the law, did little to reform the conditions that produced delinquency, such as poverty, appalling housing conditions, and the lack of opportunity that prevailed in the poorer neighborhoods of the city.

Reform forces in New York City found public support in the late 1850s and early 1860s as more and more concert saloons, cheap museums, and bars moved into once-fashionable portions of lower Broadway. While the city's elite had moved further north on Broadway, followed closely by the theaters that catered to them, they were shocked to see the disorder that had gripped their old neighborhood. Broadway was the center of respectable New York commerce and social life and was described by a guidebook from the 1870s as "the most wonderful street in the universe,"[6] while the Bowery was its dark twin, associated with poor and immigrant populations of the city. The same guidebook notes the Bowery's association with prostitution and with Jewish peddlers and later notes: "The Sunday law is a dead letter in the Bowery. Here on the Sabbath, one may see shops of all kinds—the vilest especially—open for trade. Cheap clothing stores, concert saloons, and the most infamous dens of vice are in full blast. The street, and the cars traversing it, are thronged with the lower classes in search of what they call enjoyment. At night all the places are open, and are crowded to excess. Roughs, thieves, fallen women, and even little children throng them. . . . The amusement afforded at these places ranges from indelicate hints and allusions to the grossest indecency."[7]

The appearance of theaters associated with the Bowery on once-fashionable lower Broadway triggered protests over their presence in the editorial columns of the staid *New York Times*. Support for new legislation restricting the business practices of concert saloon owners offering variety increased in the early 1860s as new recruits for the Union Army flocked to New York City. The *New York Times* began to express concerns over the morally degrading influence of low-class variety on naïve young men from rural areas. An editorial from late 1861 is typical of these protests:

> Within the last six or eight months a class of nuisance has been growing up in some of our principal streets, which demand the immediate and rigorous attention of our police authorities. We refer to the *concert saloons*, as they are called, which abound in Broadway, and which, under guise of singing and selling lager beer, are really the lowest and most infamous houses of prostitution, in which thousands of young men and boys congregate every night, and plunge into the worst excesses of ruinous and disgraceful debauchery. Some of them have licenses for theatrical performances, and resort to petty plays, gymnastic feats, dancing, &c., &c., and an additional means of enticing visitors. The *Herald* . . . is the recognized medium of advertising for these establishments, which brazen in large staring capitals their "pretty waiter girls" as among the special attractions of the place. These waiter-girls are simply street-walkers who find greater facilities for thus presenting their trade indoors than in the open thoroughfare. . . . Thousands of young men belonging to respectable families, caught by their advertisements in the *Herald*, are constantly drawn into [the concert saloons], and soon become sunk in debaucheries from which at the outset they would have shrunk with disgust and horror. The plausible cloak of music and theatrical performances blinds the eyes of parents and guardians to the real character of these places, which are thus doing their work of ruin and degradation upon the rapidly increasing number of victims, with perfect impunity and even without suspicion.[8]

Concert saloons were seen as being particularly dangerous to naïve youth because of the lure of "innocent" singing and entertainment offered by these establishments. The kinds of entertainment offered in concert saloons were not specifically at fault, but rather the business practices of saloon owners, particularly the practice of hiring young women to serve alcohol to patrons. If reformers could not control the sale of alcohol to New York residents, then they could at least ensure that the practices that enticed vulnerable young men into concert saloons were banned.

In April 1862 New York State passed "an Act to regulate places of public amusement in the cities and incorporated villages of this State," which was popularly known as the Anti–Concert Saloon Bill.[9] This act differed from earlier theater licensing laws in New York in that it specifically targeted the business practices of concert saloons. The act forbade the presence of alcohol or serving girls and waitresses in the theater auditorium, lobby, or any room adjoining the lobby. As evidenced in the protest quoted above, "pretty waiter girls" had been a distinctive feature of concert saloons in the city. The act also disallowed any individual theater owner, manager, or proprietor from holding both a liquor license and a theatrical license. This provision had a wider effect because many theaters, not only concert saloons, maintained bars on their premises. The bill also stipulated that anyone convicted of infringing the law would be ineligible to hold a theater license in the future; it also ruled out any possibility of appeal to conviction. Those convicted under this bill faced a fine of $100–$500, imprisonment for a period of three to twelve months, or both. The bill also required "every chief of police, sheriff, deputy sheriff, constable, captain of police, policeman, and every other police officer" to enforce the law through random inspections of theatrical establishments."[10]

As a result of the passage of this bill, on April 24, 1862, police conducted raids on the city's theaters, and after that date, theaters and establishments offering entertainment had to annually demonstrate their adherence to the law in order for the mayor's office to renew their theatrical license. Theater managers made an application to the office, which forwarded a request to the local police precinct. Once the police had inspected the theater, the reports on its suitability were forwarded to the mayor's office, which then issued the license, requested the theater owner to make modifications to their building to meet the needs of the law, or refused the application outright. Theaters unable to meet the requirement that there be no access to a bar from the auditorium were generally given time to meet the provisions of the bill, but even then not all theaters were able to comply. If the walls dividing barroom from the theater auditorium did not reach all the way to the ceiling, or if prostitutes actively solicited for customers on the premises, or if the regular customers were judged to be disreputable, the police could recommend against granting a license.

In 1862 many of the smaller concert saloons in lower Manhattan went out of business or converted to saloons that did not offer entertainment. Some operated illicitly without a license, but they risked being raided by police. When the law passed, George Lea, who was the manager of the Melodeon as well as other variety halls in the city, left New York and moved to Baltimore, where he opened a concert saloon called the New Idea that catered to Union soldiers and operated on a similar plan to his earlier New York theaters, offering alcohol, entertainment, and pretty waitresses to its male clientele.[11] By early 1864 he had also acquired the Canterbury Hall in Washington, D.C., from the Baltimore theatrical manager William E. Sinn.[12] Once the war was over and the soldiers who had formed a core part of his audience had dispersed, Lea returned to New York and opened a concert saloon called the Oriental in the basement of 652 Broadway. It is not clear whether Lea tried to acquire a theatrical license for this venue, although he offered low-quality entertainment in the saloon but not on a raised stage. He had operated for around two years, mostly evading the notice of the authorities, when his saloon was raided for violating the laws against serving alcohol on Sunday. This event marked the end of George Lea's career as a theater manager in New York City because his arrest left him ineligible for future licenses. But it did not mark the end of his theatrical career. He moved to Port Jervis, New York, where he opened a pharmacy and very quickly bought shares in the local theater.[13] Ironically, in Port Jervis, Lea operated completely legitimate businesses that catered to the respectable townsfolk. In a smaller town with little or no competition it was much easier to find his niche in the theatrical and entertainment scene—he managed the city's only theater—and he ran day excursions to New York City, eventually buying the branch railway line that served Port Jervis. When he died in 1902, he was a respected businessman, and the earlier, disreputable part of his career was eclipsed by his later achievements.

After the passage of the Anti–Concert Saloon Bill, the largest halls continued to offer theatrical entertainment, and they adjusted their business practices to meet the licensing requirements, firing their waitresses and walling off the saloon from the rest of the theater.[14] Because they were no longer able to rely on the revenue from alcohol sales to underwrite the cost of the bill, theater managers employed smaller acts rather than large spectaculars or reenactments. The quieter auditorium also allowed individual acts to interact with and play to audience sympathies. The stage became the focus of the evening rather than merely a backdrop to drinking and conviviality. The major effect of this act was to encourage the shift to an all-variety program and to partition the barroom within the theater so that it was accessible only from the street. Of the three largest New York concert saloons operating in 1862—the Canterbury, the Melodeon, and the American Music Hall—only the American survived into the late 1860s, but new halls emerged during this period offering variety-only formats, and many of these were operated by performer-managers who thrived in the new performer-centered environment of the alcohol-free auditorium.

With the threat of concert saloons "contained" by the legislation, most New Yorkers turned their attention to other issues, but pressure continued to be placed on variety and other theater managers by one reform society in particular: the Society for the Reform of Juvenile Delinquents. Under the provisions of the 1862 law as well as earlier theater and excise laws, this society received a portion of theater licensing fees and fines imposed for licensing transgressions.[15] The city, as a result, did little beyond a yearly inspection of theaters by local police to enforce the law. The society was the body responsible for entrapping theaters in transgressions of the law, particularly in regard to the quality and respectability of its audience and the acts presented on the stage.

The Society for the Reform of Juvenile Delinquents, and later other groups associated with the reformer Robert A. Gunn, used volunteers and employees to investigate theaters around the city.[16] Reformers ignored theaters catering to elite audiences and focused their attention on smaller theaters that appealed to the city's working-class population and on theaters offering variety entertainment.[17] Files from mayoral administrations housed in the New York Municipal Archive document ongoing efforts by these societies from the 1870s to the 1890s to revoke the licenses of theaters that had, in their view, broken the law. These documents also show the tensions between police officers and the mayor's office on one hand and the reform forces on the other. In their petitions to the mayor, reformers seemed puzzled and occasionally outraged at the mayor's lack of action in closing theaters; to the reformers the offenses committed by these theaters were so blatant that it was impossible that they would not be closed by the mayor's office. On occasion letters accused various mayors and the police of accepting bribes. Reports from the police show that the officers who visited theaters to inspect them were interested almost exclusively in the degree to which the theater complied with the law; they were also considerably less likely to describe the entertainment presented as lewd or indecent and the customers as people of doubtful character just because the theater catered to a working-class audience.

A number of cases in the mayor's files amply illustrate this point. In September 1890 the proprietor of a small variety hall and saloon known as the Whitechapel at 248 8th Avenue applied to renew his yearly theatrical license. During the preceding months the mayor's office had received a number of letters complaining about this theater. One of these, signed by the Reverend Waldo Messaros, pastor of the Free Baptist Church on 25th Street, between 7th and 8th Avenues, and twenty-two other property owners in the neighborhood, complained that the Whitechapel was "a Concert Saloon of very low type, where loose and noisy men and women congregate and where alleged singing is kept up till one o'clock each morning including Sunday. It is near a Public School and must be passed by the Congregations of several churches, going to and from service. And is in all respects a nuisance, morally a detriment to property, and perpetual annoyance to the residence of this region."[18] Several additional letters echoed these accusations, and another related hearing customers of the establishment asserting that the mayor would do nothing to shut the theater because there was an election coming up and the mayor did not want to alienate voters. This writer also asserted that the police and the political ward bosses were protecting the proprietors.

The police report addressed Rev. Messaros's accusations point by point. In his report, Captain Grant of the 16th Precinct noted:

> John A. Peterson is proprietor of Concert Hall No. 248 8th Ave., and holds concert license for said place under which he is allowed to give vocal & instrumental concerts with permission to sell wine and beer during such performances, music to cease at 12 midnight.
>
> The place is not a concert saloon of "very low type" its patrons are principally working class people of [sic] male & female.
>
> It is not true that singing is kept up until one o'clock each morning. The music both vocal & instrumental ceases at 12 midnight, the license permitting it up to that hour. As regards it being near a public school, the place mentioned is on the East side of 8th Ave., midway between 24th & 25th St., the public school is on North Side of 24th St., between 7th & 8th Aves. The Concerts are principally in the evening when no complaint have [sic] ever been made to me such as contained in enclosed communication.[19]

A second report from Daniel Englehard, first marshal in the mayor's office, confirms the police report, noting:

> I have visited this place a number of times and find that the concert consists of a variety performance, such as music singing &c. While the talent employed here may not be considered of the highest grade, there is nothing disorderly or disrespectful about the performance.
>
> The patrons of this establishment seem to be of the class of people known as mechanicks[20] [sic] and workingmen and their lady friends, ladies are not admitted without an escort—Good order seemed to prevail at all times.[21]

The difference between the complaint and the police and city reports reflects two very different worldviews that could not be reconciled. The reform forces valued not only law and order, but also hard work, sobriety, and upward aspiration, if not upward mobility. They viewed the easy fraternization of men and women in a public space with alarm and regarded all women in such a context as prostitutes. And they viewed the very presence of a variety theater within blocks of "decent" institutions such as schools and churches as both an offense and a threat to the well-being of the neighborhood. These were the values of the American middle class, and they often ran counter to those of the working class, even to members of the working class who may have aspired to class mobility. For reformers, variety halls, particularly those with bars on their premises, were quite literally an immoral and degrading influence in a neighborhood. These establishments offered the twin inducements of alcohol and sex in the form of women on the stage. Like neighborhood strip clubs or adult video stores in today's society, these theaters were viewed as bringing unsavory elements into a neighborhood and offering temptation and vice that would corrupt the children of decent working people by their very presence. That they operated within the law was of little concern to moral reformers, except inasmuch as it indicated a need to pass more restrictive laws.

Opposition to theaters came from a sometimes uneasy alliance between reform societies, local ministers, local property owners (including landlords and business owners), and even other variety managers.[22] Ministers, like the reform societies, saw variety halls as a threat to the financial and moral well-being of local residents. Business owners and landlords cared more about protecting their own income and property values, as did other theater managers, although theater managers also hoped to head off competition from cheaper halls on one hand and similar attacks from moral reformers who saw all theater as evil on the other. And, in New York City, numerous reform societies were dedicated to ridding the city of vice of all kinds. Members of these reform societies viewed politicians as being as corrupt as their constituents, and this distrust of elected authority and arms of government control—such as the police—is clear in letters of protest found in New York City records. As one scholar of American Reform movements notes, reformers distrusted the political process because it "permitted anyone, including the worst sort of rascals, to help select the nation's leaders. Reformers complained that a degraded and sinful majority, manipulated by political machines, had more of a voice in the nation's affairs than they, the godly minority, did."[23]

Unlike reform forces, the police and the mayor's office tended to view variety halls as one of many kinds of business found in the city. Unless theater managers or the performers they hired broke city laws, these establishments were of little concern to civic authorities. The policemen who patrolled the local neighborhoods in which halls were found may well have lived in those neighborhoods themselves and certainly knew their owners and regular pa-trons. Police reports tended to avoid the derogatory language of the antithe-atrical protesters, describing audiences as poor but decent; and even theaters catering to people the police regarded with some suspicion were not necessarily found unfit to operate unless the patrons were engaged in illegal behavior, such as solicitation, on the premises. In their inspections of variety halls catering to the city's working class, the police and city authorities seemed to take the view that even the poorest city residents had a basic right to leisure. It was this view that ran counter to that of the reform forces, who saw poverty as the result, at least in part, of personal weakness and the squandering of valuable resources on evils and unnecessary excesses such as entertainment and alcohol.

Police, until at least the end of the 1850s, had been paid by theater managers to maintain order in the auditorium during performances, and it is likely that police continued to call in on theaters during their regular beat patrols after this date. Policemen who walked the beat were also more likely to know residents of the neighborhoods and to be able to distinguish between respectable working-class women and prostitutes in variety halls. It is also clear from police reports on such establishments that the police did not regard the presence of prostitutes in variety halls as sufficient reason to deny a license. In 1889 a police inspector sent the following report to the Police Commissioner in response to complaints from moral reformers: "I would respectfully state, that in so far as this concerns the 2nd District, from personal observation, and the reports of the Captains comprising the 2nd District, I feel justified in saying that, while there are a number of Ball or Dance Rooms, and Concert Halls within the District, some of which are frequented by prostitutes, and other persons of doubtful character, yet all places are kept under constant surveillance, and are required to be conducted in an orderly manner, and within the restrictions imposed by the law, and in default thereof, they will, as requested by His Honor, be immediately suppressed."[24] While the presence of prostitutes and other disreputable patrons was tolerated by police, the mayoral records provide ample evidence that infractions of the law were not tolerated, and theater managers who were on the record as allowing such infractions were refused new licenses.[25]

The conflict over New York theater licensing reveals the complex relationship between the parties involved—civic authority, theater managers, and moral-reform societies. While it can be seen as an effort to impose middle-class values on working-class institutions, it is also evident that these efforts were never entirely successful. The threat of legal intervention broadened the attention of variety managers beyond the desires and needs of the men in their audiences or the performers on their stages, and they began to accommodate the views of the wider community to some degree. Some managers saw the advantage of expanding their audience to include women and children, and matinee performances targeted specifically at these groups had become a standard part of variety by the end of the 1860s. This development began a long process of internal censorship in which managers interpreted the tolerances and sympathies of their audience and the wider community and gradually enforced these standards in both the theater auditorium and on their stages.

On the other hand, the shift to cleaner and more polite variety did not eliminate the styles of performance that had invited the original legal intervention. Managers who chose to stage shows for a working-class male audience did so, but the ongoing threat of legal intervention also affected the performances they staged. For the rest of the century, managers of sexualized variety incrementally pushed the limits of decency until the civic authorities were forced to act—usually requiring the police to raid theatrical performances—and the ensuing legal battles redefined decency and set new limits for theater managers. In New York City, this process was most frustrating to the reform societies. Letters of protest in the mayor's files show that members of these societies did not understand why their efforts did not serve to eliminate variety entirely. Despite employing undercover agents to visit theaters and entrap managers in transgressions of the law, the most that these societies could do was to shut individual theaters, and even then their evidence did not always stand up in the legal process, which severely undermined the reformers' confidence in the legal process.

Despite the best efforts of moral reformers and the internal reform measures taken by managers of respectable variety, a portion of the variety audience continued to desire sexualized performance, and as long as that audience existed managers would always emerge to cater to their needs. As with the Anti–Concert Saloon Bill in 1862, the moral reformers won individual battles but lost the war against indecent performance. In the wake of the Anti–Concert Saloon Bill, respectable variety came to the fore and flourished, but within a decade sexualized variety had recovered and found new ways to operate; the passage of this law served to open the divide between these two strands of variety. While they would sometimes coexist in an uneasy alliance, sexualized and respectable variety remained fundamentally separate for the rest of the nineteenth century, growing further apart until respectable managers could claim that the two strands were entirely unrelated in the early twentieth century.

Variety in Times
of National Conflict
and Economic Turmoil

Tom Williams has opened a concert saloon in St. Paul, Minnesota, under the name of "Williams' Varieties." Fare 10 cents, but the bill of fare is not of a fair quality—though what can be expected for 10 cents, with a glass of lager thrown in.

The "peculiar institution" is working its way to the very borders of civilization; and we now find still another "Gaiety" in successful operation in St. Joseph, Missouri. . . . The foundling is a "leetle" farther "out West" than any other hall, either for purposes legitimate or ebony, on Uncle Sam's plantation, and is said to be one of the most comfortably arranged and finely fitted up concert saloons in the great West. The company consists of J. D. Murphy, stage manager; D. M. Holt, Irish and Ethiopian comedian; S. S. Purdy, bones, jig, and fancy dancer; T. H. Jefferson, banjo; A. Cooper, violinist; Chas. T. Rivers, alto singer and comedian; J. B. Preston, violincello [sic]; and Miss Sallie Dean danseuse. Thus far, business has been excellent.

—"General Summary," *New York Clipper*, November 12, 1859: 238

By the mid-1850s, variety had begun to extend its reach beyond the East Coast cities of New York and Philadelphia. Like other forms of theater, it traveled along the major transportation routes and appeared first in areas close to New York and Philadelphia, including Wilmington, Brooklyn, Albany, and Boston, but also fairly quickly in Western trading centers, such as the lake port cities of Milwaukee,

Chicago, and Cleveland, and the river trade cities of Pittsburgh, Cincinnati, and St. Louis. Variety did not always thrive in these contexts—the hall in Minneapolis mentioned in the epigraph was short-lived, due to the difficulty in attracting performers, especially in the depths of winter when river trade was impossible and overland travel extremely difficult. But it is telling that enterprising managers sought to establish variety in new contexts and that trading cities, bustling centers that attracted a population of laborers who had disposable income and more clearly defined work and leisure time, were the setting in which variety took root and flourished.

Many of the regional variety halls went largely ignored by newspapers in the cities in which they were established. Like early free and easies in New York, they relied on word-of-mouth advertising and did not pay to advertise in the local press; very occasionally they paid to be included in local city directories. As a result, regional concert saloons can be very difficult to discover, unless they met opposition from civic authorities; out-of-town managers occasionally placed advertising in the *New York Herald*, but the newspaper that carried the most comprehensive coverage of variety in this period was the *New York Clipper.* This newspaper, which was founded by Frank Queen and began publication in 1853, covered all aspects of entertainment in the United States, including sports, gambling, and theater of all kinds. While the *Clipper* was reluctant to cover variety in its first years of publication, by the end of the 1850s it carried reports on regional variety halls as well as the singers, dancers, and comedians who were coming to form the core of variety specialists in this period.[1]

The picture of regional variety that emerges from the sporadic reports in the *Clipper* from the late 1850s and early 1860s is one of a simpler entertainment that relied less on spectacle and large impressive bills than variety staged in New York City. Regional halls were closer to earlier free and easies, offering a small number of musicians, singers, and dancers for the entertainment of their drinking customers, but like concert saloons, the entertainment was presented on a raised stage. Ironically, the passage of the Anti–Concert Saloon Bill brought the practices of New York and regional variety closer together, because the New York theaters that survived did so by simplifying their bills to cut costs. During the 1860s variety developed a loose structure of two acts. The first was composed of a sequence of unrelated acts comprising singers, dancers, and novelties and was followed by a comic or burlesque afterpiece comprising the second act. This format became standard before the end of the Civil War.

By 1859 Philadelphia had seven venues operating as concert saloons or free and easies.[2] Many of these were small halls that were closer to free and easies, but both the ex-equestrian Frank Rivers and the minstrel W. W. Long ran large, respectable variety halls. Many of the small regional halls, especially those in smaller cities, were short-lived, but they demonstrated the widespread appeal of this form and encouraged other managers and performers to begin to expand away from the two East Coast centers of variety. While evidence is only fragmentary, it appears that the entertainment presented in halls outside New York relied more on the services of a small number of highly skilled and versatile entertainers who depicted characters familiar to the audience through song and dance. Some of these performers were also active in minstrelsy, but many were not, and the resulting entertainment reflected the kinds of characters found in an urban environment. This model was employed by variety during the rest of the nineteenth century.

The expansion of variety increased during the first years of the Civil War, following the expanding transportation routes to the front lines and soldiers and to conscription centers in strategic cities. While most of these developments occurred in the Northern states, Southern cities such as Richmond, Virginia, also saw the establishment of variety halls during this conflict.[3] Variety provided a welcome release from the worries of conflict for both prospective soldiers and city residents, and it was often staged at theaters that also staged legitimate drama—tragedy, melodrama, farce, and comedy—as well as newly opened variety halls. George Lea, for example, opened a hall in Baltimore during the Civil War to entertain soldiers.

At the end of this conflict, variety halls continued to flourish in trading centers along rail and river transportation routes, and the expansion of the genre had drawn a great number of men to try their hand at operating variety halls. Some of these men, like Tony Pastor in New York, Dan Shelby in Buffalo, and John Stetson in Boston, had connections to the theater, but the rapid expansion of the genre also attracted outsiders, like William Sinn in Baltimore, who was among the major entrepreneurial managers active after the war. Managers with no theatrical connections were still outnumbered by performer-managers or managers with experience in other theatrical genres. By 1870 variety had emerged as a genre in which these men engaged in friendly competition with each other as they also sought to expand their audiences and to protect the reputations of their theaters from the disreputable associations brought to the genre by sexualized variety and low-class establishments such as the unlicensed hall run by George Lea in New York City. It was important to do this not only to maintain an orderly theater, but also to attract the best possible performers to their stages.

The *Clipper* allowed performers to warn each other about the reputations of theaters and also allowed them to pressure managers into maintaining conditions most conducive for performance. No performer wanted to be caught in a raid by local police or to be forced to remain in a city after the end of their booking to appear in court as a result of an arrest. In 1871 the male impersonator Annie Hindle was arrested on a charge of public intoxication due to the disturbance she raised in a restaurant accusing Fanny Henry, a fellow actress, of stealing jewelry from her.[4] Her arrest and the subsequent court appearance disrupted a full month of her schedule, and she ran two weeks late to her booking at the Walnut Street Theater in Kansas City, Missouri, and was forced to reschedule her booking at the Race Street Varieties in Cincinnati to a later date. In this case she had caused the disruption to her own schedule, but a theater raid could be just as disruptive. As a result performers occasionally placed advertisements in the *Clipper* to warn their fellow actors and to shame managers into cleaning up their halls. The following warning appeared in 1874 and represented a very real concern over the manager's contravention of the state law: "Many Variety performers who have appeared at Acker's Varieties the past season were greatly disappointed on reaching Troy, N.Y., and seeing the establishment. For the information of those who have never appeared there, I would state that Mr. Acker keeps a LAGER BEER SALOON, and in the rear of his place has built a large wooden building without plaster or ceiling, which is called 'Acker's Theatre.' The entrance to the same is through the saloon."[5]

The sheer number of new halls and the influx of new performers resulted in the need for support services and an infrastructure designed to facilitate the booking process. Chief among these were agents who represented both theaters and performers, but other services such as advance agents and bill printers and posters that served the wider theatrical world also expanded to include variety. Agents were instrumental in connecting variety performers with the managers who hired them. Before the advent of agents, performers found bookings by individually writing to managers and detailing their skills. Managers occasionally placed advertisements urging the most sought after and highly skilled performers to contact them, but there was no systematic or easy way to contact traveling performers, especially if their schedule was unknown. And, even if the manager managed to make a booking with a star performer, it was most likely for a future date—the most prominent performers could be booked two seasons or more in advance.

Before the Civil War, an informal booking system that relied on personal contact between the performer and the manager had been the standard practice to some extent in all regional theater regardless of genre. Managers assembled a stock company in New York, but performers also frequently wrote to individual managers requesting work. Correspondence to the theatrical managers Sol Smith and Noah Ludlow includes a letter from the dancer and pantomimist J. F. Schinotti. In this letter, Schinotti describes his many skills that may be of use to the managers. He begins by describing his skills as a painter of scenery and an expert in "Ballets, Combats Dances, &c" as well as in constructing the stage machinery used to create illusions in melodramas and pantomimes. He requests that the managers pay him $30 a week, and in return he would be "generally useful, paint, make properties, play Harlequin, Monkey, Wild men and Old men &c. in comedy."[6] Managers, too, communicated with performers they wanted to recruit for their theater, often placing at the bottom of their advertising in the *Clipper* short requests that specific performers write to them.

Agents facilitated the booking process, especially in the late 1860s and the early 1870s, a period in which variety moved into more and more cities in the Midwest and South, and there was a huge demand for skilled variety performers. This rapid expansion and a relative shortage of performers drove up the wages of the star performers, those individuals who spent the majority of each year traveling from theater to theater taking short engagements of one or two weeks.[7] Performers also sometimes booked a date and then failed to arrive because they had found a better paying engagement. In the early 1870s the *Clipper* occasionally noted performers failing to appear for performances or double booking a particular date. When this occurred managers were left with an empty spot on their bill that they had to scramble to fill at short notice, often with a less able performer. Theater managers forwarded prepaid rail fares to performers in order to ensure their appearance, but this did not always provide enough of a guarantee. When managers used an agent they had access to the agents' clientele of performers and some assurance from the agent about the reliability of the individual. Performers also retained the services of the agent as a guarantee that the theater would be respectable and that they would be paid. In a world that was rapidly expanding, close personal relationships between actor and manager were becoming less possible. While some actors and managers clearly maintained these relationships, many newer performers and managers did not, and agents allowed both parties some measure of security in an increasingly competitive genre.[8]

All sorts of men became agents, but they shared an extensive knowledge of the theatrical world and connections to both managers and performers active in different genres—few agents represented clients in only one branch of the theater. Older, more experienced actors sometimes represented younger performers, and theatrical managers also took on this role, managing bookings for individual actors and actresses and also for theaters in other nearby cities in order to create informal regional circuits—the circuit formed by Spalding and Bidwell in the South was an early example of this, and it linked theaters in Mobile, New Orleans, St. Louis, and Galveston with smaller theaters in intermediate towns in order to attract good performers to theaters in this region. Dr. G. R. Spalding, like George Lea, had started his career as a pharmacist, but he had acquired a circus as part-payment of a loan and had been drawn into managing the enterprise. His business acumen proved useful and his circus flourished. His partner, David Bidwell, was drawn into theater after working on boats and in restaurants. He was an investor in Spalding's circus, and in 1853 he opened the Academy of Music in New Orleans. At the time, Spalding was the manager of the Olympic Theatre in St. Louis, and they exploited the river route between the two cities by running show boats on the Mississippi and gradually expanding their influence to other nearby cities.

Regional variety circuits involved managers from a wide range of genres. Theater managers who rented out their halls to touring dramatic companies featuring a star performer also began to host minstrel companies in the pre–Civil War period and variety troupes during and after this conflict, especially during the summer months. In the 1870s new circuits were formed, guaranteeing touring managers a certain number of weeks' business in any given region. In some cases, these circuits represented a number of managers working cooperatively in order to attract the best possible entertainments to their region or state, but in other cases one or two powerful managers with interests in several theaters were instrumental in forming the circuit. This was certainly true of Spalding and Bidwell in the South, and in the early 1870s the Baltimore variety manager William E. Sinn held interests in theaters in Baltimore and Brooklyn and apparently also worked cooperatively with other variety managers.[9] There were similar circuits linking theaters in smaller cities in Pennsylvania and Michigan.

The 1870s also saw the advent of full-time agents whose entire business centered on arranging theatrical bookings. Probably the most prominent variety agent of the 1870s was Col. T. Allston Brown, who had begun his career as a theatrical correspondent for the *Clipper* in 1855.[10] Brown's early experience reporting on theatrical activities in Philadelphia for the *Clipper* and the local newspaper, the *City Item*, helped him forge connections to the theatrical world, and these were further cemented when he worked as an advance agent for Henry Cooper's English Opera Company in 1860 and then as a treasurer for Gardner and Madigan's Circus for several years after that. After three years of working inside the theater world, he returned to the *Clipper* as an editor of the drama section, which required him to attend all kinds of theater in New York, and he remained in this position until 1872, when he formed his own dramatic agency. Brown's connections in theater paralleled those of the *Clipper*, and he represented a wide range of performers, few of whom were active in spoken drama; the vast majority of his clients worked in variety, circus, and minstrelsy. Brown also represented the leading variety theaters of the period, including Tony Pastor's in New York and William Sinn's theaters in Brooklyn and Baltimore.

Theatrical agents acted as unofficial booking agencies in an era before such services existed, and they frequently represented both actors and managers who were in competition with each other. For example, Brown represented both of the leading male impersonators of the early 1870s, Annie Hindle and Ella Wesner, for several years and advertised heavily for both performers. Brown also represented managers who competed with each other for customers, such as the Theatre Comique and Tony Pastor's Opera House in New York City or all three of the major theaters in Pittsburgh.[11] It is evident from the routes of Tony Pastor's tours of this period that a number of his performers were Brown's clients, and he often played at theaters represented by Brown, but this was not exclusively the case. This attitude was typical of variety in this period, in which rivals frequently helped each other out by referring bookings or providing other support during difficult times. Unlike the United Booking Office, founded by the Keith Organization early in the twentieth century, Brown did not seek to monopolize the booking process, but rather sought to facilitate all sorts of theatrical activities, including those in which he had no financial interest. Actors and managers used Brown's services because of the personal relationships he maintained with a wide range of people engaged in the American theater.[12]

Variety was flourishing in 1873 when the national economy collapsed, plunging the United States into a depression that lasted through the end of the 1870s. Despite early optimism, within a year the effects of the depression were being seen in the theatrical world. The rapid expansion of variety was slowed, and agents became even more important to both performers and managers. More than ever, performers needed a guarantee they would be paid, and managers needed to secure the services of the best possible talent at the lowest price. In order to cut costs, regional managers disbanded their stock companies and ballet corps and increasingly relied on touring variety combinations and minstrel companies to fill their bills. If anything, touring companies required even more infrastructure than individual performers, because all of the arrangements of the route and the costs of touring were borne by the troupe manager, who was responsible for transporting, accommodating, and paying the members of his troupe regardless of the income earned. To facilitate bookings, troupes used the services of New York agents, like Allston Brown, but they also employed advance agents, who traveled ahead of the troupe to secure additional bookings in small towns, place advertising in local newspapers, and make arrangements for the troupe. This introduced one more level of infrastructure into variety, and bookings were increasingly arranged through negotiations between agents and managers, or two managers, introducing a distance between performer and manager that had not existed in early variety.

Touring variety troupes predated the financial collapse of 1873, but until this period they had operated primarily during the summer months when the regular season was over and the theaters shut due to the hot weather. Managers rented their theaters out to out-of-town managers and closed their venues when there were no bookings. Late summer was when regular maintenance and renovation of the theater occurred, so that the improvements could be featured at the beginning of the next season in late September or October. Minstrel troupes had begun to tour during the 1850s, while legitimate theatrical combinations had done so even earlier, and variety managers followed their lead by the early 1860s.[13] Robert Butler and his troupe visited Boston for the first time in July 1863 and performed at the Boston Museum for three weeks. He returned during the next two seasons, extending his stay to approximately five weeks, beginning in the week after July 4 and ending in early August.[14] Butler took advantage of the fact that the other Boston theaters were closed by mid-July, and during his 1864 and 1865 visits his troupe was the only theatrical entertainment available in the city. Despite the hot weather, Butler could attract an audience due to the lack of competition and because his troupe offered a novel form of entertainment. While legitimate theater, pantomimes, and minstrelsy were popular in Boston, there were no concert saloons in the city in this period.[15]

In the late 1860s Tony Pastor, who had been part of Butler's Troupe, continued the tradition of touring during the summer months. He expanded his route to visit towns in Pennsylvania, upstate New York, Connecticut, Rhode Island, and Massachusetts and also lengthened the duration of these trips. During the 1870s Pastor's tours covered more and more territory, and by the mid-1870s he visited Midwestern cities such as St. Louis, Cincinnati, and Chicago annually, usually staying for at least two weeks in each city, often to the distress of the local variety halls. His tours in this period lasted through the entire summer season, from April to September or October. No financial records for these early troupes survive, but Pastor's account books from the early to mid-1880s do, and they reveal the extent to which a support infrastructure had grown up around variety as well as the many miscellaneous expenses borne by the variety manager.

During the 1870s large legitimate theaters such as the Boston Museum or variety halls such as the Griswold Opera House in Troy, New York, most often hosted touring companies. These theaters already held a theatrical license and could provide support staff, although troupes traveled with a small group of backstage support staff and musicians because they also played venues that could not provide needed personnel.[16] Some legitimate theaters and halls, particularly those in smaller cities, rented out their facilities at a flat rate. Pastor's account book for his 1882 touring troupe indicates, for example, that when he played at the Music Hall in Albany, New York, he paid the theater $70 per night in rental and kept all of the door receipts. His account books show no expenses for a license, stagehands, or ushers, but he paid for advertising in local newspapers, for the printing of posters and bills, and for bill posting to advertise the event around town. In smaller cities, managers booked into halls-for-hire, which provided no services at all. When Pastor played in Poughkeepsie, his expenses for a single night's performance included $60 for the hall, $23 for a theater license, $5 for stagehands, as well as advertising costs. In this case Pastor's expenses were justified as he attracted a large audience to the theater and grossed nearly $550 in one night, while incurring $166 in expenses.[17]

Pastor's account books also indicate that the manager of the touring troupe paid all transportation costs for not only the sets, costumes, and other baggage, but also for all of the performers and support staff, including the company's advance agent who traveled ahead of the troupe to arrange performance details. Railroad fares and carriage hire routinely appear in Pastor's account books. Pastor also paid the fares of performers joining or leaving the troupe once the tour was underway and for accommodation costs, although the latter expense occurred only when they played for two or more days in any city because the troupe traveled at night.

A third kind of arrangement, and one that occurred most frequently between Pastor and the managers of theaters in large cities, was paying for the hall rental with a percentage of the ticket sales. In this case the manager of the host theater assumed all of the costs of advertising and all or most of the costs of bill printing and posting, which was not an inconsiderable weekly expense, and he occasionally also paid for a share of the bandwagon that transported the troupe from the railroad station to the theater in a lively street parade. Given the advertising value of this event and the fact that the host manager's profits increased with a larger audience, his willingness to help pay these costs is understandable. During the early 1880s Pastor gave up as much as 50% at large theaters, such as the Grand Opera House in New York City, but more typically he took 70% of the door and the local manager received 30%. This kind of arrangement with the manager of the Providence Opera House, George Hackett, netted Pastor $963.90 for two evening performances and a matinee, while Hackett got $413.10. Pastor's expenses for those two days were

$232.32, including hotel costs and railroad fares, but not salaries, which he calculated as a weekly expense and took out of the week's profits.[18]

Advertising accounted for an increasing part of the variety managers' budget. Managers had placed advertising in local daily newspapers in order to attract customers to their halls from as early as the 1850s, but during the 1860s and 1870s these advertisements grew larger and more complex. Variety managers, and the advance agents for touring managers, placed advertisements in all of the local daily newspapers. When local newspapers included a theatrical report, agents may also have offered them prewritten reviews of the show, an early version of the press kit sent to media to advertise entertainment today. Reviews of performances, particularly those in dailies from small cities, echo the advertising copy for the show almost verbatim, and it is entirely possible that the newspaper sent no one to the theater and composed the review based on the advertising copy. Managers usually placed advertising for a week or more before their performance to create excitement and anticipation, and Pastor's account books from 1882 show that he spent $140 placing newspaper advertisements in his first week on the road. In smaller cities such as Poughkeepsie and Paterson, New Jersey, these costs were less than $18, but in Newark they were nearly $45, and in Albany they were over $60. During the 1880s these costs rose considerably as the numbers of newspapers and magazines increased.

Touring managers also paid the cost of printing and posting theatrical bills and the occasional rental of a billboard. Job printing costs were relatively low in this period—Pastor's account books for 1882 show him spending just $1–$2 per day on these costs. But, like the cost of advertising in local and national newspapers, these costs rose precipitously during the 1880s. Local job printing offices, often run by the printer of local newspapers, were used to print tickets and coupons for the performances, but printing companies in larger cities produced the handbills and posters that were carried by the advance agent; larger charges appear occasionally in Pastor's accounts for "Michigan Job" or "Boston Job."[19] By 1886 Pastor was spending larger amounts on both newspaper advertising and bills. In this season he added $12 per week to advertise in the dramatic newspapers, and his bill for printing had risen to almost $120 per week.[20] Bill posting was also a recurring expense, particularly in cities in which Pastor was responsible for his own advertising. The cost for this service was approximately $20 per city.

The expansion of variety had encouraged the existing theatrical infrastructure to extend its support to the new genre and to develop services specifically suited to its needs. This process began in the wake of the Civil War, but it continued through the 1870s and was further refined in the face of the devastating economic collapse of the mid-1870s. The introduction of layers of management into variety irreparably damaged the relationship between performers and managers. Performers were willing to accept reduced wages in the economically difficult 1870s, but as conditions improved performers expected their wages to rise again. The lower wages had become an integral part of the managers' new business models, and they were unwilling to abandon a strategy that earned them increasing profits. The introduction of an infrastructure had industrialized entertainment paralleling the developments in manufacturing earlier in the century.

82

Managers of regional theaters were also able to displace more and more of their operating costs onto the managers of touring troupes, which enabled them to survive and sometimes prosper during the difficult economic climate of the 1870s and early 1880s, but also forced touring managers to keep their expenses as low as possible. This development in variety also inserted an even greater distance between performers and theater managers than had been the case in the early 1870s, and it allowed regional theater managers to identify more with the local community than with the wider theatrical world—when managers had to personally negotiate bookings with actors and actresses. Connection to that world gave them an advantage, but with the advent of well-connected agents, personal connection to the theater world became less necessary. The development of infrastructure that provided a level of security to theatrical professionals also allowed entrepreneurial managers with few or no connections but considerable business acumen to enter variety. William Sinn is an early example of this kind of manager, and the 1880s saw a number of similar managers entering variety from the business world and introducing business models designed to maximize profit.

The performers responded to this shift in the same way as industrial workers—by agitating to unionize. In 1880 an advertisement appeared in the pages of the *Clipper* protesting the unfair pay rates offered by managers and attempting to organize for the mutual benefit of all performers:

> Aggressive Capitalists in the Amusement World, as elsewhere, taking advantage of the necessities of people in the profession who work for wages, have already forced the salaries of performers and others far below a living basis. . . .
>
> The stage must not be permitted to degenerate through the machinations of unscrupulous managers, who take no pride in the profession except in reaping the shekels earned by others.
>
> To elevate and extend this great power by a harmonious action which shall cause every worthy performer to feel himself as much a man as his employer . . . a movement has been inaugurated, and is already powerful,

looking towards the arbitration of a just relationship between Capital and Labor, and a more equitable division of the earnings.[21]

The language of this call echoes the language of organized labor, which was also increasingly active during this decade. It is clear that managers and performers no longer felt connected to each other. Actor-managers such as Tony Pastor were now rare, and entrepreneurial theater managers sought to maximize their earnings in a similar way to industrial capitalists. This early effort at unionization failed, as did a second attempt by the same group in 1886.[22] Vaudeville performers did not succeed in unionizing until the early twentieth century, when the White Rats was formed, and even this union was largely ineffectual in fighting Keith, who was emerging as the preeminent vaudeville manager.

Managers had the ultimate power in this conflict as they had the option of refusing to employ actors who were involved in labor unions. Those involved with the early unionizing efforts were aware of this. In their second attempt to form a union in 1886, Carl Weber and Will Ingersoll stressed that the membership of this organization would be secret so that members would not "jeopardize" their livelihood, but could still reap the benefits of membership. Despite this precaution, the Universal Amusement Bureau failed, most likely because, as with industry, nonunion performers were always available to undercut the effectiveness of potential labor action. That, and retaliatory efforts taken by managers, also brought about the demise of the White Rats in the early twentieth century.

The expansion of variety away from the East Coast during the Civil War had brought increased opportunities for performers and managers, but it also pushed the limits of the business models that had developed in the decades before the war. The reliance on personal contact between managers and performers was impractical given the numbers of people engaged in variety. The infrastructure that developed benefited everyone because it provided some measure of guarantee to both performers and managers, but it also made it easier for businessmen with no previous theatrical experience to enter the field and to compete as equals against experienced performer-managers. The rapid rise in wages at the beginning of the 1870s shows that these men employed the same tactics that George Lea had used a decade earlier—buying the best performers available with high wages. Had the economy not crashed in 1873, there would almost certainly have been a move within variety to curb wages, because the high wages paid during 1870–72 were unsustainable.

The economic failure allowed managers to impose lower wages, and it also encouraged entrepreneurial managers from different regions to cooperate with each other in order to maintain their prominent position as local managers. In 1876 theatrical managers formed an association whose members worked cooperatively in booking and production in order that all could benefit. This association worked to bring imported stars and plays to the American stage, set wage levels so that managers would not have to outbid each other, and cooperated in booking. While most of these managers were associated with narrative drama, the list included a number of prominent managers who booked variety acts, including David Bidwell of New Orleans, Ben De Bar of St. Louis, and Col. W. E. Sinn.[23] This kind of agreement between managers was instrumental in developing both the business practices and infrastructure that were crucial to the emergence of vaudeville later in the century.

The entry of businessmen into variety also shifted management away from men who understood the working-class audience that the genre served and were attuned to their needs and desires. The performer-managers of the prewar period were intimately familiar with their audiences, and while they sought to accommodate the introduction of new laws and head off pressures of moral reformers, they also responded to the demands of their audience, literally interacting with them from the stage and joking with hecklers. Entrepreneurial managers active in respectable variety, on the other hand, did not tolerate hecklers and were also more likely to police the content of the acts appearing on their stages to bring them into conformity with middle-class ideals of decency. Sinn, for example, prominently advertised that he did not hire cancan dancers or tableaux vivant artists.[24] This proved to make good business sense, and it also helped to head off the attentions of moral-reform forces, whose focus returned to variety entertainment during the economic crisis.

Just to Please
the Boys
Seriocomic Singers

Then don't be shy,
 for single life's a sin;
Fair lady, as the proverb says,
 Faint heart did never win,
Then don't be shy,
 But do the best you can,
And when you go a courting,
 Why speak out like a man.

—"Speak out like a Man," in *Jennie Engel's Bouquet
of Melodies Songster* (New York: R. M. De Witt, 1873), 39

I n March 1864 the young seriocomic Jennie Engel traveled from New York City, where she had been working in concert saloons and very occasionally in other kinds of theater as an olio singer, to Washington, D.C.[1] She had secured a three-year contract to perform at the concert saloons run by George Lea, who operated halls in the capital and in Baltimore. While Lea had carved himself a lucrative niche running sexualized museum shows in New York City, his halls in Washington and Baltimore were run as respectable variety halls. The Anti–Concert Saloon Bill had shut him out of the New York market, and ever the canny businessman he had headed south to take advantage of the thirst for diversion from the serious war news in the strategically important city of Baltimore, and Washington, which was the political center of the Union. Jennie Engel and Dora Dawron, along with the resident ballet company, were the featured acts on a bill that also included male comics and singers and a minstrel quartet. Engel received top billing in Lea's advertising, and the theatrical reporting stressed her youth and beauty as well as her accomplished singing.

Dora Dawron had begun her booking at Lea's theater a week before Engel arrived, but while both women were singers they performed very different kinds of acts. Engel was a seriocomic who sang sentimental songs, ballads, and light comic songs in the soprano range that depicted a young woman not unlike herself. Dawron, on the other hand, was a serious singer who had more considerable vocal skills than Engel, but she appeared as a novelty act, dressed in a costume that combined a man's suit on one side of her body with a woman's dress on the other. Billed as a double-voiced vocalist, Dawron performed ballads and duets in which she sang both parts, alternating between tenor and soprano as she turned the appropriate half of her body toward the audience. She was incredibly popular with audiences and had frequently found employment with P. T. Barnum, who exhibited her in his theater, as well as in concert saloons. But reviews and advertising make no mention of her appearance beyond noting her unique costume. Dawron's appeal lay in the wonder she elicited in her audience as she accomplished the apparently impossible task of embodying both male and female. While this skill won her popularity, it also put her into an entirely different class of act than the seriocomic Jennie Engel.

Young and pretty, seriocomics represented an ideal femininity to the men in the audience; she was the girl of the city, sometimes feisty and teasing, often able to take care of herself, but always desiring a young man to call her own and to take care of her. Songs depicted American-born characters almost exclusively, although sentimental Irish characters were also the province of female singers. Few of her songs were comic, and even the comic Irish songs sung by seriocomics fell far short of the cutting humor characteristic of Irish songs sung by men; they avoided the heavy dialect characteristic of men's songs, relying much more on sentiment and charm. The billing of seriocomic became more common after 1860. In the 1850s very few women had appeared in free and easies, and those who did were most often related to the proprietors of these venues or to male performers who appeared on the same bill; this helped guarantee their safety and their reputation—no decent women were present in the saloon, which was a male space.[2] The crowded and noisy auditorium of the large concert saloons made them an inhospitable performing context for all singers, and it must have been an intimidating environment for young women. Despite this, the numbers of female singers in variety had increased by 1860, and they increased even more after the passage of the Anti–Concert Saloon Bill. Some of these young women had begun their careers as dancers and cultivated their singing ability as a way of remaining on the stage into their 20s; others were supporting performers active in burlesque, operetta, spectacular, or other branches of the theater who were tempted to move across to variety by the chance to take a leading role and earn better wages; and some were immigrants from England who had been active as singers in music halls.

The ideal for women that emerges from songs sung by seriocomics during the 1860s and 1870s falls a long way from the middle-class ideal for femininity and gives insight into the kinds of behavior deemed acceptable in working-class culture. Female characters depicted in women's songs were as active and flirtatious as men. They were quick to advocate for themselves, defend themselves against men—usually revealing the men as inadequate in the process; they were also quick to sing the praises of the men to whom they were attracted. The songs sung by women echoed the sometimes contradictory views of women held by men in this period. On one hand, women used their appeal to men for their own benefit. While men viewed this trait as dangerous and insidious, women's songs depicted it as pragmatic. Men's songs frequently depicted women working, usually as waitresses or in manufacturing, and the woman's job was viewed as part of her identity or at the very least explained how the male protagonist came to meet her. Mentions of work or a career are absent from women's songs, although many songs depicted young women wandering freely about the city and even the countryside, often alone.

In many ways these songs depict characters not unlike the working-class women who appeared in the pages of the *Police Gazette* who engaged in paid employment when it was needed but whose major concerns were domestic. The women depicted in variety songs were also more focused on life and enjoyment and particularly on flirtation and marriage. While seriocomic singers depicted a more independent, robust, and even earthy or knowing femininity than the middle-class ideal, they did not seek to dispense with men, nor did they wish to challenge their superiority. Men in women's songs were always in charge, even when they were behaving badly, and when women won, it was because men realized the error of their ways and allowed them the victory. While women in variety were not expected to adhere to middle-class ideals of the period, there was also an unwillingness to allow women to appear as grotesque or ugly. In variety, the depiction of grotesquely comic immigrant characters by women did not occur until well into the 1880s. During the 1860s and 1870s old, ugly, or comic women were most likely to be portrayed by cross-dressed men following the traditions of burlesque and other comic theater.

The vocal training of the earliest singers in variety was most likely informal and their vocal skills limited, although surviving sheet music shows that young women were expected to have greater musical skill than male singers.

The vocal range called for by most women's songs was not much more than an octave, but women actually sang these songs, while men could also employ a spoken delivery style; women occasionally interpolated short segments of spoken commentary into their songs, but these were limited and most often served to either introduce the song or to segue into the chorus. The audience's expectation of the seriocomic was that she be pretty and tuneful; but while good looks were of primary importance, audiences did not tolerate bad singing for very long. Reviews of Jennie Engel's performance in the *Washington National Intelligencer* described her as "young and accomplished" and a "vocalist of superior ability."[3] The reviewer clearly considered her youthful beauty and singing ability as being equally important. This expectation is also reflected in reviews found in the *New York Clipper*. When a woman sang in a weak voice or out of tune, reviews noted that fact and generally found the performance inadequate. They were less critical only when the singer was very young and presumed to be lacking in experience, and then reviewers usually advised the theater manager to mentor and train the young woman, giving her smaller supporting roles to play first so that she could gain the skills and confidence needed for a soloist.

After the Civil War, Jennie Engel emerged as one of the leading seriocomics active in variety. She was part of Tony Pastor's summer touring troupe in 1872 and 1873, and she also frequently worked with the variety managers Josh Hart and John Stetson. Engel's career reached its peak in the mid-1870s, and she was prominent and well known enough that the music publishers began to use her image on the covers of sheet music and to publish songs from her repertoire. After more than a decade working as a seriocomic, Jennie Engel had outlasted most of the women who were her contemporaries. Women active as singers in variety had careers that lasted less than a decade—young women worked from about the age of 16 into their early 20s, and most left the stage when they married. The performance reviews in the "Variety Halls" column in the *Clipper* chronicle literally hundreds of female singers active in the 1860s and 1870s, but few were noted as exceptional by this newspaper's reviewers, and only a small proportion of these women sustained careers of more than two or three seasons. Female performers who married within the profession were able, in some cases, to form double acts with their husbands, but the greater impediment for seriocomics was advancing age—there were no roles for old women in this genre—and seriocomics who sustained careers did so only as long as they were able to maintain a youthful appearance.

Engel's career path shows the problems facing female performers, whose value lay in their youth and good looks as much as their performance skills. During the 1860s Engel was active primarily in and around New York City, developing her skills in the context of concert saloons and early variety. She worked for the leading managers of the period, including Hitchcock, Butler, and Pastor, and by the mid-1860s was also taking part in the afterpieces that ended variety bills. While it is not clear when Engel was born, she was most likely in her late teens by 1860 because she was never billed as a child performer. A number of songs featuring images of Jennie Engel on their covers survive from the 1870s, and the pictures show a rather somberly dressed woman in her late 20s or early 30s.[4] This photograph, and earlier drawings that appeared on sheet music covers, presented Engel as a respectable singer whose appeal did not lie in revealing her legs or other parts of her body to her audience—she is shown in profile, her hair in long ringlets piled onto her head and flowing over her shoulder, wearing a dark colored dress with a lace collar. Engel appears no different than any respectable middle-class women, who were presumably part of the audience to whom the publishers of the sheet music sought to appeal, and there was nothing about Engel's sentimental repertoire that made it unsuitable as parlor songs. A later picture of Engel from sheet music printed in San Francisco in 1878 depicts her in a very different manner. Engel is shown in a similar black dress and with long curly hair swept up at the back of her head, but in this drawing she looks directly ahead in a coquettish way with her head slightly to one side and a small smile on her face; here, the appeal is sexual.

Engel's career took a similar turn at the end of the 1870s. Engel continued to appear in variety theaters that presented the cancan and other sexualized acts, even though the most fastidious and reform-minded performers were beginning to avoid these bookings. While she appeared at theaters run by Tony Pastor, Josh Hart, and Col. William Sinn as late as 1878, Engel had also begun to take bookings at theaters such as the Volksgarten and Harry Miners's Bowery, both of which catered to the working-class and increasingly ethnic population living in lower Manhattan. Engel also performed at Thomas Snelbaker's Vine Street Opera-House in Cincinnati during 1879 when Snelbaker was increasingly raising the ire of local authorities in that city. In retrospect it is easy to view this as a decline in Engel's career, but at the time it was more likely that she was willing to take whatever bookings allowed her to continue to work. If Engel was a fading star in the most respectable of variety circles, she still possessed skills valued by managers who catered to an all-male audience, and Engel appears not to have significantly changed her act in this setting. The variety world was in the process of renegotiating its values, and either Engel did not recognize this or she did not care. Engel's choices and her increasing age did matter, however, to the most respectable theater managers, and after 1880 when Engel performed in New York she did so to Bowery audiences rather to the more respectable and upward-aspiring audience of Tony Pastor's Tammany Hall Theater in Union Square.

The problem Engel increasingly faced during the 1870s was competition from younger singers, who lacked her performing experience but had youth and good looks on their side. By the mid-1870s, variety was able to attract talented singers with training who came from more affluent backgrounds. Lillian Russell, who was from a middle-class family and the daughter of an early feminist, began her career on Tony Pastor's stage in this period. Russell had trained as a singer and possessed the skills to succeed in operetta. Trained singers who worked as supporting actresses in burlesque companies also took bookings in variety as a way of gaining more experience and to fill time between bookings in narrative theater. Jennie Hughes was one of these singers, and her career shows the degree to which variety had changed in just a decade. Hughes came from a good family from Fair Haven, Connecticut, and learned music as part of her education at Boston Grammar School, while Engel almost certainly came from a working-class New York family with ties to the theatrical world.[5] After finishing school Hughes studied singing for a year with Signor Ernani, who had also taught the singer Minnie Hauck. Her first role on the stage was at Niblo's Garden, where she performed a page in the drama *Ruy Blas* in January 1870. She continued to perform at Niblo's and supplemented Lydia Thompson's Troupe later in that season.[6]

After just one season performing in operetta and burlesque, Hughes moved to variety, winning immediate success because of her singing skills, youthful good looks, and repertoire based primarily on Irish ballads. Hughes was an ambitious young woman apparently dissatisfied that she had been constantly relegated to supporting roles, and particularly pants roles, in the burlesques staged at Niblo's. Variety offered Hughes the starring role she desired, and she flourished in this genre, quickly becoming one of the leading seriocomics of the period. Her vocal training gave her an advantage over untrained singers like Engel—while the men who patronized variety halls generally did not attend opera performances, they did appreciate strong singing skills. Opera was increasingly financially out of reach to working-class patrons, but serious and trained singers found a warm reception on the variety stage, and all singers were held to high standards.

Hughes's vocal training also allowed her the career mobility that Engel lacked. While Engel slipped gradually into low-class variety during the late 1870s and 1880s, Hughes was able to move back into roles in burlesque, building on her success in variety. In 1876 she played the role of Zeena in *Amour, or the Arabian Nights* in Philadelphia, and the following year she played Idex in *The Naiad Queen* at the Boylston Museum in Boston. For the next several seasons Hughes moved between burlesque and operetta and variety, sometimes leading her own touring company, which played both genres.[7] She returned permanently to operetta when she joined the Cinderella Opera Company in 1880 and was later hired by D'Oyly Carte as part of his American Company to perform *Billee Taylor.* In her 30s Hughes increasingly took matronly roles such as aunts and mothers in these productions, but she continued to work steadily. Reviews indicate that Hughes had gained weight during her 30s, and her advancing age made these roles more appropriate. Tracing the end of Engel's long career, on the other hand, is difficult. She apparently remained on the stage through the 1880s, although there is little record of her activity; a single advertisement from 1899 suggests that Engel had moved into musical theater playing eccentric roles—she was billed as part of "The Clever Company" performing in the play *Why Smith Left Home.*[8]

Both Jennie Engel and Jennie Hughes gained enough prominence within the world of variety that publishers used their names and images to sell music and to publish repertoire associated with them. The first piece associated with Engel is a song sheet published by Henry De Marsan during the early 1860s. In 1868 the St. Louis publisher Compton and Doan issued a series of songs associated with Engel and featuring her portrait on their cover. Between 1870 and 1873 six songsters containing Engel's songs were published in New York, and in 1874 the Boston publisher G. D. Russell and Co. also issued a series of songs under the title "Miss Jennie Engel's Favorite Songs." This collection gave Engel credit as lyricist of three songs, and in one case composer also, and it indicates that she had garnered enough success that publishers were willing to take a risk publishing songs she had written and not just use her image to market songs by professional songwriters.[9]

Engel's success can best be gauged when compared to other female singers of the period. Most of the songsters bearing the images of women had titles such as *Our Girls Songster, Black Crook Belle Songster,* and *The Bewitching Girl Songster* and contained a mixture of songs associated with blackface minstrelsy, variety, and touring burlesque troupes.[10] These songsters delivered a similar appeal to sexualized variety and the growing trade in photographic images of burlesque actresses, but the songs they included were overwhelmingly associated with male performers. While women, or at least the visual appeal of women, were central to variety, female singers were not among its leading performers, and with a few exceptions, there was little to distinguish them from each other. It was not until the 1870s that a small number of seriocomic singers, including both Jennie Engel and Jennie Hughes, had gained enough popularity with their audience to have their own songsters printed, but even these included songs by male singers too.[11] Engel's and Hughes's success put them into a class of female performers who were treated in similar terms to male performers by managers and other people associated with the entertainment world.

Jennie Hughes had less published music associated with her, primarily because of the depression that occurred soon after she entered the profession. I have found three songsters that bear her name, two of which were published in 1872 and the last in 1874.[12] The economic collapse brought a temporary halt to the production of these books of songs, and by the time business had recovered, Hughes had returned to operetta. But the three songsters that bear Hughes's name contain over 200 songs, most of which were associated with her—the *Rose of Erin Songster* alone contains over 130 songs and is three times as large as either of the other songsters bearing her name or any of those associated with Engel. Few other women of the period had this level of popularity, and most were lucky to have a single song included in songsters associated with leading male performers.

Despite the differences between the vocal skills and training of Jennie Hughes and Jennie Engel, the repertoires of the two women are remarkably similar. Irish sentimental songs formed the core of both women's repertoire. These songs often centered on loss and longing for the homeland and for loved ones far away. In some cases they depicted young women waiting in Ireland for a beloved to return, and in others the homesickness of the immigrant in a new country. "You'll Soon Forget Kathleen," sung by Jennie Engel early in her career, at the American Theatre, 444 Broadway, is an example of the former.[13] While the song sheet does not give the author, it describes the inspiration for the song in an introduction: "The circumstances which gave rise to this beautiful ballad, occurred during the visit of a friend of the Author to the North of Ireland, and was most feelingly related to the Author by him. It was the parting of a young tenant-Farmer from his betrothed, on going to seek his fortune in some distant land." The lyrics that follow are in the voice of Kathleen, pleading with her beloved not to leave and doubting his promise that he will never forget her:

> 'Tis vain that you tell me: you'll never forget me
> To the land of the Shamrock, you'll ne'er return no more
> Far away from your sight, you will cease to regret me
> You'll soon forget Kathleen, and Erin Go Bragh!

This song, which closely entwines the love of a woman and a nation, is heavily sentimental.

Songs describing homesickness are equally sentimental and were intended to unite the audience in tearful sentimentality. "Erin My Country" is one of a number of similar songs in *Jennie Hughes' Rose of Erin Songster* that depicts remembered Irish landscapes, distant friendships, and a carefree youth:

> Oh! Erin, my country, though strangers may roam
> Thy hills and thy mountains I once called my own
> Thy lakes and thy valleys no longer I see
> But warmly as ever my heart beats for thee
> Oh! "Cushla Machree" my heart beats for thee
> Erin! Erin! my heart beats for thee.[14]

This song, and many of the Irish songs in the repertoires of both women, combines a potent mix of sentimentality, homesickness, and a nostalgia for rural landscapes and close community that was accessible not only to the Irish in the audience, but also to urban working-class populations. Unlike comic songs, which united the audience in shared laughter at the expense of a racial or ethnic group, sentimental songs such as these united everyone in the audience—the loss expressed was familiar to all regardless of ethnic background—and these Irish songs performed a similar function as English folk songs such as "Down by the Old Mill Stream." The women who sang them allowed all of the men in the audience to transcend their differences and shed a tear to songs that would also not have been out of place in a middle-class parlor.[15]

Apart from the sentimental fare, both women's repertoires included songs that represented life in the city for a young working-class woman. The subject that predominates is men and marriage, and many songs sang the praises of men who would make the perfect mate. Military men featured prominently in these songs, and their uniforms and bravery were greatly admired, even after the Civil War. "The West Point Cadet," the lyrics to which were written by Jennie Engel, who also performed the song, depicts the young soldier in idyllic terms.[16] He is attractive because of his bravery and his willingness to sacrifice himself for a patriotic cause. The narrative depicts the woman remembering her meeting with a cadet in her youth and their waltz at a ball, where his brave gallantry added excitement to the romance of the dance. The character is represented as an ideal but also in the past, and the song carries the implication that he died during the war. The central character in Engel's song "Marching with the Band" took a more pragmatic approach to falling in love with a soldier.[17] Her beloved plays trombone in the army band, and the song details her delight in his appearance and in going to see him marching on parade. The narrative of this song is one that ends in marriage rather than love sacrificed to war. The West Point cadet represents ideal love because he did not live to disappoint the girl, while the trombone player is depicted as a good, steady, and reliable spouse.

Men were the primary focus of songs sung by seriocomics, and songs often praised the qualities of the ideal man. "Show Me the Man," which was sung by Emma Alford and others during the 1870s, spells these qualities out in its four verses.[18] The first verse stressed the importance of a love of fun, joking, and leisure:

> Show me the man who loves a jest,
>   Oh show me such a one
> Who's not above a jolly lark,
>   At honest hearty fun
> Who never pull a lengthened face,
>   At mention of a spree
> When such a man presents himself,
>   Why that's the man for me
> Chorus: Show me the man, that is if you can,
>   Whatever his rank may be
> I'll love him for life, and make a good wife,
>   But show such a man to me.

The following verses called for courage and honesty, a man who was not looking for a fight but could defend himself if needed. She also wanted her man to take her to balls and concerts, buy her jewelry and pretty bonnets, and not abandon her at home alone once they were married. And, finally she wanted a man to be her partner and to share, as equals, the bad as well as the good in life. The last verse is telling, because it shows that the central character understands that life is full of hardship. She does not, however, want to be rescued from the bad times, but rather wants a partner who will share them with her, in the same way that she wants to continue to share fun and leisure with her husband after marriage. The relationship that is depicted as the ideal in this song is not companionate marriage as it would be practiced by the middle class in the later nineteenth century, but rather a union of near equals who were both employed and worked together for mutual benefit. At the same time, the woman depicted in this song does not expect to be fully the equal of her husband.

Songs in Jennie Engel's and Jennie Hughes's songsters and printed sheet music echo similar desires from women. And, both women also sang songs in which the central character took an active role in courtship, manipulating their suitors and encouraging physical contact. "Squeeze Me, Joe," sung by Jennie Hughes, relates a tale of a young man's courtship of a young attractive widow. In the repeating chorus the widow expresses her delight, not only at the courtship but also at the physical affection the young suitor shows:

O squeeze me, Joe, O squeeze me, Joe,
　　It makes me feel so jolly you know
O squeeze me, Joe, O squeeze me, Joe,
　　And if you love me, tell me so.

Clearly, the woman in this song is just as active a participant in the process
of courtship as the man and vociferously encouraged him to overcome his
shyness and to propose to her.

Jennie Engel's song "Speak Out Like a Man" acknowledged the games
played by young women in courtship and encouraged men not to be intimi-
dated or fearful of women or to be put off by a young woman's reluctance to
accept his advances. The song text suggests that shyness and modesty were
merely a pretense that women hid behind, but that a persistent man who
continued to woo his beloved would be rewarded because marriage was in
her best interest:

When at your kind attentions,
　　We appear to take offence
Pray don't be disconcerted,
　　That's merely a pretense
If to wring your ears we threaten,
　　We of course mean no such thing
It's merely a suggestion—
　　We ourselves should like a ring.

In this song, the woman's primary concern is marriage, and she refuses the advances of her suitor only to make sure that he is serious about marrying her. The
lyrics gently chastised men for being too easily discouraged, and Engel's advice
to them, "And when you go a courting, Why, speak out like a man," reminded
the men in her audience that they were supposed to be the superior sex.

This kind of song, along with comic songs that related the stories of court-
ships gone wrong, offered advice to the men in the audience on love and
marriage, which were topics that elicited great anxiety for men—including
the men depicted in songs sung by both women and men in the context of
variety. Courtship and love was a realm in which women seemed supremely
confident. While most women's songs seemed to center on love and marriage,
these women were not sheltered or chaperoned in their courting, nor were
they limited to a domestic setting. Women's songs rarely if ever commented on
work, but a significant number of songs depict working-class women wandering through the city and country alone. Jennie Engel's song "Gushing on the
Cars" related the joy of traveling through the countryside by train, and while
a young male companion is mentioned in the final verse of the song, the first

two verses focus only on the thrill of speed and the joy of exploration as the central character passed through the countryside:

96

> The joy of all this life,
>   Is riding on the cars
> For those who love excitement,
>   Your sense it never mars
> It makes the pulses quicken,
>   And the heart to throb and beat
> It causes pleasant feelings,
>   As with time you do compete
> Chorus: Yes, rattle, rattle,
>   all the way by rail
> Down upon the level,
>   Yes across the plain
> Over hills and mountain,
>   And the flow'ry dale
> Crossing bridge and brooklet,
>   Gushing o'er the rail.

The joy and freedom in these lyrics is echoed by the melody of this song, which was also composed by Jennie Engel. The last line of the chorus ascends over an octave to express the excitement of the singer. The thrill of travel and free exploration was one that was familiar to Engel, who had been traversing the nation as a performer since her late teens. While this experience was not typical for working-class women in this period, travel was often a necessity for men, who followed seasonal work and also traveled in search of fortune or at least a better living. Engel's song makes a necessity into an adventure and allowed her a moment to bond with the men in her audience through a shared experience. This song, along with a number of motto songs that encouraged class solidarity, is of a type not found in the repertoire of Hughes, and it signals a shift that had begun in variety during the 1870s as new performers, including those like Hughes from middle-class and nontheatrical families, entered the profession. Jennie Hughes's repertoire relied more heavily on Irish and sentimental songs than Engel's, and, while she did sing songs that depicted women taking an active role in courtship, the women she portrayed sought less independence and were less mobile than Engel's characters.

This subtle shift was part of a larger change in female performance aesthetics in the mid- to late 1870s that disadvantaged older women in variety, who were accustomed to interacting freely with their audience. It also explains why any number of both male and female variety performers did not find success in vaudeville; by the 1890s even men were expected to censor their material to accommodate women in the audience, and if they were unable to remove the raunchier material from their routines they suffered. The audience for high-class variety or vaudeville of the 1880s, 1890s, and later adhered more closely to middle-class values and no longer took pleasure in coarseness or vulgarity. While men had to censor parts of their acts, this change affected women to a greater extent. Both men and women had interrupted their songs with spoken interpolated commentary into the 1870s, but during the 1880s female performers abandoned this practice, perhaps under pressure from managers. Keith certainly began to regulate the content of acts, as well as the costumes worn by young women, from the 1890s. Female variety performers also found themselves competing with imported English acts beginning in the 1880s. English performers were viewed both as greater novelties and also as being more refined than their American compatriots. This placed American performers at a disadvantage, and in some cases it also resulted in younger American performers modeling their acts on those of the English rather than on the older generation of Americans.

97

Dutch, Irish, Minstrels,
and Other Characters
Male Comic Singers

Oh, I like to speak right out my mind
    When I got a chance you see,
If I keep myself awake you'll find
    Dat you don't got over me!
Von der Germany I don't been long,
    Und I like dat Uncle Sam;
So you play me for a "flat" you're wrong,
    Und dat's der kind of mans I am!

—*Dats der kind of man wot I am*, words by Master Barney,
music by W. F. Wellman Jr. (New York: W. F. Wellman Jr.,
1871)

I f the primary role of women on the variety stage was to be pretty and tuneful, then the primary role for men was to be funny. In a world before stand-up comedians, songs provided the platform on which comedy was built, supplying a central character, a narrative full of comic events, and an opportunity to interpolate longer comic monologues or commentary within the song. Songs were flexible and designed to accommodate multiple interruptions, and most relied on comic improvisation rather than on refined singing skills. Comic songs formed the core of men's repertoire and were based on specific character types familiar to the variety audience. These types were shared by variety and minstrelsy, as well as other popular theatrical genres, and were based on the kinds of people found in East Coast cities and particularly New York. Workingmen, upper-class men, the

Irish, the Germans, and African American characters were all staples of these forms, and the major difference was in proportion rather than performance style. Variety was distinguished from minstrelsy primarily because African American characters did not dominate the stage, although they were always present. For this reason, it can be difficult to distinguish these forms in their early days, and the ties between these genres were both deep and complex. Because there were so many different types of men on the variety stage, this chapter will focus on dialect comedians and specifically men who portrayed Irish, Germans, and African Americans, and men whose acts relied on ballad singing and portraying workingmen with no specific ethnic identity will be discussed in the following chapter.

In the mid-nineteenth century, singing, or rather the presentation of character through song, was an important means of presenting comedy. The song became the means by which performers shaped their comic persona. Some performers presented multiple types in the context of a single act with only minimal adjustments to costume, such as a change of coat, or the addition of props, such as different hats or walking sticks. But performers who specialized in a single character type had emerged by the early 1850s, and the most common types in variety were blackface minstrels, the Irish, and the Germans, also known as Dutch comedians. Most of the Irish and blackface performers moved freely between variety and minstrelsy, performing fairly similar acts regardless of the context. Dutch comedians were more common in variety than in minstrelsy. The focus here will be on three men: Charley White, a minstrel performer and sometime manager; Phil Gannon, an Irish singer and jig dancer active in the 1850s and 1860s; and the Dutch comedian Gus Williams, whose career extended into the later nineteenth century.

Phil Gannon and Charley White were both active in variety and minstrelsy before the Civil War, but Gannon's career ended before variety flourished in the 1870s, while Charley White managed to sustain his career until his death in 1891.[1] Gannon was born in New York in 1830 and found employment as a boy with a city merchant. His free time was spent avidly attending public exhibitions. Gannon was very much part of the urban working-class male population that free and easies catered to, and he used his skills as a jig dancer to win employment in venues offering miscellaneous amusements.[2] In 1849 he was pitted against James Summers, the Champion Dancer of England, and won, and was billed as a champion jig dancer whenever he appeared after that. By 1850 he had moved into minstrel performance, performing in blackface as a dancer, and within three or four seasons he moved into concert saloon performance as an Irish jig dancer and comedian. Gannon drew on his family's Irish heritage in his act, portraying a range of Irish characters from comic country bumpkins and recent immigrants, to savvy urban residents, to soldiers and sailors and even occasionally women. His repertoire was less cruel in its depiction of Irish characters than many of the songs sung in variety and minstrelsy.

Early Irish songs dating from the 1850s and even into the 1860s include a large number of cruel parodies of the Irish in which the Irishman was depicted as a drunkard and a fool. The tone of these songs suggests that the Irish were either not present in the audience or in the vast minority. Nonsense was a dominant feature of these songs and is present on a number of levels. Nonsense syllables, delivered in a heavy brogue, were present in song lyrics in both the chorus and the verses. Songs also often related a narrative that was plainly fanciful and suggested that the character depicted was drunk or delusional. The depiction of the Irish changed subtly during the later 1860s and early 1870s, and while cruel parodies continued to be present, the number of sympathetic depictions of the Irish grew, deepening and softening the earlier stereotype. Gentler depiction of the Irish had begun to appear by the end of the 1850s as Irish immigrants and their children entered minstrel and variety performance, and Phil Gannon was very much part of this trend. Later during the Civil War, songs that praised the courage of the Irish began to appear, and after the war songs encouraged communal pride and the formation of a hybrid identity in which ethnic and American identity were melded and also firmly located within an American setting.

The least sympathetic depictions of the Irish were not unlike the least sympathetic minstrel songs of this period in that the central figure was depicted as an unsophisticated man who spoke in a heavily dialect that was intended to heighten the comic effect. Song sheets dating from the very early 1860s, such as "Paddy McFadden" sung by Harry Fox and "August the One" sung by M. Cox, present this kind of character.[3] Both of these songs rely heavily on nonsensical lyrics, particularly in the chorus. For example, "Paddy McFadden" begins:

> Paddy McFadden was lazy and fat
> And the hair of his head grew out of his hat
> He had but one son and he christened him Pat
> Musha whack Fadden, Fadden ni ah.

The words of this and subsequent verses make little sense, and each verse ends with the same nonsensical line. The chorus is similarly nonsensical and also ends with the same tagline. "August the One" relies on a similar kind of lyric:

It was on August the first of Novimber
And June the second of May
The parties all did assemble on Monday
Or some other day
Whack fol de rol rol de ri do.

While this song lacks a chorus, it also relies on a repeated nonsense tagline, and by the third verse the lyrics clearly identify the central character as Irish.

The presence of regularly recurring lines of nonsense syllables is not peculiar to songs about the Irish. Songs depicting native-born characters such as "I Spy Your Little Game" and "The Suit of Corduroys" both employ choruses comprising nonsense syllables, and in neither case does the chorus reflect stupidity or lack of judgment on the part of the central character.[4] But both of these songs are comic songs, and the nonsense choruses reinforce the comic situations presented in the text and may also be closely related to the convivial bonding associated with audience participation in singing. Nonsense choruses and repeating taglines allowed audience members to join in and provided a momentary riotous escape on the part of the audience that was also safe because it was firmly contained by the structure of the song and could not get out of hand.[5] In the context of a cruel parody in which nonsense was a characteristic of the verse, a nonsense chorus compounded the effect of the song by providing the audience an opportunity to join in the singing if they desired.

While Phil Gannon's songster includes a small number of songs with nonsensical choruses, they are vastly outnumbered by sympathetic songs; of the thirty-five songs and sketches in the songster, only three employ nonsense choruses, and of these only one portrays its central character cruelly. While Irish characters were central to Gannon's act, the songs portray him as an "everyman" whose only distinguishing feature was his accent. Gannon's act relied not only on comic songs, but also on extended monologues that allowed him to more fully develop his character. Gannon's songster includes a five-"act" burlesque of Richard III set to a medley of preexisting airs, including "Bow Wow Wow," "Paddy Casey," and "Yankee Doodle," among others, that condenses Shakespeare's play into seven pages of text and song. Nothing about this sketch transforms Richard into an Irishman, and the comedy lay in the translation of the play into vernacular language and the associations brought by the tunes to which the texts were set. A second sketch, "The Irish Janus," relates the story of Patrick Shakespear O'Brien from his birth in the Irish countryside, through his travels to Dublin, to England, and then finally to Philadelphia. While there are funny events related—such as his teaching Queen Victoria to dance the Irish jig—this character retains his dignity, and by the end of the sketch is depicted as an American patriot, albeit one with a heavy Irish accent:

> But the star Spangled Banner is the Banner for me
> She has Stripes for the Tyrants and Stars for the Free.

This shift in tone reflects the increasing numbers of Irish performers on the stage and in the variety audience, but even then performers most likely maintained a small number of cruelly comic songs to perform if they found themselves playing to an audience that was hostile to the Irish—even for an Irish performer, it was more important to please the audience than it was to uphold ethnic pride or dignity.

By the 1870s the Irish had come to form a core part of the variety audience. This is indicated by the increasingly sympathetic portrayals of the Irish during this decade, which also saw the urban Irish dramas of Harrigan and Hart staged at the Theatre Comique in New York City. In this decade, little distinguishes Irish songs from other seriocomic songs depicting native-born white men, except for the names of the characters included in the song and almost inevitable references to St. Patrick's Day and the use of dialect, which was most likely supplied by the performer even when it was not indicated in the text. Joseph P. Skelly's song "Clear the Way! (Parade Song)" is an example of this more sympathetic kind of song.[6] Like the songs celebrating Irish heroes of the Civil War, it constructs an Irish American identity that maintains links and fondness for Ireland but is firmly rooted on American soil:

> Hark the drums are sounding near us,
>> Flags are waving ev'rywhere,
> Thoughts of home come back to cheer us,
>> Shamrocks in our hats we wear.
> Now we're going to fall in line,
>> We're the boys can cut a shine,
> We'll forsake the hod and spade
>> For old Erin's grand parade.
> Chorus: Clear the way! Clear the way!
>> Irish boys are marching;
> Shouts of gladness you will hear,
>> Martial music front and rear.
> Clear the way! Clear the way!
>> Erin's flag is waving;
> Down the street we're sure to meet
>> A loud and hearty cheer.

The following verses describe other aspects of the St. Patrick's Day celebrations, including drinking, the mingling of young men and women, young men playing pranks, the bond formed through shared memories of Ireland and the voyage across to the United States, and the dance staged at Hibernian Hall. This celebration is depicted in positive terms as a communal occasion full of good cheer, celebration, and community pride. Within a period of twenty years, the depiction of the Irish on the variety stage had moved from hostile to accepting, although anti-Irish songs never disappeared completely. In the 1870s and 1880s, as in earlier decades, when facing a nativist audience, singers needed to be able to accommodate their anti-Irish feelings. These same songs could be shaped and softened through spoken interpolations and a milder use of dialect when playing to a more sympathetic crowd.

The Irish and the blackface character from minstrelsy were two male character types particularly associated with sentimental singing, and in many ways the songs sung by these two character types were similar. While the black character longed for the safety and rural life of the plantation in blackface sentimental songs, the Irish character longed for the green fields of Erin. None of the songs of this kind that I have found were overtly disparaging, but the association of sentimentality—which was the province of female singers—with the Irish may well have signaled their inferior manhood, even as it allowed their audience to enjoy the emotional pull of the song. The meanings and functions of these songs were just as open to interpretation as those of comic songs, and both were equally affected by performance style to shape the audience reading. In both cases songs could be performed earnestly, with the emphasis placed on sentimentality. But burlesque and parody were also possible with the use of exaggerated physical gestures and eye rolling that reduced the central character to a pathetic figure of fun.

The song "My Good Ould Irish Home" was part of Gannon's repertoire, and the published song text notes that it was sung to the melody of "My Old Kentucky Home," providing a further link between the black and the Irish sentimental characters. In this song the Irish immigrant misses his homeland and longs to return to it. This character does not express any affection for his new home, nor does he comment on his life away from Ireland. The three printed verses dwell instead on Ireland and the things there that he misses. The song begins:

> Och my heart still yearns for my good ould Irish Home,
> > Though grieving may all be in vain
> Bad luck till the day that I ever through to roam,
> > For I'll never see my counthry again
> Methinks I can see my own little cabin door—
> > The thought makes my poor bosom swell

But sad is my fate—I will never see it more—
    So my good ould Irish home fare thee well.
Chorus: —Thin spake no more of comfort;
    oh, spake no more I pray
For my heart still turns to the home I've left behind,
    To my poor, but happy home far away.

This song can be seen as sympathetic to the longing of the immigrant, but it could also be seen as disparaging to the Irish by depicting them as effeminate in their sentimentality. The longing of the Irishman for the famine and poverty of his homeland may be viewed as irrational, but he is not as irrational as the black character in the original song, who longs for slavery. This kind of ambiguity is not uncommon in variety songs; indeed songs that allowed multiple interpretations were preferable because they opened performance to the widest audience possible.

While Charley White began his career in minstrelsy like Phil Gannon, he made his career portraying a character with whom he had no connection. White was one of the many men active in blackface minstrelsy in the 1840s and was among the pioneers who formed independent minstrel companies in that decade. Born in Newark in 1821, White had entered minstrelsy before the mid-1840s and may have begun performing in blackface in the context of circus by the age of 20.[7] While White was a skilled minstrel, he seems to have had little patience for the itinerant life of a touring performer, and by 1846 he had opened his own theater, the Melodeon, at 53 Bowery.[8] Even though White's early career had been in minstrelsy, he always offered a more diversified entertainment at his theater, and he spent the rest of the 1860s and 1870s moving between minstrelsy and variety performance and also working in management positions in variety.

During the 1870s White's career foundered, and he continued to move in and out of variety management, with his theaters almost inevitably failing. While he was a skilled performer and acknowledged as a skilled stage manager, White lacked the management skills necessary to run a theater. By the end of this decade, his name had begun to appear primarily in nostalgic reports of early minstrelsy as the men active in the first generation of performers died. White began to appear in lower-class variety halls and was also the recipient of a number of benefit performances, and he might have slipped into an impoverished obscurity in the 1880s except that he was cast as "Uncle Job, the Preacher" in a production of the *White Slave* staged at Niblo's Garden in January 1883. This was a blackface role that allowed him to use skills honed in a career in minstrelsy, and he continued to perform in various productions of this piece until his death of pneumonia in 1891.[9]

The material White performed in variety differed very little from the kinds of songs performed in minstrelsy. He sang comic minstrel songs in which the central character told a fanciful narrative or sang the praises of his beloved. The comedy lay not only in the heavy dialect of the lyrics, but in the style of dress and the physical movements, including grotesque dance and exaggerated facial gestures such as eye rolling and grimaces that accompanied the song. Some of the songs written and sung by White were comprised almost entirely of nonsense. The song "Kitty Kimo,"[10] which was written by White and sung by Dan Emmett, relies on an antiphonal structure, with the repeated line "Sing song, Polly, won't you ki me oh," which could be repeated by the whole group of performers, or the audience, or both. The chorus is pure nonsense and is similar to the cruelest of Irish songs:

> Camo, kimo, daro, war, my high, my ho, my rumsti-pumididdle
> Soot bag, pidly-winckem, linck 'em, nip cat
> Sing song, Polly won't you ki me oh.

Even the chorus employs the repeated tagline.

Many of White's songs focused on courtship and on the loss of a beloved to a romantic rival. These were not sentimental songs of love, but rather songs that placed the blame squarely on the central character. The narrative of lost love was not uncommon in songs of this period, but in these cases the loss was played for broad comedy, which reinforced the idea that the central character was foolish or violent or inadequate. The song "Bless Dat Lubly Yaller Gal" relates the tale of a man whose love has left him. The nonsense in these lyrics is less obvious than in "Kitty Kimo," but no less problematic. In the first verse, the central character bemoans the fact that his beloved has left him, but a slow interjection suggests that the reason she left was the threat of violence:

> Oh now she's gone and left you
> for fear dat you might harm her
> To day after tomorrow, she's gone to Alabama.

After the second verse, in which the central character sings of the attractive qualities of his beloved, this melody is repeated but with new lyrics:

> Oh now she's gone and left me,
>   my heart is fill'd wid sorrow
> I'll find some oder yaller gal,
>   An I'll marry her to-morrow.

This character is so quickly consoled over his loss that any sentimentality disappears, and he is reduced to a foolish figure who elicits little sympathy. While this depiction of African Americans was also part of minstrelsy, in the context of variety, black Americans could appear only as foolish and as lesser beings. Sentimental songs that allowed the audience to empathize with the singer were increasingly the province of the Irish, and when White appeared in sketches in blackface his character was most often relegated to the lowest rung of a social hierarchy in which ethnic characters and Anglo-Americans jockeyed for advantage in a crowded urban environment. In the context of variety, blackface characters were crucial in constructing whiteness on the stage—in comparison to these characters, all other ethnic types present in the 1860s and 1870s could be constructed as white—and because African Americans were not part of the variety audience, there was no reason to soften or moderate the depiction of this character, as was the case with the Irishman.

While the occasional African American performer, such as the dancer Master Juba, was valued in the context of minstrelsy, there was no such tolerance on the variety stage. I have found no evidence of African American performers in variety before 1900, and even after that date only a small number of black performers seem to have been active in vaudeville.[11] The original context for variety performance—the working-class saloon—may be one of the reasons for the absence of African American performers. Working-class men were not well disposed toward African Americans, or immigrants for that matter, viewing them as unwelcome competition who drove down wages in the labor market. The persistent presence of women as performers in variety may also have been a factor in the exclusion of black performers. The flexible format of variety bill, and the practice of performers assisting each other in sketches, meant that there was no way to ensure that a woman would not share the stage with African American performers. Given the reaction to performers such as Bill "Bojangles" Robinson and Bert Williams appearing on stages with white actresses in the context of early-twentieth-century revue, it should not be surprising that variety was segregated before 1900.

While both blackface and Irish characters came into variety from minstrelsy, the German character was one that developed most fully in the context of variety. Germans were not a significant part of the early variety audience in the same way as the Irish, primarily because of the language barrier. Only a small number of songs featuring German characters date from before 1870, and these are associated with singers from Philadelphia, most likely because of the concentration of Germans in that city and possibly also due to the involvement of Germans in early variety in Philadelphia. The "Lager Bier Song," sung by Jerry Merrifield, Sanford, and Rochez at the Arcade Concert Saloon in New York City in the mid- to late 1850s, is the earliest example of a German character song I have found.[12] The structure of the text shows that the song was sung by a soloist and chorus, who sang antiphonally:

> Now ladies and gentlemen, just in time
>   Chorus—Swilly willy wink um boom,
> To come and listen to mine rhyme
>   Chorus—Swilly willy wink um boom,
> My clothes is made of cash-e-mere,
>   Chorus—Swilly willy winkum, hire a saw,
> By dam I likes mine lager bier
>   Chorus—Swilly willy wink um boom,
> Chorus—Ri tu re an na, tu se an na,
>   Swilly willy winkum, hire a saw,
>   Ri tu re an na, tu se an na,
>   Swilly willy wink um boom.

The verse that follows relates the story of a German man who likes to drink beer, and his habit eventually kills him. The text is in dialect and has elements of nonsense and slapstick (for example, the German is constantly being hit in the head, first by the barman for not paying his bill, then later by his wife). The nonsense sung by the chorus is not significantly different from that in the Irish songs discussed above and also allows the opportunity for group singing while reinforcing the comic nature of the song. Later German songs published in the 1870s use "Dutch" dialect, but I have found none that employ nonsensical lyrics such as these; Irish songs, on the other hand, continued to include nonsense and dialect in subsequent decades. This suggests that this might be a very early example of a German dialect song, which started by being modeled on existing Irish or minstrel songs and gradually grew distinct from them in the later 1860s and 1870s.

The American-born children of German immigrants were the first to enter variety entertainment. Some, like Jennie Engel, were of mixed American-German parentage, but others grew up in immigrant households learning to speak both German and English and being comfortable in both contexts. German-speaking audiences did not patronize variety theaters, but preferred German entertainment venues that operated alongside variety halls. Beer gardens and other German venues offered similar kinds of entertainment to variety halls, although the emphasis tended to be placed more heavily on musical performance by brass bands and on art singing than on sung comedy. While German communities were largely separate from English-speaking society, the position of Germans as small business owners and craftsmen meant that a stereotype based on the most obvious features of Germans—broken English and a love of beer—soon emerged in popular theater.

At the same time, Germans were not subject to the same hostility as the Irish. German immigrants tended to be better-educated professionals who did not actively compete with unskilled and semiskilled laborers, who were at the bottom of the labor hierarchy and had more competition for work. Also, Protestant German immigrants were able to integrate relatively easily into the wider Protestant American population and were easily understood by them. For this reason songs depicting the Germans made fun of their problems with the English language and their love of beer, but the humor rarely if ever sought to dehumanize Germans in the same way as songs depicting the Irish or African Americans. The "Dutch" character type moved into a wide range of theatrical genres and could still be found in the early twentieth century when the linguistically challenged, beer-drinking German character made his way into film.[13]

The German performer Gus Williams had the longest career of the three performers considered here. He entered variety in the late 1860s as a comic singer, but soon moved to portraying German characters exclusively. Williams, whose real name was Gustav Wilhelm Leweck, was born in New York in 1848, and he enlisted to serve in the Union Army in 1862.[14] At the end of the war he joined a theatrical troupe in Huntsville, Alabama, and by 1868 was performing regularly with Tony Pastor in New York and John Stetson in Boston. By the mid-1870s Williams was among the highest paid variety performers in the country, earning $150 a week.[15] While Williams was a dialect comedian, the charm of the characters he created was that they were essentially little different than Anglo-American men. Most of his songs centered on love or courtship, on life in large American cities, and on work and making ends meet in hard times. The only thing that distinguished his character was his accent and comedy based on the challenges of learning to navigate the world in a second and unfamiliar language. Unlike the Irish or African American characters of minstrelsy, the German character in Williams's songs was allowed dignity, and he did not sing longingly of his love of his distant famine-plagued homeland or the idyll of plantation life; the German as constructed in variety songs was a good and enthusiastic migrant, seeking to take full advantage of the opportunities offered him in his adopted country.[16]

Several songs associated with Williams give a sense of the character he created. "A Dollar and Fifteen Cents" is a comic song that depicted a man so in love with a waitress at a saloon that he eats a huge meal without realizing it. Like many of Williams's songs, this piece came in two versions, one in standard English and the other a "Dutch" version that he performed. In the nonethnic version the chorus details the list of food consumed during his meal:

Roast beef, boiled ham, pickled beets, and pie and cheese
Plum pudding, wine sauce, which she said was "immense,"
Small beer, sausages, fried eggs and butter toast,
Which added up together, makes a dollar fifteen cents.

This list of food is distinctly English, and it is served by a waitress described as a Yankee girl. During the second verse the protagonist flirts with the waitress, and by the third verse they are husband and wife. The narrative of the German version is essentially the same except that the action takes place in a lager bier saloon and the waitress is German. The diet is also typically German, which no doubt added to the humor:

Roast pork, boiled pork, bickled [pickled] eels und sweitzer kase,
Blood puddidg, sauer-kraut, vich you said vos immense,
Rhine-vine, sausages, smear-kase und liver wust,
Dat, added up togeder, makes a dollar fifdeen cends.

Despite the slightly different setting of the German version of the song and the very different food consumed, the basic narrative of the two versions is the same. In each the central character meets a pretty girl and flirts with her, and in the final verse of both versions he is married to her. While the Anglo couple lives on Shawmut Avenue in the Flatbush section of Brooklyn, the German couple lives on South Fifth Avenue, New York, which was then an immigrant neighborhood.

I have found a number of examples similar to this in which the song either comes in two versions, one Anglo and one German, with essentially the same narrative, or is a German version of an older English song. Williams was one of many singers, including Tony Pastor and Ella Wesner, who performed a version of "The Belle of the Ball," which exposes the many deceits practiced by women to maintain their beauty into middle age. He also sang versions of "Champagne Charlie," "Moët and Chandon," and "After the Opera"—all songs that were part of the repertoires of a number of singers of this period—and there is little about much of his repertoire to distinguish it from his contemporaries who portrayed American characters. In "The Finest Police in the World!," which was sung by Williams in the context of a sketch with the same name, Williams portrays a city policeman who is brave and dedicated to his job and to enforcing the law:

We're the finest police in the world,
    And our praises are sung in the papers
When we find a disorderly man,
    Very soon he is cur'd of his capers

We are the pride of the nation wide,
    And around out footsteps, no law is defied
The rogues all fear us on ev'ry side,
    We're the finest police in the world.[17]

This song is typical of much of Williams's repertoire, which did not specifically identify his character as German. What transformed any song sung by
Williams into a German character song was his performance style—his use of
dialect and interpolated commentary to flesh out the central character.

Williams's experience with John Stetson placed him in an environment
in which he was able to develop a wider range of theatrical skills. Variety in
Boston was a more mixed affair than it was in New York City, and even after
the Civil War theaters were more likely to combine variety with narrative
theatrical pieces than stage a show that was comprised exclusively of variety
acts.[18] Williams most often worked at the Howard Athenaeum, which routinely
staged one or two pantomimes and a variety olio each evening. This experience
allowed Williams to learn skills associated with narrative theater, and he was
able to further hone these skills when he toured with Stetson's Star Dramatic
Company, a variety and burlesque company that also featured the pantomimists Maffit and Bartholomew and the burlesque actresses Adah Richmond and
Lillie Hall among others.

In 1878, despite his success in variety, Williams began taking roles in narrative pieces. He stepped in to replace Mr. Leffingwell in the role of Maid
Marion in the burlesque of *Robin Hood*, although the reviewer complained he
was unsuitable for the role and that he was too "coarse," and after several more
performances he left the role.[19] Despite his early lack of success, Williams persisted and during the following season had a comedy custom written for him.
Entitled *Our German Senator*, this piece was built around Williams's trademark
German character and was a huge success with audiences, although reviewers
periodically complained about its lack of substance and literary merit:

> The piece proved to be an elaborated variety sketch, thinly guised as a
> farcical-comedy. There is extended through three acts material that is not of
> greater specific gravity than could be compacted into one act of reasonable
> length. . . . The piece is without literary merit, and certainly can lay claim
> to no excellence as a work, either for its comedy of dramatic attributes.
> Yes this compound affords Mr. Williams some excellent opportunities for
> the presentation of his peculiar abilities as a character comedian. His great
> superiority in his line make it easy for him to please an audience, even when
> offering little. As the easy-going, somewhat stubborn German, he makes a
> laughable creation, a highly commendable performance. But he is out of
> his element when distributed throughout an evening's performance. The

edge, the zest, is taken from his work. In short, Mr. Gus Williams, as the star of a three-act play, is by no means as diverting, as funny, as enjoyable as Mr. Gus Williams of the variety stage, restricted to a crisp fifteen or twenty minutes. All his work is done equally well, and apparently satisfied the audience, but it was nevertheless genteel variety.[20]

Despite the critic's complaints, this piece and the several that followed it attracted audiences, signaling a divide between the aesthetic expectations of the audience and theatrical reviewers. Reviewers admired Williams's performance skills, but they agreed he was out of place on the narrative stage. Reviewers' expectations were shaped by more serious narrative drama, and they expressed dismay at the free-wheeling improvisatory nature of much of Williams's comedy. On the other hand, audiences clearly loved Williams in these pieces, and they allowed him to sustain his career into the 1890s, when he used his success on the narrative stage to transition into vaudeville, finding bookings in Keith's theaters. Williams was one of the few old-time variety performers who managed this transition, primarily because he had spent the 1880s in light narrative comedies.

Williams's career shows the flexible nature of musical theater as it expanded in the late 1870s and 1880s. The move to musical comedy was one that a number of variety performers attempted, but few were as successful as Williams. Ella Wesner twice attempted to move into similar pieces that centered on her trademark character, but they quickly failed on each occasion. The Irish duo Harrigan and Hart expanded their variety sketch comedy into full-length topical urban comedies that were hugely successful but in many ways did not seek to expand variety's audience beyond the working class. Unlike Harrigan and Hart, Williams toured widely around the country, appearing for a minimum of two seasons in each new show he undertook. He did not play to the traditional variety audience, although the theaters he played in were generally midrange houses whose cheapest seats were well within the reach of a working-class audience. Williams appealed to an audience that aspired upward and yet had not abandoned their desire for the free-wheeling fun of the variety hall. When B. F. Keith hired Williams to play in his respectable vaudeville houses in the 1890s, he did so because he wanted to tempt this same audience—the grandchildren of Williams's original audience from the 1870s who now identified themselves as middle class—back to the diversified entertainment their grandparents had enjoyed.

Just Ordinary Workingmen
Seriocomic Songs for Men

Some say that Central Park's the place,
    For fun of every kind;
On Broadway and Fifth avenue
    Much pleasure others find.
But I'm a different sort of chap
    No fun in that I see,
For when I want enjoyment
    The Bowery for me.
In the Bowery, in the Bowery,
    For beautiful girls with bright eyes and dark curls
In the Bowery, in the Bowery,
    That's where I reside when I'm home.
—"In the Bowery," in *Tony Pastor's Opera House Songster* (New
York: R. M. De Witt, 1873), 38

W hen Tony Pastor began his variety career around
1860, he entered a form of theater that, although
relatively new, had already developed fairly well-
defined character types for performers. Many of these, like the blackface or
Irish characters, were present in other forms of theater. Before he reached
his teens, Pastor performed with a minstrel troupe that included veterans like
Charley White, learning the conventions of that form as a tambourine player.[1]
He also apprenticed as an acrobat with Nathan's Circus and later performed
as both a clown and ringmaster with a number of different circuses. In his
variety performance, Pastor drew on his role as the singing clown more than
any other, and this character was central to his performances for the rest of his

career. Pastor's character had no specific ethnic identity; while his father was an Italian musician, Tony and his younger brothers had been born and raised in New York, and the characters he portrayed reflected that experience.

In his act Pastor performed a mix of comic and seriocomic songs that represented a native-born American character, not unlike the men in the audience. Like seriocomic songs for women, the primary aim was to move or amuse the audience with the poignancy or sentiment of the song. The narratives often centered on lost or failed love, but the mood remained generally light rather than heavily sentimental or maudlin; in these cases, the situations revolved around misunderstandings and misbehavior rather than death or other tragic circumstances, and the overwhelming message of the songs was "learn from my mistakes." Pastor's repertoire was large and varied—a newspaper article published in the *New York Times* near the end of his life estimated that he had memorized 1,500 songs during his career—and it included a wide range of types, including Irish and German.[2] Most of his songs represented ordinary men, mostly working-class men, but some also portrayed upper-class men and men of leisure who could enjoy all of the pleasures the city had to offer.

Because of his long career, dozens of songs from Tony Pastor's repertoire are readily available in the form of song sheets, printed sheet music, and also in archival sources, but much less is known about how he, or any of the performers active in variety, performed these songs. In an era before sound recordings, there are no comprehensive descriptions of performances offered in memoirs or in newspaper reviews printed in the *Clipper*, even of a prominent and successful performer like Pastor. Few other newspapers reviewed performances, including those that carried variety advertising, and even the *Clipper* offers little more than fragmentary snippets that need to be pieced together and added to surviving printed music from this period. The features of Pastor's act that emerge most clearly from these fragments are his engaging personality and his ability to charm his audience. These sources have less to say about the quality of his singing voice or the finer details of his act, and despite Pastor's long career, which spanned from the 1840s until just after the turn of the century, little of his early repertoire has survived in published form. The same is true for songs sung by other variety performers of this period. The ephemeral nature of the product, combined with the marginal position of the working class as consumers, means that many of the songs referenced in performance reviews in the *Clipper* cannot be found.

Most of the sheet music that survives from the 1850s was intended for a middle-class audience of home music makers, and these songs are vastly different from the comic song sheets—single pages of lyrics, some with melody, but most only indicating the "air" to which the satirical words were to be sung—

that survive from the 1860s. In the late 1850s, songster collections associated with variety performers began to appear, but again, these rarely contain more than the lyrics and sometimes the air to which they were sung. Song sheets and sheet music of songs from the earlier 1850s are largely absent. Surviving evidence from later in the 1800s, along with a consideration of the history of music publishing in the United States, suggests reasons that little or no repertoire from the earliest period of variety survives. Music publishing in the early part of the nineteenth century was closely allied not only with sellers of music and musical instruments, but also with book publishers who published large numbers of popular songs in the form of songsters or song sheets.[3] Songs were published in full score by music sellers who catered to customers who had the financial resources to buy musical instruments and to learn to read musical notation, and this repertoire was predominantly sentimental or religious or based on opera and popular dance forms of the period, such as the polka and the schottishe. It took at least two more decades for commerce to fully appreciate consumer power of the working class, and popular songs in full score did not appear in large numbers until the last decade of the nineteenth century and the first decades of the twentieth century, when the ownership of a piano came to be a mark of upward social mobility.

For professional variety performers, music was part of an aural tradition that involved some degree of written transmission but was by no means bound by the notation. Songsters from the 1860s reveal that many of the songs sung in variety were set to preexisting melodies, and this is true of a large proportion of Pastor's repertoire from this period. In some cases these tunes were folk songs, particularly in the case of Irish character songs that often used well-known Irish melodies such as "Irish Washerwoman" or "Rosin the Bow." Older commercial popular song tunes were also used, sometimes alone and sometimes in medleys with folk songs.[4] The use of preexisting songs, as well as parodies and reply songs, suggests that this music relied to some degree on audience members knowing the web of associations invoked by the reuse of tunes. This was particularly true when a singer substituted new lyrics to the verses that commented on the original song, but retained the original chorus—in performance the two songs were, quite literally, in conversation with each other. These multiple associations, along with the language of songs that relied heavily on puns and other wordplay as well as topical and local references, support the idea of the early variety audience being a relatively homogenous group sharing a common tradition of English language and humor. There were also a large number of English popular songs in American variety, particularly in the late 1860s and early 1870s as the genre expanded. Songwriters such as G. W.

Hunt and George Cooper and Alfred Lee who wrote music for English music hall singers are extremely well represented in songsters from this period.

In this period, music publishers sometimes bought songs from performers, using their name and their image on the cover to attract sales. In this process, the performer might be credited as the author of the song, particularly if it was a folk song that the performer had adapted to meet his own needs. The song "Ten Thousand Miles Away" was among a number of pieces the ballad singer Charles Vivian sold to the San Francisco publisher M. Gray in the early 1870s, and the sheet music attributes it to Vivian. This song was, in fact, an English folk song that related the story of a young man whose love was transported to the Australian penal colony and who commits a crime so that he can join her. The melody and words of Vivian's 1872 version are almost identical to a version found in a collection of Australian folk songs published in the 1960s.[5] Given that Vivian was a ballad singer and had emigrated to the United States from England in 1867, it is not surprising that he had this song in his repertoire. When Ella Wesner performed this same song, reviews note that she did so in a convict's costume to make explicit what is implicit in the song text, and Tony Pastor further transformed it by using the melody with its associations of imprisonment as the melody to which he set a parody about a prisoner being sent to Blackwell Island in New York. This illustrates the degree to which the appeal of these songs lay in the skills and personality that each variety performer brought to its performance.

By the mid-1870s American songwriters such as Joseph P. Skelly, Edward Harrigan, David Braham, and others had also begun to publish songs they had written to be performed in variety, and the use of folk song and older popular song melodies decreased, at least in the printed texts included in songsters. Given that the general infrastructure supporting variety had increased through the 1860s and 1870s, it is likely that songwriters and publishers had also come to see the value of this genre to contribute to their income. Advertising placed in the *Clipper* suggests that in this period songs were supplied to performers by songwriters, who also supplied orchestra parts.[6] Performers then further adapted this material to their needs, adding verses, changing or adapting melodies, and possibly also reselling these modified versions to publishers, who preferred material associated with specific performers because it increased their sales.[7] The many thousands of songs that survive from the 1870s and later share a similar structure, simple accompaniment, and limited melodies using simple rhythms, and they were designed not to be musically complex or interesting, but rather to provide the foundation for performance. When it came to popular song, the ability to sing a new melody was less important than the comic and topical lyrics delivered through song and the appeal of the interpolated commentary added in the context of performance.

The one element of songs that printed forms—song sheets, songsters, or even sheet music—cannot capture is performance. It cannot be assumed that the performers strictly adhered to the melody as given in the notation. Late-nineteenth-century recordings of English music hall singers indicate that comic performers often presented the text in a kind of heightened speech that occasionally lapsed into melodic singing, and songs were also interrupted by comic monologues performed over a vamped accompaniment. Reviews of American variety performers, and song texts from songsters published during the 1860s and 1870s, suggest that these practices were also employed in the United States. It should also not be assumed that the performers followed the texts printed in songsters—even those with long comic interpolations—as given in the printed form. Performers often added verses to songs to keep them topical, and in a number of cases variant forms of songs—both the music and the text—made it into print in different cities when performers sold their material to publishers for additional income.[8] Comic interpolations were most likely also constantly updated to include local and topical references to please specific audiences or to suit specific situations, and the interpolation printed in the songster was a model that was just as malleable as the rest of the song.

Performers, for the most part, seem to have relied on handwritten or published scores and orchestra parts that they carried with them in their travels. Several sets of Tony Pastor's repertoire books survive in the collection at the Harry Ransom Center at the University of Texas, and each of these includes over one hundred songs, in most cases scored for two violins, flute, trumpet, trombone, and drums.[9] These books are made up of manuscript sheets that had originally been loose but were bound together at a later date. Some pages are quite worn, and not all of the pages are the same size. The songs are numbered, but not arranged in any alphabetical order, and occasionally new items were inserted to become, for example, 19½, which fell between 19 and 20. Insertions tend to be written onto the back of another song, and very occasionally one also finds a crossed-through part on the back of a song.[10] All of the parts are handwritten, and each instrument had its own book of scores, bound together. The name of a city and date is occasionally noted at the bottom of songs, most likely indicating the date and place of first performance, and the fact that music from several years in no chronological order appears in a single volume also supports the fact that they were bound later.

The vast majority of the songs in Pastor's song books are not included in large archival collections of sheet music such as the American Sheet Music Collection at the Library of Congress or the Lester S. Levy Sheet Music Collection at Johns Hopkins University. Of the 102 songs in the books marked "Tony Pastor's Opera House," which include material sung by Pastor but also songs sung by other acts that performed at his theater, fewer than a quarter were found in these collections.[11] An even smaller proportion of the songs in the books entitled "Tony Pastor's Comic Songs" were found.[12] The Tony Pastor Opera House books contain a number of English songs, many of which were not published in the United States. Given that these books appear to date from the late 1880s, a period in which English performers frequently appeared in American variety, it is likely that these songs were acquired from touring acts that played at his theater. If they did not travel with arrangements or had arrangements that were unsuitable for Pastor's ensemble, it may well have been easier for the musical director to make his own arrangements of the English material. In contrast there are only a small number of English songs in the books marked "Tony Pastor's Comic Songs"; most of the material is American and much of it appears not to have survived in printed form.

The repertoire in these latter books appears to have been Pastor's alone and is a curious mix of comic, topical, sentimental, and seriocomic.[13] It includes a number of folk songs such as "Irish Washerwoman" and "Garry Owen," and there are also a number of titles that suggest the song was a parody or an alternate version of another song. For example, the song "Young Chap Dressed in Blue" was probably an alternate version of "The Dark Girl Dressed in Blue," made popular in the English music halls by the singer Harry Clifton and published in the United States by Oliver Ditson in 1864.[14] Irish songs or songs depicting Irish characters form a core of the repertoire, although there are a number of songs such as "Schönes Mädchen" that reference German characters, and also some such as "New Yhork Volunteers" that reference local New York characters such as the Bowery B'hoy. The songs were also written over a broad span of time; the earliest date from the 1840s and 1850s, while the latest are from the late 1870s and early 1880s. Pastor's personal repertoire included a greater number of older songs than the repertoire of his theater, which makes sense given the length of his career.[15]

If performers did not rely on printed sheet music, it may seem problematic to consider it as an indication of anything other than the growing recognition by printers of the consumer power of a working-class audience and the appeal of variety performers to a music-buying public. But, in many cases the printed sheet music or the songster bearing the performer's name is the only surviving record of the material sung in the context of variety. As a result I often use this material, but never consider the published songs as more than a rudimentary framework on which the performance was built. Evidence gained from reviews in the *Clipper* and other newspapers, as well as contemporary photographs where they exist, needs to be considered along with the notation, and even then the reconstruction of performance can only be speculative in many cases.[16]

When comparing songs sung by variety performers to other printed sheet music of the period, and in particular to songs associated with burlesque and operetta troupes, the limited singing skills of variety performers are immediately evident. Songs sung in variety, particularly those sung by comic male performers, stayed within an octave range and sometimes employed a range as narrow as a sixth. The melodic motion is conjunct and rarely moves chromatically, and there is also very little rhythmic complexity or vocal ornamentation indicated. The songs associated with members of Lydia Thompson's Burlesque Troupe, on the other hand, have wider ranges of at least an octave and employ disjunct and chromatic motion more consistently throughout. The songs are marked by rhythmic variety and require the singer to sing long phrases, sustained pitches, and complex cadenzalike embellishments at the ends of verses or choruses. All of these features indicate that the acts of male variety performers generally relied less on singing and more on acting skills and comic timing.

Spoken interpolations are not uncommon in both sheet music and songsters, particularly those dating from the 1860s and 1870s. Spoken interpolations are indicated in the music or text between the verse and chorus or at the end of the chorus and the beginning of the following verse. A spoken interpolation before the chorus allowed the performer to control the pace of performance, particularly if the audience joined in singing the chorus; in this case a spoken introduction to the chorus prevented the audience from entering too early and rushing the performer. The prevalence of audience participation in the United States is unclear. I have found no reviews that specifically mention audience singing, although in free and easies the use of the term "glee singing" in advertising, as distinct from other kinds of songs presented by professional performers, most likely indicated audience participation.[17] The practice of the spoken interpolation before the chorus may have come into variety through the many English music hall songs that were also performed in the United States.

Even though songsters lack music notation, they provide greater insight into the spoken interpolations with which performers interrupted songs than published sheet music, which generally provides only a limited space to additional dialog and indicates it only at transition points, such as between the verse and the chorus. Texts in songsters routinely included long, spoken monologues that interrupted songs and allowed the performer to complicate the narrative. These printed interpolations, which are generally placed between verses in the songster text, rely heavily on puns and references to other songs, plays, or topical occurrences and may now be unintelligible. For example, the first verse of the song "I'm the Ladies Beau Ideal" in *Ella Wesner's King of Trumps Songster* makes reference to both the Grecian Bend and the Roman Fall. While the Grecian Bend clearly references a style of women's clothing fashionable in this period, the Roman Fall is a reference to another song of Wesner's in which she challenged men not to allow women to triumph in having the most ridiculous clothing because they might feel superior. Her suggested fashion for men was a suit she called the Roman Fall.[18] Wesner's audience who knew her repertoire would have caught this reference, but it is less easy to understand now. I suspect that this was the nineteenth-century version of the "answer" song and that spoken interpolations in comic songs reference all manner of popular songs, plays, characters, and events that are now incomprehensible to us.

Tony Pastor's repertoire included a number of songs that depicted the Irish and German characters even though he did not specialize in these types. Irish character songs in Pastor's repertoire were sympathetic to the Irish, including a number protesting anti-Irish bigotry, among which were "The Irish Volunteer" and "No Irish Need Apply." "No Irish Need Apply" is written in dialect and relates the story of a young man newly arrived from Ireland who faces hostility and discrimination as he seeks work in the United States. Verses five and six note the generosity and decency of the Irish, and the final verse celebrates their contribution to America as soldiers for the Union:

> Ould Ireland on the battle-field a lasting fame has made
> We all have heard of Meagher's men, and Corcoran's brigade
> Though fools may flout and bigots have, and fanatics may cry
> Yet when they want good fighting-men, the Irish may apply
> And when for freedom and the right they raise the battle-cry
> Then the Rebel ranks begin to think: No Irish need apply.

While the text of this song uses dialect, it is not strong—occurring only on occasional words, such as "dacint" rather than "decent"—and there is also no use of nonsense syllables. The character depicted in this text is not comic but rather sympathetic and patriotic, and it is a serious and stirring song. It depicts the Irish as decent workingmen, not unlike American-born workingmen, and most likely represents the steady presence of Irishmen in Pastor's audience during the late 1860s and 1870s; no variety manager in this period could afford to alienate his patrons.

"The Irish Volunteer," also sung by Pastor, relates the bravery of Colonel Corcoran and his troupe of Irish volunteers in fighting for the Union. Corcoran is depicted as a brave hero, fearsome in leading his men into battle, refusing to retreat, and when finally captured, sharing all he had with his soldiers to sustain them. The fourth verse depicts him in prison, condemned to die, and swearing vengeance on the Confederacy, not only by the Northern forces but also from Ireland. The fifth and final verse celebrates his release and anticipates his return to New York City:

> But now a bright sunshine has followed the rain
> And back in New York we'll soon have him again
> At the head of his regiment then he'll be seen.
> And as such a valor and worth he displayed,
> A Brigadier-general he's sure to be made
> Then the insults he met from the vile rebel crew
> He'll pay them all back; aye, and interest too
> Or he'll die for the Stars and the banner of green.

Like the song "No Irish Need Apply," this song constructs the Irish as honorable, brave, and patriotic Americans. On the other hand they do not lose Irish identity, but rather merge the two into a statement of Irish American pride.

While songs offering a sympathetic portrayal of immigrants were part of Pastor's repertoire, the largest proportion of his songs were seriocomic. Seriocomic songs were also a significant part of the repertoires of male ballad singers like Charles Vivian. While much of Vivian's repertoire was comprised of seriocomic and comic songs, he was a skilled enough singer that later in his career he took parts in Gilbert and Sullivan productions in Chicago, and his singing skills were what distinguished him most from comic performers such as Pastor, Williams, and White. While the latter were actors who used song as the foundation for the characters they portrayed, Vivian was primarily a singer who had an engaging personality.[19]

The son of a clergyman, Charles Vivian was born in 1846, and, after his father's death, he began to appear in English music halls.[20] Vivian was both an ambitious and an enterprising man, and it is likely that he decided to emigrate to pursue his career in the United States, away from the fierce competition of skilled English singers, including George Leybourne, Alfred Vance, and Harry Clifton, who were active in music halls. When Vivian arrived in the United States in 1867, he quickly found success in variety, and his act relied heavily on English material associated with Leybourne, Vance, and Clifton that he could never have sung in England because music hall performers had exclusive performance rights to their songs in that country. Both Leybourne and Vance were billed as "lions comiques" in English music halls, and they represented fashionable men of the day, known as "swells," in song. Vivian also sang these songs but he was of a very different type than his English counterparts, and swell songs comprised only a small part of his repertoire and were vastly out-numbered by motto and seriocomic songs.[21]

In all of Vivian's songs the central character is not marked as ethnic or racial, and in many cases he appears to be a white workingman like the men in his audience.[22] Even though Vivian was English by birth, he did not highlight this in his advertising, nor did he sing songs that specifically referenced English characters in their texts. A large number of the songs he sang had been sung in English music halls in the mid-1860s, in the years just prior to his departure for the United States. Music hall performers had exclusive rights to the songs in their repertoires in England, but there was nothing to stop other singers from performing that repertoire in American variety. In America performers constantly acquired music from each other, sometimes through networking and other times through appropriation, and I have found numerous cases where multiple singers sang the same song.[23] The English music hall songs that Vivian performed in variety were quickly acquired by other performers, who made them their own.[24]

Vivian's repertoire was fairly typical of performers who did not impersonate ethnic or racial characters. Many of his songs dealt with love and courtship or leisure or both. A small number of songs encouraged working-class solidar-ity, reminding those who were successful to remember their origins and to share resources with the less fortunate. These tended to be motto songs that featured a repeated tagline at the end of the verse and chorus that might also have encouraged audience singing. Despite the anti-immigrant sentiment that could be expressed through comic character songs, songs that protested social inequities and called for the fairer treatment of the working class did not place blame for economic difficulties on immigrants but rather on the middle and upper classes, who were depicted as hoarding resources and of being corrupt and greedy. "Crime" was an English song adapted to the American context by R. Steirly and was sung by Harry Vandemark.[25] This song notes the wealth of the nation and wonders at the greed of politicians and the rich in hoarding and guarding that money when it could be more equitably distributed to the poor. The reference to crime in title and at the end of each verse has multiple meanings. First, it blames the increase of crime in the nation to poverty and desperation, but it also accuses the rich of crime. The final verse is far from subtle in this accusation, addressing the wealthy directly:

Just think while you're drinking your wine sir,
    How the poor of our nation are fed
While you with your rich folk can dine sir,
    'Tis a Godsend for them to get bread
Just visit the home of the poor sir,

Such a sight you will rarely behold
The fever dens go and explore sir,
   And scatter your hoardings of gold
When a little would soon burst asunder,
   The chain that the poor suffer under
Go and list to that great pang called hunger,
   And never more wonder at crime.

Songs also warned of the many dangers associated with living in an urban landscape in which there were myriad ways in which a workingman could be parted from his hard-earned money; these included confidence schemes, thieves, unscrupulous business owners, and even friends who borrowed but never paid back. Song texts did not criticize those who sought upward mobility, indeed they often encouraged it; instead they warned the audience not to be blinded to confidence schemes by a desire for economic and social advance and pleaded that those lucky enough to succeed should remember their community and share their good fortune with them.[26]

Class cohesion was a theme that ran through a number of Vivian's songs such as "Where There's a Will There's a Way" and "I Will Stand by My Friend," both of which encouraged the audience to persevere and to encourage and support their friends and community.[27] "I Will Stand by My Friend" noted that success was generally won with support from others and that, even though it was difficult, true friends stood by each other in both bad and good times. The song warns against fair-weather friends, but also advises that true friends deserved support:

A friend in need is one indeed
His heart and hand he lends
How different when we have to say
Oh save us from our friends
With many friendship's but a name
No sympathy they lend
They bid good day, but never say
I will stand by my friend.

These songs come closest to expressing a sense of working-class solidarity, although it was never as clear or as cohesive as English working-class identity in the same period.

Despite their more focused message, songs stressing class solidarity were a small but persistent part of the repertoire of male performers, and also that of male impersonators, during the 1870s and early 1880s but gradually fell out of favor in the mid-1880s, most likely because they no longer resonated in the same way with the emerging vaudeville audience. In the face of increasing immigration, the white, native-born working-class audience, as well as the German audience, was now increasingly identifying with the values of the middle class and no longer appreciated the cutting class critique and calls for class solidarity in this style of song. During the 1880s the number of ethnic character types on the variety stage increased, reflecting both the increasing diversity of the variety audience and potentially also the conflict between different immigrant groups and between immigrants and the native-born. Songs offering a class critique may well have maintained their popularity into the 1880s because immigrants were never their target. But there came a point at which targeting the middle class also lost its appeal, and that was the point at which these songs largely disappeared. This shift can be seen most clearly in the songs depicting men around town, or the "swell" song.

Swell songs could offer class critique, although often their meaning was more ambiguous because of their unabashed celebration of leisure and fashion. These songs were popular in English music halls, and many songs of English origin found popularity in American variety also. The central character in both English and American swell songs was an upper-class man-about-town. He was marked by his fine taste in clothing and particularly in wine. Peter Bailey notes that English swell songs took several approaches to depicting the swell; some songs expressed frank admiration of his finery and leisure pursuits while others showed that he was essentially a fake.[28] American swell songs also provided class critique, either by casting doubt on the manhood of the central character or by showing him to be a hypocrite. While many male performers sang swell songs as part of their repertoires, these songs were only a small part of that repertoire. In the case of male impersonators, on the other hand, swell songs formed the core of their repertoire, and other kinds of songs played a much smaller role. These songs will be discussed at length in the following chapter on male impersonators, but it is notable that the tenor of these songs changed in the mid-1880s, and the most pointed class critique also disappeared from their texts.

Women also posed a real threat to a man's disposable income because courtship inevitably involved the expenses associated with an evening of leisure, such as eating out or going to the theater and gifts for the young woman. Once a man was married, his wife expected to have some control over the household expenditure, curtailing his ability to spend freely and his ability to indulge in leisure in the way he had before marriage. The anxiety and ambivalence expressed about courtship and marriage in men's songs is notable, especially when contrasted with women's songs on the same subject. Women seemed entirely comfortable with these topics and supremely in control of the situation, but while men desired marriage, they also dreaded the threat to autonomy and freedom it represented. The sheer number of songs sung by both men and women that address courtship and marriage suggests that these topics were of central concern for the audience.

Songs about love were almost inevitably seriocomic songs. Not all of the texts depicted happy scenarios. While some songs described the sweetness of love and pleasures of courtship, others had comic twists that showed the singer failing to win his beloved's hand in marriage or marrying her only to find out that she was more than his equal. These songs functioned as a primer for young workingmen who were inexperienced in courtship and lived and worked in a largely homosocial world that gave them only limited access to marriageable women. Songs in which the central character was successful gave hints about how to conduct a successful courtship. The others warned of the many dangers, including inappropriate objects of affection and missteps in courtship, while allowing the audience to laugh at another man's failures as they learned from his mistakes.

"Pretty Jemima" was a song sung by Charles Vivian that focused on courtship and its attendant anxieties as the central character tried to find the courage to ask his beloved to marry him. It followed his courtship of Jemima and ends with her acceptance of his proposal. Originally published in England in 1868 and sung by Alfred Vance, the song was performed by Vivian soon after his arrival to the United States, at Butler's American Theatre at 472 Broadway.[29] This narrative is repeated in vast numbers of similar songs written in this period, although not all of the courtship narratives were successful. "I Can't Understand It at All," written by J. P. Skelly, is a seriocomic song that depicts failure in love.[30] The central character of this song falls in love too quickly and inevitably has his heart broken. The first two verses of this song introduce the character and his dilemma, and in the third he faces asking his sweetheart for her hand in marriage:

> My last lady-love is a sweet little dove,
>   Her charms I can never define;
> To-night I shall go my devotion to prove,
>   And ask her at once to be mine;
> I'll speak very plain, for her love I must gain,
>   I'll go there to conquer or fall;
> But, somehow I'm filled with a prospect of pain,
>   O, I can't understand it at all.
> Chorus: I can't, O, I can't understand it at all;
>   'Tis remarkably strange, and I sigh for a change.
>   When my hopes are most high, they are certain to fall,
>   O, I can't understand it at all.

The chorus of the song provided ample opportunity for comedy in its repeated tagline, and the song makes it clear that the central character is essentially a failure. It holds him up to ridicule, reinforcing the idea that the ideal man was careful and measured in love, but decisive in courtship and marriage, taking his place as the superior partner in the union.

There were also songs that warned the men that women could be fickle and abuse men's devotion. A number of seriocomic songs in Tony Pastor's repertoire show the central character being misled by his beloved and finding himself in trouble as a result. "Isabella with the Gingham Umbrella" depicts a young man who falls in love with a young woman who leads him on before cheating on him with another suitor. "The Sewing Machine" also depicts a man courting a young working-class woman, but in this song she is also a pickpocket, and she abandons him to face the charge of robbery when she is caught lifting pocketbooks at Barnum's Museum.[31] As a result he is sentenced to three months in prison at Blackwell's Island. The final verse warns the men in the audience:

> So, single men, I pray: beware!
>   And of my song take heed;
> Of Sewing-Machine girls pray take care,
>   or you'll be lost indeed.
> Avoid their fascinating glance:
>   if you do not, I ween
> You'll surely get in trouble with them
>   or their Machine!

While the central character in these songs is held up to ridicule because he is not clever enough to avoid being exploited by a woman, women are also depicted as being manipulative or even criminal rather than representing an ideal. This is a very different view of women than the one offered in women's songs, but like women's songs many men's songs also depicted women as active participants in flirtation and courtship as opposed to passive objects of affection. On the other hand, men's songs never showed their central character deceiving a woman in courtship; men were always the victims of women.

While the performance of song was central to variety entertainment throughout its history, the uses to which song was put and the kinds of characters represented in song changed significantly. From the 1860s to the 1880s there was a consistent move toward more and more formal presentation of song, even by male performers, and a shift in emphasis from song to sketch as the basis for comic material. The earliest singers active in the free and easies were close to their audience in a number of ways—they were people who had similar backgrounds and similar experiences, and they led their audience in collective singing. The use of contrafacta into the 1860s and 1870s suggests that this was the prevailing practice in the earliest years of variety, and the use of familiar Anglo-Irish folk songs and other popular melodies facilitated this group expression. With the founding of larger concert saloons, singers came to be one of the many kinds of acts presented on the variety stage, and changes to the law encouraged singers to emphasize the presentation and development of archetypal characters through song. In this period, singing took a backseat to acting in comic performance, and this would continue to be the case into the early twentieth century. Over time song took a smaller and smaller role in the presentation of comedy, and eventually the presentation of songs came to be the province of serious singers and women.

Champagne Charlie

The Fantasy of Leisure
for the Workingman

I am the swell of the day—as you see—
    All other swells are but models of me;
You must have heard of the names which I bear,
    Surely you must, for I'm known everywhere;
Girl are enchanted when I am in view,
    Gents are bewildered, and gaze at me too;
Some criticize me and stare, while they say,
    "Oh, ain't he nobby, that swell of the day!"
—"The Swell of the Day," words and music by J. P. Skelly,
sung by Alecia Jourdan, in *Ella Wesner's King of Trumps
Songster* (New York: A. J. Fisher, 1875), 48

In August 1868, as the new theatrical season was about to begin, a small advertisement in the *Clipper* announced the success of a series of new motto and comic songs along with the impending arrival of Annie Hindle, the young English woman who performed them. Over the next several editions short items appeared in the "Music Halls" column of this newspaper, further building the anticipation of her arrival but never describing her act. When she finally began to perform at the end of that month, Annie Hindle wore a perfectly fitting suit of male clothing and sang comic repertory more typical of male singers in a deep alto voice. No one had seen an act like this before, and she caused a sensation, as well as a scramble to name this new specialty. Initially, Hindle billed herself in advertising as "the great London sensation"; there was no name for her act in her advertising, which stressed her comic skills and her flawless impersonations of "men and manners of the day (with instantaneous change of costumes)."[1] For her first two seasons in the United States, Hindle maintained her position as the only female performer of male characters, but by 1870 she had inspired a number of other women to perform similar acts, and they were billed variously as "character-change" singers or "protean" singers because of the quick costume changes they performed in the wings of the stage between songs. Eventually the term "male impersonator" came to denote Hindle's unusual specialty, and by then around a dozen women were active in variety performing similar acts.

Little is known about Annie Hindle's life before she arrived in the United States, although it is certain that she was born around 1847 in England.[2] Hindle had been adopted as a child by Mrs. Ann Hindle, who traveled with her to the United States and settled in Jersey City, New Jersey, providing a home base for her adopted daughter until her death in 1884. Annie Hindle was active in English music halls as a child, and her early advertising in the *Clipper* shows that she understood the importance of marketing herself to a new audience. The stress of adapting to a new culture and travel through an unfamiliar country seems to have had some effect on Hindle, and in mid-September 1868, just two weeks after her arrival, she married the English ballad singer Charles Vivian while they were performing together in Philadelphia. She placed the management of her career in his hands, and for the next six weeks the couple performed and traveled together.

What was remarkable about this pairing is that Hindle and Vivian performed practically identical acts that presented a series of male characters through song. Both sang a mix of comic and seriocomic songs, and both stressed their skills in impersonation and mimicry; the only difference was the inclusion of ballads in Vivian's repertoire that required more substantial vocal skills. It is likely that professional rivalry developed between the pair, with Vivian resenting his wife's greater success. Vivian drank, often to excess, and Hindle later claimed that the marriage had failed because he had severely beaten her.[3] That Vivian headed to the West Coast when the marriage dissolved and that his rare return visits to the East Coast were greeted with snide commentary by the *Clipper*, particularly when he and Hindle appeared together on the same bill, tends to support her claim.[4]

Once the marriage had ended, Hindle was once again on her own, and during the next two seasons her career thrived. She was in constant demand by variety managers, and in 1870 she employed Col. T. Allston Brown as her agent. There was little to distinguish Hindle from the other successful female performers in variety except for the peculiarity of her specialty, and by 1872 she was no longer the only male impersonator active in variety; several other women had been inspired to perform similar acts. The first woman to copy Hindle was Ella Wesner, who performed on the same bill as Annie Hindle for three weeks at the Waverly in late August and early September 1869 before she left New York for the season to join the theatrical stock company in Galveston, Texas. There were suggestions in the 1890s that Wesner had worked as Hindle's dresser, but I have found no evidence that this was the case, although she may have assisted Hindle during their brief booking together.[5] Even so, when Wesner launched her career as a male impersonator in 1870, she sang Charles Vivian's repertoire. At that point Vivian had been absent from the East Coast for close to two years, and Hindle was most likely Wesner's source for these songs; perhaps she gave them to her as the basis for the olio act she was hired to perform in Texas. The third male impersonator, Augusta Lamoureaux, began performing in this style in late 1871; like Ella Wesner, she had begun her career in ballet and worked briefly as a singer in variety before changing specialties. By 1872 Blanche Selwyn, a seriocomic singer who also had seen Hindle perform while she was married to Jas. Porter, the manager of the Metropolitan Music Hall in Washington, D.C., took on this specialty too.

Like female acrobats, male impersonators defied gender-appropriate behavior, even for working-class women. Despite this, they were not merely tolerated but greatly loved by their audience, in part because of the service they provided to men. In their acts male impersonators appeared to perform a kind of magic in which a female body was transformed into a realistically male character. Reviews of the women active in this specialty in the early 1870s noted the realistic fit of their suits, their low singing voices, and their believable masculinity with wonder. The acts of Hindle and Wesner, the two leading performers in this style, set the standards for reviewers, and younger performers who failed to meet their realism were criticized. But, despite their realism on stage, the audience was fully aware that they were watching women perform, and the acts of male impersonators exploited this knowledge to cast aspersions on the men they represented through song. In a very real sense, the acts of male impersonators active between the late 1860s and the mid-1880s can be seen as reinforcing working-class manhood by actively undermining middle- and upper-class ideals in performance and in depicting socially more powerful men as failing to meet standards of working-class manhood.

While male impersonators sang a broad range of material, from seriocomic and sentimental songs to comic and character songs, swell songs that depicted the urban man-about-town formed the core of their repertoire. As Peter Bailey notes in his work on swell songs in English music halls, there were two persistent variations on this character: the genuine upper-class swell and the fake swell, a man who was either aspiring to upward mobility and imitating his social betters or trying to pass himself off as the genuine thing.[6] For the audience, these figures provided a model of upper-class behavior and allowed men to glory in the excessive leisure enjoyed by the higher classes. But on occasion the songs also allowed the men in the audience to feel superior to these men, by revealing them as fakes, or as hypocrites, or as weak. On the British music hall stage, swell songs were sung primarily by male singers known as "lions comiques," although by the late 1860s and early 1870s young women, most of whom were in their teens, had also begun to perform similar material. As a child performer, Annie Hindle must have been among the first women in music halls to imitate the English lion comiques.

Women had certainly appeared on the American stage in male character before Hindle's arrival, particularly in serious spoken drama. In that context, highly skilled actresses such as Charlotte Cushman took male roles in order to find more challenging roles than those typically written for women; Hamlet and Romeo were two Shakespearean roles not infrequently performed by actresses on the nineteenth-century stage. Women also appeared in male roles in the context of sexualized performance and particularly English burlesque as performed by Lydia Thompson's Troupe in the late 1860s, but the costumes worn by a burlesque actress were scanty and often showed the full length of her legs and also highlighted her tightly corseted waist. The intent in these cases was to display the woman's body to male view, which is why this form elicited such fervent opposition, not only from clergy and moral reformers, but also from the feminist actress Olive Logan.

Male impersonation in variety was very different from cross-dressed roles in narrative drama because performers were not limited by a script and could shape their act through improvised comic interpolations in response to their audience in the same way as male comic singers. It was also different from the "sister acts" performed by singers such as the Foys or the Richmond Sisters in which one woman dressed in male clothing, and the two women sang seriocomic duets—often songs depicting courtship—with each other. The male costumes worn in sister acts were not as tight or revealing as burlesque costumes, but they left little doubt that the person wearing the pants was a woman. Generally, these women also did not cut their hair, but hid it under hats or caps, and their appearance remained feminine despite their male clothing. In addition, both women in the sister act sang in the style of female seriocomic singers—in a soprano range and with only minimal spoken interpolations. Male impersonators, on the other hand, were quite masculine women, particularly in the early 1870s, when the ideal for this performance style was set by Annie Hindle and Ella Wesner, both of whom were mature women with slim figures, short cropped hair, and alto singing voices. Reviews, as well as lyrics in song-sters and published sheet music, also suggest that male impersonators adopted male performance style, speaking through their songs and interrupting them with lengthy spoken interpolations like their male counterparts.

The first swell songs performed on the American variety stage were English songs, such as "Champagne Charlie," that were imported from English music halls. English performers like Charles Vivian and Annie Hindle sang them, as did Tony Pastor and Gus Williams among others. In many ways "Champagne Charlie" represented the prototypical swell in both England and America, a wealthy and fashionable man concerned only with drinking and socializing with his friends:[7]

> I've seen a deal of gaiety throughout my noisy life,
>> With all my grand accomplishments I ne'er could get a wife,
> The thing I most excel in is the P. R. F. G.[8] game,
>> A noise all night, in bed all day, and swimming in Champagne.
> Chorus: For Champagne Charlie is my name,
>> Champagne Charlie is my name,
>> Good for any game at night my boys,
>> Good for any game at night my boys,
>> Champagne Charlie is my name,
>> Champagne Charlie is my name,
>> Good for any game at night my boys,
>> Who'll come and join me in a spree.

The lyrics of this song paint a picture of a young man living on inherited wealth with little to do but indulge in leisure and particularly alcohol. Transplanted to the United States, a country in which upward mobility was not only desired but also possible, this figure became an escape fantasy for men, promising an easy life of excess leisure, free from the daily grind of work.

Follow-up songs, such as "Moët and Chandon," continued to sing the praise of fine wine and drinking, while others such as Joseph Skelly's "I'm out for a Lark" focused on the freedom of young single men to engage in the range of leisure available in an urban environment.[9] Skelly's song transforms leisure into a more universal male preoccupation, no longer reserved for the ultrawealthy and off limits only to married men:

> I sympathize with married men who must remain at home
> They lose their life of joy and fun, no more at night they roam;
> But I am free, without a care, to ramble gaily ev'rywhere,
> With jolly friends the hours to share, I'm out for a lark, for a lark!
> With jolly friends the hours to share, I'm out for a lark, for a lark!

Spoken: Sometimes the old gentleman is anxious about his festive
  son and heir and wants to know where I am going? But I tell him
  candidly—O, that's all right governor—
Chorus: I'm out for a lark, I'm out for a lark
Come boys with me and we'll have such a spree
We'll kiss all the girls and then I'll remark,
Don't be alarm'd love, it's only a lark!

This song not only equated freedom and fun with youth, but it also refused to be deferential to age or status. No respect is shown to the parental figure, who might just as well be a moral reformer, an employer, or any man of higher status as a father figure. The old gentleman here is middle-class patriarchal authority, and the song depicts pleasure-seeking as the birthright of all young men regardless of social status. The texts of American songs often lacked the class critique of the English songs, but they also left more room for identification by all men in the audience, particularly those who were young and single.

The swell's love of fine clothing and his concern with his appearance made this character a figure of fun, even in English music hall performance. As Peter Bailey notes, the dandy, and particularly the effete fop, had been a figure long held up to ridicule in English theater, and the swell can be seen as continuing this tradition.[10] American swell songs also make fun of these tendencies, sometimes gently and sometime sharply, particularly when they combine class hostility and hostility to the English and foreigners in general. A similar ambivalence can be seen in newspapers such as the *National Police Gazette*, which was resolutely nativist in its sympathies. The *Police Gazette* delighted in pointing out the moral misdeeds of both the middle class (and particularly clergymen) and the European actors and actresses who were the darlings of the elite audiences, concluding that the middle- and upper-class love of dissolute foreigners signaled both their hypocrisy and their gullible nature. These nativist and class sympathies are also evident in swell songs of the 1870s.

A relatively kind depiction of the swell can be found in J. P. Skelly's "Charley the Masher."[11] The central character here is concerned more with fashion and flirtation than with riotous drinking:

I'm Charley the "Masher," a swell super-fine,
My garments are made in the latest design,
I wear a large diamond and gloves rather small,
My manner so graceful, is pleasing to all.
I'm just like a Count, or a lord, or a duke,
But some vulgar fellows will call me a "fluke";
I'm sure they don't know me, just walk on Broadway

And all the young ladies will instantly say:—
Chorus: I'm Charley the "Masher," the gayest of swells!
I play the Piano and chat with the belles;
Wherever I go, I'm the girls "little pet!"
I'm Charley the "Masher," now don't you forget!

Despite Charlie's preoccupation with his appearance, nothing in the narrative of this song suggests that he is lacking in virility. He is a young, well-dressed man intent on ingratiating himself with women, and someone that, in the second verse, makes one young woman's brother distinctly nervous for her virtue. On the other hand, his desire to be with women, rather than engaged in drinking and leisure with a group of young men, renders him somewhat suspect, and his flashy style and boastfulness hint at him being a fake.

Edward Harrigan's song "Hildebrandt Montrose" offers a less kind depiction of the swell.[12] The young man in this song is wealthy and well dressed and draws the attention of all the young women, which is not so different from other swells. But this song suggests that the young man is essentially impotent, and his breeding, his highfalutin ways, and his delicate nature are all signs of this. The brothers of young women do not bother to watch this young man, who is a "pet" of society women. He speaks French ("francais vooley parley"), he carries a silk umbrella, his hair is in auburn ringlets, he sings in a soprano voice, and he prefers soda water to alcohol. In every way, this man fails to qualify as a real man, and through doing so he becomes a figure of fun. Skelly's song "Fifth Avenue George"[13] depicts a similar young man, and while the humor of this song, which was sung by Tony Pastor, was more gentle, the central character was no more virile:

He wears a "Knox" hat, made to order,
    And his diamond can vie with the sun
A gold headed cane he keeps twirling;
    As a swell he is "A, number one!"
He can waltz like a girl in the ballet,
    And sing like a signor from Rome
In every grand parlor or ballroom,
    Fifth Avenue George is at home.

This song is also careful to locate this figure in high society, and he is particularly attractive to society women, indicating the gullibility and lack of judgment of the social elite. The skills that make him attractive are also clearly associated with femininity (dance) and foreigners (operatic singing), carrying the suggestion that he fails the true tests of real American manhood—drinking, fighting, sport, and leisure.

The swell was also frequently depicted as failing to win women who saw through his fine manners and clothes and detected his inadequate manhood. In Ella Wesner's song "I'm the Ladies' Beau Ideal," a young swell boasts of his good looks and clothing and then relates the story of his courtship of a young woman, who he believes is attracted by his fine appearance.[14] It becomes clear, however, that this is not the case, and the central character is left, in the last verse, to smooth his ruffled feathers and to seek consolation in leisure. The impression left by this song was that for the swell a young woman was little more than an accessory like kid gloves, and the song revealed him as foolish and shallow. An undated song sheet, "The City Beau," depicted a similar character who was sung by the minstrel performer Cool White.[15] This man is also a well-dressed man of leisure who flirts with young women, but in this song they rebuff him immediately:

> He thinks the ladies dote on him,
>   And fancies all the while,
> A snare in every glancing eye,
>   A trap in every smile.
> But smiles and fancies turn to rage,
>   When that decided no;
> Tells how the dashing city belle,
>   Can scorn the City Beau
> Tells how the dashing city belle,
>   Can scorn the City Beau
> Chorus: For he's the beau, for he's the beau,
>   For he's the City Beau.

The swell song gained additional meanings in the United States, a country in which the boundaries that marked social distinctions were incredibly porous. The class tensions between the wealthy and the working class were different from those in England, where a more fixed class system allowed only limited social mobility. For this reason American swell songs needed to be open to a broader range of meaning during the 1870s, a decade marked both by an economic boom and a crash. When these songs were part of the diverse repertoire of male comic and character singers such as Tony Pastor, Charles Vivian, or even Gus Williams, the class hostility may have been muted, but when performed by women the doubtful manhood of the swell—which was intimately connected to his class affiliation—was brought into sharper relief.

The successful male impersonators of the 1870s—Annie Hindle, Ella Wesner, Blanche Selwyn, and others—used their audience's knowledge of their female body beneath an apparently male exterior to cast doubt on the manhood of the characters they portrayed. Wesner had a number of songs in her repertoire in which she depicted a drunk upper-class man, and the character of a drunk sailor became such a staple of her act in the 1880s that she was known as "The Captain" for the last decade or more of her career. Songs depicting drunks showed these men as failing in a number of ways. First, in becoming drunk, often too easily, they failed to meet the standards of working-class manhood, in which a man was ideally able to hold his liquor without losing control.[16] Second, they failed to meet the middle-class ideal of temperance and control, revealing themselves, and potentially all middle-class men, to be fundamentally hypocrites.

135

Wesner's song "I'm on the Teetotal" is particularly eloquent on this latter point. This song depicts a middle-class temperance advocate who had recently signed the pledge and given up alcohol. But, in spoken interpolations, he informs his audience that his doctor warned him to "ease off it gently" and recommends that he limit himself to a "noggin of gin at breakfast, and your Irish hit at lunch, and your bottle of port at dinner, and you'r [sic] brandy and cayenne at bed time . . . be moderate."[17] The verse that follows this interpolation further reveals the hypocrisy of this character:

> Your worst rogue makes your holiest saint, and that's the reason clear
> I'm down upon the moderate man whom I catch sipping beer;
> I call him sundry awful names, and urge him to repel
> The deadly poison; if he won't he'll sign his own death knell.

In the rest of the song, the character is shown tippling from bottles of liquor hidden in various coat pockets and becoming progressively drunker and drunker. His final chorus declaring that he is on the teetotal is transformed into a drinking song:

> For he's a jolly good fellow—total, total good fellow—
> I'm on the teetotal—and so say all of us.

This song, performed with increasingly slurred speech and the physical comedy of the character tippling from multiple bottles hidden in pockets all over Wesner's costume, provided a particularly effective critique of middle-class ideals that many in the audience suspected even the middle class failed to meet.

While one of the primary functions of male impersonators was to reinforce working-class manhood by depicting the flaws in the middle-class ideal, male impersonators also portrayed working-class male characters, particularly during the 1870s. Many songs sung by Wesner and Hindle were seriocomic narratives of courtship similar to those sung by Vivian and Pastor that warned men of the many pitfalls inherent in the process of wooing a woman. A number of these songs provided basic courtship advice aimed at young men with relatively little experience. Wesner's song "There's Danger on the Line" equated courtship with railway signals, advising men to move slowly and cautiously through the process rather than rushing into a situation that might prove disastrous and result in injury. "As I Strolled along the East River" also depicted a courtship, but in this case the young woman is married and the young man realizes his mistake too late, despite the young woman's many hints that she is not interested in his advances. In this song the central character is left unharmed, but is made to look like a fool.[18] The song "Pretty Jemima,"[19] depicting a nervous young man's anxiety over asking his beloved's hand in marriage, was part of Hindle's repertoire as well as that of Charles Vivian. All of these songs were designed to allay the anxiety reflected in men's seriocomic songs about courtship, and it is telling that they were sung by women. I have found less evidence of similar advice in songs by men, whose songs were more ready to find humor in failed courtship or to shrug off failure in a similar manner to the swells depicted in songs. While these songs formed only a small part of the repertoires of male impersonators such as Wesner and Hindle, they are important because of the service they provided to both the young men in their audience and the women they would later court.

The message "learn from my mistakes" is not uncommon in a number of Wesner's songs, and like the songs associated with male comic singers, Wesner's repertoire gave plenty of room for comedy. Probably the funniest of these is "The Gymnastic Wife," which was also sung by Tony Pastor.[20] This song, in which a man relates episodes from his marriage, provided ample opportunity for acting and physical comedy. The central character is depicted as a timid man who has fallen in love with a strong, athletic woman who is more than his equal. The first verse describes his attraction to his wife's physical prowess, and in the second he is depicted as being humiliated at his wedding breakfast when his wife lifts him off the floor by his hair. As the song progresses, the figure of the wife grows more fearsome, while the central character appears more and more a figure of fun. The chorus advises:

> My wife's so strong, and all day long
> She frightens me out of my life
> Whatever you do, oh! whatever you do
> Don't have a Gymnastic Wife.

It is important to note, however, that this song, and the vast majority of songs I have found sung by Wesner and Hindle, did not find fault with the woman's behavior. Despite the comedy of this song, the central problem is not the gymnastic wife but rather her husband's inability to match or exceed her strength.

Just as the variety audience accepted male impersonators as exceptional women, so too does this song suggest that there was a place within working-class culture for strong assertive women. The song implies that the most suitable husband for such a woman was a strong and assertive man, which serves to reinforce the expectation of male superiority.

137

The repertoires of male impersonators also included a small number of sentimental songs, as well as a mix of motto and seriocomic songs. Annie Hindle, for example, sang "Don't You Put Your Foot on a Man When He's Down," a motto song designed to encourage class solidarity and the sharing of scarce resources.[21] Overall the repertoires of these singers more closely resembled those of men; the primary difference lay in a slightly greater number of sentimental songs than was typical for male comic performers. Like their male counterparts, male impersonators active in the 1870s also sang songs advocating working-class solidarity and protesting class inequities, and they depicted a broad range of characters, including old and young men. The character on which their act centered, however, was the swell.

During the 1880s and 1890s the swell song became even more important in the repertoires of male impersonators, and the emphasis of these songs changed subtly. While the swell and his style of dress and behavior became more important to male impersonators, the class critique inherent in these songs diminished. Even the more mature performers such as Wesner and Hindle placed greater emphasis on their appearance and the fashions they exhibited; while Hindle's billing had been as a seriocomic and impersonator of "fast young men" of the day in the late 1860s, a decade later her billing was as "le roi de la mode" or the king of fashion. This shift in emphasis from manners and behavior to appearance is significant because it eliminated or at least muted the class critique that had been embedded in earlier swell songs.

The mid-1880s was also a period in which a new kind of swell made a brief appearance in popular song. The "dude" was even more effete than the swell of the 1870s had been and was less interested in women and more obsessed with his own appearance. While a number of these songs appear to parody Oscar Wilde, who had toured the United States in 1882, or the Gilbert and Sullivan character of Bunthorne from the operetta *Patience*, the dude can also be seen as a more extreme form of attack on middle-class manhood by working-class performers whose status within variety was under threat. Annie Hindle featured the dude in her act, and in 1883 Ella Wesner scored a hit with the introduction of a song that featured the "Dreadful Dude."[22] While I have not been able to locate this song, I have found a number of songs from the mid-1880s that feature the "dude," and all describe him in a similar way. The song "It's Dudish, You Know!,"[23] published in 1885, presents the least flattering depiction of the dude. The central character of this song boasted of his fine and delicate figure, his lack of stamina, his expensive clothing, and the women who adored him. His preferred diet was angel cake, he avoided steak at all costs, and lastly, he boasted about his pet poodle. In five verses, the dude emerges as a figure so effete he is almost indistinguishable from the women who adore him. He also closely resembles the more modern stereotype of the effeminate gay man.

138

The contempt shown for the central figure in this song reflects the growing fear of feminine behavior in men, as well as the growing tendency to equate such men with women. As Rotundo notes in his landmark study of American masculinity: "Early nineteenth-century charges of effeminacy were usually applied to abstractions ('effeminate virtue,' 'effeminate indulgence'), not to people. But new forms of figurative language connecting men with femininity became popular in the late nineteenth century, forms that unsexed a man, made him bisexual, or turned him into a woman."[24] The appearance of the dude in popular sheet music of the mid-1880s signaled not only the growing fear of feminization among American men but also the appearance of sexual subcultures as a visually identifiable part of urban life. George Chauncey notes that male homosexuals constituted a recognizable subculture in the largely immigrant Bowery district in New York City by the 1890s and had been offered as part of the entertainment and sex business present in this district since the 1870s.[25] While none of these songs explicitly identify the dude as homosexual, this reading is readily inferred from their texts. And, the dude is also clearly linked to the swell, and through him to upper- and middle-class masculinity, by his love of clothing and a social life and by his popularity with society women. While the dude dressed like a swell, this song depicts him in stereotypical terms that are reminiscent of the descriptions of "fairies," young male prostitutes and entertainers who worked at a number of Bowery clubs, including Armory Hall and the Slide. In fact, Chauncey notes that homosexual men were also in the audience at these establishments and that they could be identified as such by their fashionable clothing and rouged cheeks.[26]

In equating middle- and upper-class men with male homosexuals, these songs practice a tactic that was familiar to many working-class men at that period. Among single working-class men, particularly those engaged in seasonal labor or in other forms of transient work, manhood was not constituted through income, profession, or family, but through the participation in male rituals that included work, but also included drinking and the ability to "treat" one's comrades to a "round," boxing, gambling, and other competitive displays of strength or skill. While manhood could be attained through participation in these rituals, it also needed to be constantly proved, most often through fighting or through winning competitions.[27] Just as working-class men might physically attack a lone middle-class slummer or an unprotected homosexual man in their neighborhood in order to prove their own manhood, these songs also attack middle-class men, stripping them of their manhood and depicting them in derisive terms. Given the attacks by middle-class reformers on working-class culture and the slow but certain shift toward middle-class standards in performance aesthetics, this increasing hostility, signaled by the recourse to fighting language from older performers and the songwriters who provided their material, is not surprising. This was, however, a last-ditch stand on the part of old-timers, and within a few years these songs disappeared, to be replaced by the charming young English swell.

The shift in repertoire was not peculiar to American male impersonators, and even touring English male impersonators adjusted their material to accommodate the sympathies of the American audience. Male impersonators active in English music halls had continued to impersonate clerks, soldiers, and policemen—men not unlike those in their audience—while American performers increasingly focused on upper-class leisure, but there is evidence that when touring America sentimental fare and songs depicting upper-class swells were more popular. Vesta Tilley, for example, abandoned current songs and revived her early material from the 1870s when touring the United States at the end of the century. By the end of the nineteenth century, the men in the American audience no longer had any desire to see themselves portrayed by women, preferring to see depictions of the excessive leisure of the superwealthy. The vaudeville audience took upward mobility seriously; it was no longer the joking matter it had been in the early 1870s. The shift in emphasis in billing from behavior to fashion during the 1880s marks the beginning of this change, and it was a change that ultimately brought about the end of the more realistic American style of male impersonation. As working-class gender roles were redefined in the last decades of the nineteenth century, there was less and less room for the exceptional woman, who in many ways was the precursor to the mannish woman who also caused increasing social anxiety in the first decades of the twentieth century during the final push toward women's suffrage.[28]

Performance style for male impersonation also changed gradually during the 1880s. Male impersonators active in the 1870s were held to standards that came closer to those expected of men on the variety stage. Wesner often suffered from vocal problems caused by illness and too-frequent performance in the early part of her career, and reviews noted her hoarseness and the rough quality of her voice, even as they praised her performance. These women were also expected to appear realistically male—to have a slim build, no obvious female curves, short-cropped hair, and an impeccable wardrobe of clothing in the latest men's fashions. By the end of the 1870s reviews placed increasing emphasis on the clothing worn by the swell, and advertising stressed that these women modeled the latest men's fashions. By the mid-1880s male impersonators depicted few characters beside the swell. The importation of English male impersonators, beginning in the late 1880s, also drastically shifted the emphasis of this specialty from realism to a more feminine aesthetic.[29] These women did little to disguise their feminine curves, and all appear to have sung in the soprano range. They were all considerably younger than their American counterparts and depicted young men who were adolescent and who could not believably indulge in the many behaviors they described to their audience. The popularity of English male impersonators and changing audience sympathies resulted in a significant shift in performance style for male impersonators. Like female singers, male impersonators were now expected to be able to sing pleasingly and in a believably female range, and their songs presented less class critique and placed greater emphasis on fashion and leisure.

The shift in repertoire and performance style of male impersonators came as the relationship between these women and their audience was also being redefined. By the late nineteenth century, actresses active in all branches of the theater increasingly opened their offstage lives to their public in order to prove that they were fundamentally no different than women in wider society—articles in the many theatrical and women's magazines that circulated stressed the normal home life of actresses, their love of fashion and furnishings, and their disinterest in men's topics such as politics and particularly women's suffrage. This marked a profound shift in theatrical culture from the province of men to that of women. While the first generation of male impersonators was hugely popular with their audiences during the 1870s, there was little interest shown by readers of theatrical gossip in local newspapers in their lives off the stage. Gossip columns generally ignored variety performers, and it was not until the late 1870s and 1880s that small items relating to their professional lives were featured in newspapers other than those catering to the theatrical profession. Male impersonators were no different, and as a result the *Clipper* is the primary source of information about these performers; for performers such as Selwyn and Lamoureaux, Alecia Jourdan, Maggie Weston, Minnie Hall, and others, this newspaper included information relating only to their professional lives. Hindle and Wesner, the two most successful performers of the period, appeared in this newspaper more frequently, not only because their careers overshadowed those of other performers in this style, but also because events in their personal lives were deemed of interest to the profession at large.

Both Annie Hindle and Ella Wesner were exceptional women—women who pushed the boundaries of even working-class femininity—in the theatrical world, and their popularity and success helped them sustain this position for most of their careers. The exceptional woman could be accommodated within the variety world because she was exceptional. So while some women were strong, or masculine, or forceful, or ambitious, or highly skilled, most appear not to have aspired to such a role. In most cases women left the variety stage after marriage, even when they married within the profession. There were provisions for women to continue working after marriage, and when women married fellow performers the family partnership could also result in a professional partnership, either as a husband-and-wife act or as the core of a traveling troupe. Blanche Selwyn frequently appeared on the same bill with her second husband, Ben Gilfoil, and Gilfoil's act even included a parody of Selwyn's act, which consisted of Gilfoil in blackface burlesquing Selwyn, who in turn impersonated and parodied middle-class masculinity.

Even though women could, and did, continue to perform after marriage, child-rearing interfered with their professional lives, and the itinerant life of a performer was not the optimal environment in which to raise children. Before the mid-1870s female performers with children may well have opted to join local stock companies, exchanging higher pay rates for a more stable life. Their husbands could continue to tour if they chose, sending money back to the family, or they could also perform in stock companies and perhaps move from there into management positions. If the marriage dissolved, women returned to performance or possibly took backstage support roles, but few moved into management. The relatively small number of older women who remained in variety, and the even smaller number of women who sought to move into management, suggests that most women were happy to retire from performance and to assume the traditional role of mother and wife.

Even the roles that appear to challenge gender construction of this period did not seek to upset the prevailing gender hierarchy in which men were superior to women. It was only at moments where the actions of a woman seemed to call that superiority into question or to seek male privilege that negative and sometimes vicious responses were expressed from within the theatrical world. The individual histories of Hindle and Wesner show the limits to the acceptance of exceptional women. Both of these women performed similar acts, both were ambitious and highly paid, and both women were involved in public scandals that were similar in nature. The reactions to these events are telling and expose the limits of acceptance within the variety world.

Hindle's name regularly appeared in the "Music Halls" column of the *Clipper*, which noted her professional engagements, but it also appeared elsewhere in this newspaper. During the 1870s Hindle published poetry, most often on the topic of love and loss, in the pages of the *Clipper*, and all of her love poems were addressed to a female subject and also written in a female voice. By the mid-1870s the *Clipper* had also begun to include odd humorous items about Hindle that carried the suggestion that she was not an entirely conventional woman. In 1871 it carried a report of Hindle being arrested on a charge of public intoxication due to the disturbance she raised in a restaurant accusing a fellow actress of stealing jewelry from her.[30] There was nothing remarkable about this report except for the public nature of the dispute—theatrical people frequently found themselves in disputes, fueled by rivalries and jealousy. A dispute between two actors had, after all, initiated the Astor Place Theater riot. In 1873 the newspaper carried a second arrest report for Hindle, who had been detained in Michigan, en route from Bay City to Toronto, on suspicion of being a man traveling dressed as a woman. With more than a little amusement, the reporter noted: "The sheriff, having examined her throat and not finding Adam's apple there, became satisfied she was of the female persuasion and released her."[31] When Hindle's second marriage to the minstrel performer W. W. Long was noted in the "Fact and Fancy Focused" column, which was more often the source of humorous gossip for the profession, theatrical people would have understood the humor in this domestic arrangement, especially when the same column later ran a report that Hindle was being sued by her former dresser "to recover the value of jewelry alleged to have been pawned by the plaintiff for the benefit of Miss Hindle when business was bad."[32] This report carried the suggestion that the relationship between Hindle and her dresser, Augusta Gerschner, had gone beyond that typical of an employer and employee.

While the *Clipper* happily included coded snippets of gossip about Hindle's irregular personal life in its pages for the amusement of the profession, it did not censure her behavior on or off the stage. The reviews of her performances in the same period show that she was highly respected for her skills and in great demand. The next scandal relating to Hindle was reported by the *Clipper* in 1886, and on this occasion even the *Clipper* could not remain neutral about Hindle's behavior, which not only transgressed gender roles of the period, but also showed that Hindle regarded herself as deserving of male privilege. On June 6, 1886, Rev. Brooks of the Second Baptist Church in Grand Rapids, Michigan, married Annie Hindle and her dresser Annie Ryan in Hindle's room at the Barnard House, a local hotel. The marriage was witnessed by Gilbert Sarony, a performer in Hindle's specialty company, and Loran Osborn, a clerk at the Grand Rapids National Bank who was, most likely, a passerby pressed into service as a witness.[33] In the wake of the marriage and the scandal it caused, the company collapsed and Hindle was forced to retire from performance for that season.

The first newspaper reports of the wedding appeared in local Grand Rapids newspapers, and all of them had problems choosing the correct pronoun for Hindle. The consensus was that the marriage indicated that Hindle was actually a man. The *Telegram-Herald* ran a lengthy report of the wedding, and upon reading this story it becomes clear that the reporter had hounded the couple into the early hours of the morning, when Hindle finally agreed that she was a man mostly, I suspect, to make him go away.[34] That the marriage also caused a stir in the theatrical world is indicated by the fact that the *Clipper* was the first national newspaper to carry the story. Typically, theater reviews and reports from correspondents appeared up to two weeks after the event in the *Clipper* columns; only local New York news made it to press more quickly. But in this case, the *Clipper* reported the marriage on June 12, just six days after it had occurred, printing the following telegram, dated June 8: "On Sunday night, Annie Hindle, under the name of 'Charles Hindle,' was quietly married to Annie Ryan, of Cleveland, O., who for the past five years had been traveling with her or him as maid. They left immediately for Cleveland."[35] The following week it confirmed the marriage and commented that it had been "a surprise to everyone, especially female variety-artists, many of whom had occupied the same dressing-room with Hindle. He was married in male attire, but resumed female garments on leaving the city."[36]

143

News of Hindle's marriage reached the nontheatrical press almost a month later. In early July the *National Police Gazette* ran the following in its "Stage Whispers" column: "Since the marriage of Annie Hindle to her maid the question arises, 'Is she he?'"[37] More than a month later, this newspaper declared that Hindle was a man: "Annie Hindle(?) or Charles Hindle(?), recently married in Cleveland, says that she married Vivian, and that when he discovered her sex he wanted to masquerade with her, but not having such a feminine appearance failed to make a success. Hindle further claims to be the illegitimate child of Ellen Terry, Henry Irving's famous partner. She denies that the woman with whom she lived and whom she called mother in Jersey City was anything but a foster mother. A Western reporter states emphatically that Hindle is a man."[38] This is incoherent, even by the *Police Gazette's* standards, and it gives some indication that the writer was not sure how to discuss Hindle after her third marriage. Annie Hindle is variously referred to as "he," "she," and the gender neutral "Hindle," which ironically is the term Hindle most often seemed to choose in her own advertising. The source for the *Police Gazette* was clearly the *Telegram-Herald* report of the event, rather than items published in the *Clipper.*

What is most interesting about the *Police Gazette's* reaction to Hindle's marriage is that this newspaper had previously denounced a number of women active on the American stage for their romantic interest in other women. Three years before Hindle's marriage, the newspaper had loudly decried the affection that the Swedish soprano Christine Nilsson lavished on her female friends.[39] This paper was also quick to denounce women, particularly educated and professional women, who sought equality to men. While the *Police Gazette* was happy to denounce the foreign-born opera stars and actresses and the daughters of New York's elite society, it was less certain of how to make sense of Hindle's marriage, and her skill as a male impersonator combined with her affection for women was seen by the writer as proof that she was a man. The writer found it easier to view more than a decade of Hindle's performances as a fraud than to confront the implication that, just possibly, some working-class women were not content to occupy traditional roles.

The case involving Ella Wesner suggests that the cause of the scandal associated with Hindle's marriage was her usurping of male privilege rather than her intimate relationships to women. In 1872 Ella Wesner had become romantically involved with Helen Josephine Mansfield, a sometime actress who had gained a certain measure of notoriety by 1870 as the well-known mistress of Col. James Fisk, the owner of the Erie Railway Company and the manager of the Grand Opera House in New York City. In January 1872 Fisk was assassinated by Edward S. Stokes, who had been a friend and business partner of Fisk's until it was discovered that Stokes was having an affair with Mansfield. In late 1871, largely as a result of their jealous rivalry over Josie Mansfield, Stokes and Fisk filed lawsuits against each other over business matters, and on January 6, 1872, Stokes lost his claim against Fisk. Stokes then ambushed Fisk in the Grand Central Hotel in New York and shot his rival, fatally wounding him. Stokes was arrested for the murder, and Mansfield was unable to leave her home for fear that she would be attacked by those sympathetic to Fisk or hounded by the newspapermen who were camped out on her doorstep.

The New York newspapers devoted pages of coverage to the Fisk shooting during January 1872. The *Sun's* entire front page and a second page editorial gave every detail of the shooting and Fisk's death on Monday, January 8, and Fisk's funeral occupied most of the front page the following day. By the end of January, however, Mansfield's name had disappeared from the newspapers. Mansfield and Wesner had mostly likely become acquainted because of Fisk's many connections in the theatrical world. In early May, Wesner joined Tony Pastor's summer tour that traveled through the Northeastern states and Midwest, and by the end of that month local correspondents to the *Clipper* were beginning to note Mansfield's presence with the company even though she was not performing.[40] Wesner was booked to perform at the Theatre Comique during the week beginning October 7, and when she returned to New York, Wesner placed an announcement in the "City Summary" section of the *Clipper* indicating that she and her "friend" Josie Mansfield were staying at the St. Julian Hotel. Wesner gave every indication that she intended to appear at the Theatre Comique, visiting the theater at the end of the week before she was due to perform. The following day, however, Wesner and Mansfield left New York for France.

Josie Mansfield's departure from the United States went unnoticed by the New York daily press, but the *New York Clipper* covered it extensively primarily because of Wesner's sudden and unannounced departure from the city. The *Clipper* cared little about Mansfield, but it was concerned with Wesner's irresponsible and unprofessional behavior: "Although [Wesner] was billed and advertised to commence an engagement at the Theatre Comique this evening, Oct. 7th, she took no pains to inform the manager of her departure. On the contrary, we are reliably informed that she visited that theatre on Friday P.M. last, and assured the management that she would be ready for her engagement on Monday. Such conduct is highly reprehensible, and, beyond the pecuniary loss to which managers in such cases are subjected, it creates a feeling of distrust between managers and performers, from which entirely innocent parties are liable to suffer inconvenience."[41] And in the review of performances at the Theatre Comique during the week of October 7–12, the reviewer noted: "Notwithstanding the elopement of Miss Ella Wesner to Europe with Miss Josephine Mansfield, the business at the Theatre Comique did not suffer in the least during the past week."[42] Clearly, the relationship between performers and management was of greatest interest to this newspaper, and there was no moral outrage at the relationship between the two women. By mid-November, advertising placed in the *Clipper* sought to place Wesner's "elopement" in a more positive light, claiming that she was touring "the principal cities" of Europe "in search of novelty" and would "return from Europe with a full repertoire of new songs in time to join Tony Pastor's touring company" in the spring.[43]

Hindle's wedding attracted the public notice that Wesner's escaped for a number of reasons. First, by the mid-1880s the national press had begun to notice the actions of variety performers, and a growing number of newspapers across the country regularly ran theatrical gossip in their pages. Second, Hindle's relationship with the profession was very different than Wesner's. During the 1870s Hindle had frequently changed agents—her experience with Charles Vivian had apparently taught her that men could not be trusted to guide her career. Hindle also attempted to take on variety management on a number of occasions and was most likely an independent woman who preferred to take charge rather than rely on the men around her to take care of her interests. As a result, when her marriage came to public attention, she lacked the support network to step in and repair the damage. On the other hand, Ella Wesner's career was saved by the speedy intervention of Col. T. Allston

145

Brown, her agent, and Tony Pastor, who had employed Wesner on a number of occasions and at whose theater she had debuted as a male impersonator.[44]

Hindle's marriage to Annie Ryan did not end her career, but it did relegate her to performing in second-rate variety halls and with female minstrel troupes. Hindle's first engagement after the scandal had died down was with the Ella Hill Burlesque Company, touring through New England. A review of the performance in the *Bangor Whig and Courier* described it as "on the whole, one of the best variety entertainments that has come this way for a number of years." The review also signaled out Hindle for praise, noting that she was a performer "whose fame as a personator and change artist precedes her" and that she had "surprised and pleased the audience."[45] Clearly news of the scandal had not reached this reviewer. Hindle continued to find similar bookings into the 1890s, and in 1892 she signed the female agent Bijou Price to represent her. Hindle's professional associations with women during the last decade of her career suggest that there was an informal support network provided by women in the profession to each other.

Unlike Hindle, Wesner had been content to leave the management of her career in the hands of her agent, even though she was older than Hindle and had more experience in American theater. This continued to be the case throughout the rest of her career, and at the end of her career she struggled to find bookings because she had outlasted many of her male supporters in variety and had not managed to forge the same connections with the younger generation of entrepreneurial managers. It is worth considering that a childhood spent working in the theater had conditioned Wesner to accept the status quo and not to seriously challenge the primacy of her male colleagues in theater, while Hindle, a foreign-born performer with weaker ties to the American stage, may have felt less bound by tradition.

Baby Bindley, dressed in stage costume with musical glasses. Advertising card with biography on back,
produced by her father and manager,
Prof. Bindley. Unknown photographer, ca. 1875. Author's collection,
acquired with funding from the
Center for 21st Century Studies,
University of Wisconsin–Milwaukee.

BABY BINDLEY,
The American Child Actress, Character-
Change Artist, and Musical Phenomenon.

Gus Williams, "Dutch"
comedian active in variety,
vaudeville, and musical comedy. Photograph by Dana,
New York, ca. 1875. Author's
collection.

Tony Pastor, variety performer and manager. Photograph by Newsboy, New York, ca. 1880. Author's collection.

Charles Vivian, English ballad singer active in variety. Unknown photographer, ca. 1870. Author's collection.

Ella Wesner, male imper-
sonator active in variety.
Photograph by Napoleon
Sarony, New York, ca. 1872.
Author's collection.

Ella Wesner, dressed in principal boy's costume, taken late
in her career when she was
performing at Koster & Bial's
Music Hall. Cigarette card,
Dixie Cigarettes, with thumb-
tack holes at top and bottom,
ca. 1890. Author's collection.

"The Great Hindle," Annie Hindle, the first male impersonator active in variety. Unknown photographer, probably Napoleon Sarony, ca. 1880. Minstrel Show Collection, Harry Ransom Humanities Research Center, the University of Texas at Austin.

Lydia Thompson in burlesque costume for a male character, with axe. Unknown photographer, ca. 1870. Author's collection.

Lydia Thompson.

Grace Sherwood in burlesque costume, dressed as Robinson Crusoe. Photograph by Newsboy, New York, ca. 1880. Author's collection.

Mabel Santley, burlesque actress with the Rentz-Santley Troupe, in suggestive pose. Tinted stereoview, Stereoscopic Gems, ca. 1880. Author's collection.

Colonna Troupe, English ballet dancers and burlesque actresses who formed the core of the first Rentz-Santley Troupe. Stereoview by unknown photographer, ca. 1870–75. Author's collection.

Sustaining Business in Difficult Times

What's in a Name?
Vaudeville vs. Variety in New York and in Regional Theater

PARISIAN VARIETIES, Sixteenth street and Broadway.
EVERY EVENING AT 8 O'CLOCK. MATINEES every Tuesday, Thursday and Saturday at 2. Favorite resort for gentlemen and strangers. Choice specialties, brilliant novelties, musical morceaux, spicy, sparkling, voluptuous, Frenchy, but artistic.
—Advertising, *New York Clipper*, May 6, 1876: 48

In the years after the Civil War, variety flourished in New York, and small, low-class theaters opened to cater to the city's returned soldiers and workingmen. Like the early free and easies, these halls did not place much advertising, and they received little attention from local authorities unless they were the cause of public disturbance or drunken rowdiness. But the economic failure of 1873 brought all sorts of commercial entertainments, including variety, back to the attention of the city's moral reformers, and they almost immediately focused on the cancan and other mass displays of women, both of which were characteristic elements of sexualized variety.[1] Contemporary thinking connected personal failure to national failure, and in the midst of economic crisis and on the cusp of the centenary, anxiety about the nation's moral health ran high. The depression years saw temperance campaigns and campaigns against prostitution and other forms of urban leisure, not just in large cities, but all over the country. In New York City, the police raided the Metropolitan Theatre in 1874 for staging the cancan and arrested the manager, the dancers, and the orchestra of theater, jailing them overnight. Similar raids occurred in subsequent years in the Midwest, and by 1879 moral reformers in Cincinnati were engaged in a prolonged battle to change the theatrical licensing laws of that city to eliminate variety halls that staged this dance.

While changes to the law in New York had driven George Lea from the business of variety, they did not completely eliminate sexualized variety. Ballet corps had provided titillation for the male audience through the late 1860s and early 1870s, and after the success of the *Black Crook* and Lydia Thompson's British Blondes in 1868, the cancan was a dance that was increasingly associated with variety performance. There were few complaints about this dance until the mid-1870s. The cancan was incredibly popular with male variety audiences, as were other mass displays of women, including the "Amazon chorus" and other displays of formation marching known as "Zouave Drills." In many ways, these displays prefigure the choreography of Busby Berkeley in the early twentieth century or the choreography of the Rockettes. But, while these forms of dance are considered family fare, the performances in variety halls were not, and the primary difference was context. Unlike respectable variety theaters operated by Tony Pastor and Col. William Sinn and others, these halls did not seek to accommodate women in their audience. While the law prevented them serving alcohol in the auditorium, few other changes had been made to a show that resembled the rough-and-rowdy shows of the earlier concert saloons.

As the economic situation worsened during 1874, managers of smaller New York theaters whose existence was always tenuous chose to stage the cancan in order to guarantee a large audience—their advertising often noted the number of consecutive nights the cancan had been staged for the audience. The Metropolitan Theatre, a small low-class variety hall in New York, began offering the cancan and a "Lady Gymnast" to its patrons during the summer of 1874, and other theaters followed suit when they saw its popularity. By the end of the summer season both the Metropolitan Theatre and Robinson Hall offered the cancan to their patrons nightly.[2] The *New York Times* noted this fact with some disgust, declaring that the performance "not merely overleaps the proprieties in a slight measure, but . . . is strongly objectionable."[3] By the end of that month the dance had attracted enough notice that the police were forced to act, and on August 31 they raided the Metropolitan Theatre, where the cancan was given with what the *Clipper* called "questionable embellishments."[4] Forty-two people were arrested, including the dancers, the orchestra, the proprietor, and the stage manager, and they were all held overnight. At the court the next morning only the proprietor, Mr. Shapter, was jailed and fined, while the others were released.[5]

These arrests did not end the performance of the cancan in New York, but managers now knew how far they could modify the dance before offending the authorities. Given that the proprietor of the Metropolitan Theatre was fined $500 for keeping a disorderly house, managers had a real incentive to maintain some minimum level of decency at their performances. Both the Metropolitan Theatre and Robinson Hall continued to stage the dance after the raid, and the cancan maintained its popularity in subsequent years. In advertising managers tended to stress the French, and therefore sexually sophisticated, nature of the dance. The cancan raids in 1874 reinitiated the complex dance between civic authority, moral reform, and variety managers that had abated in the wake of the Anti–Concert Saloon Bill in the early 1860s, and managers once again were adept at remaining within the letter of the law, while transgressing against its intent.

In 1875 George Robinson reopened his hall at 16th Street and Broadway as the Parisian Varieties and advertised that it was a "Temple of sensational art" offering "the most elegant entertainment in New York" consisting of a "grand olio of song, dance, ballet, farce, sketch, musical gems, gymnastic wonders, and the cream of specialty, novelty and variety."[6] Nothing about these claims distinguished the theater from the many other variety halls in the city, but the names of the personnel listed beneath suggests that Robinson had decided to rely on something other than the presentation of first-class variety to attract an audience to his hall. Adverting named ten women and eight men who comprised the variety stock company and also included the names of eighteen and later twenty female ballet dancers. The large number of women at this theater is notable in a period in which many variety halls had dispensed with their ballet corps and men tended to outnumber women on variety bills by approximately two to one.

The proprietors of the Parisian Varieties had learned over a number of seasons operating this venue as a rental hall that all-female entertainment consistently drew a good audience. But the cancan arrests in 1874 had taught them just how far they could go both in their advertising and on the stage. Advertising placed by the managers of these halls now stressed elegance, taste, and decency, but playful turns-of-phrase also hint that some fun was being made of these concepts. For example, an advertisement for this theater placed a month after it opened described the theater and the entertainment it offered as: "Home of the beautiful. Palace of Delight. Grand Olio of Artists every night. We give the gems of art without offence, to captivate the fancy, charm the sense, most delightful attractions ever attempted in New York. MELANGE DE FASCINATION, of voluptuous dances, beautiful women, living tableaux, spicy sketches, gorgeous ballets, brilliant novelties and NO COARSENESS OR VULGARITY.

An enchanting medley of all that is charming and tasteful in art by the prettiest women and accomplished actors in America."[7] The emphasis placed on the number of women on the stage continued to escalate in the first few months of operation, and by late December the theater was advertising twenty acts and fifty performers. The scale and grandeur of the entertainments described in this advertising is reminiscent of advertising placed by George Lea two decades earlier, and both theaters also made a feature of the presentation of suggestively titled tableaux vivants. During the next year, the language used in advertising placed by this theater continued to skirt along the edge of suggestiveness, including phrases such as "spicy and piquant" and "spicy, sparkling, voluptuous, Frenchy, but artistic."[8]

At the same time, the few existing reviews of this venue suggest that these managers staged a fairly standard variety show that placed more emphasis on women than was typical, but that was not particularly obscene. Robinson even defended his hall against obscenity charges; when the reformer Anthony Comstock requested that the singer Harry Montague remove a song with indecent lyrics from his act, Robinson fired the singer.[9] Except for the large number of women on the bill, there was little to distinguish the performance staged at this venue from Pastor's variety hall. In March 1876 the company from the Parisian Varieties toured towns in Connecticut and Massachusetts, and a review from Bridgeport noted that "in spite of a heavy storm, [they] were greeted with a good house, consisting chiefly of males, who were attracted thither with the expectation of seeing something 'broad' in the entertainment; but nothing of the kind, in any great degree, was offered, the show being of the usual style, and somewhat better than variety shows in general."[10]

The managers of the Parisian, Robinson and Woodley, presented a show based on a standard variety format. Neither man performed as part of this show, while most of the variety theaters against which they competed were managed by performer-managers, who could draw the leading performers of the period through personal connections.[11] Rather than trying to compete directly with other variety halls such as the Globe, the Olympic, Tony Pastor's New Opera House, or the Theatre Comique, the Parisian used the promise of sex to attract men to its audience and hoped that a solid, well-presented variety show with more emphasis than was typical on women would be sufficient to keep them. And this is where the major difference between respectable and sexualized variety lay—in the composition of its audience. At a time when variety managers increasingly sought to attract women and children to their audiences, these managers clung to a traditionalist view in which the audience was comprised entirely of men.

Unfortunately for the managers of this hall, tastes were rapidly changing, and this tactic was unsuccessful. By their second year of business under the name of the Parisian Varieties, the managers had begun to resort to novelties such as Greco-Roman wrestling matches to bolster their audience.[12] The continuing stress on women caused problems with the hall's neighbors, some of whom complained to the police. The theater was raided again in October 1876, and all of the performers as well as the ballet master, Giuseppe Cardella, and the proprietor, George Robinson, were arrested.[13] The raid appears to have marked the beginning of the end for this venture, because the Parisian Varieties disappeared in early 1877.

The cancan and sexualized variety remained attractive to male audiences in regional theater, especially in areas that attracted large populations of laborers. Managers of sexualized variety met this need by forming touring troupes that played in variety halls that could not afford to bring in first-class touring troupes like Tony Pastor's. Pastor most often played in the legitimate theater in regional tours, staging his show in opposition to the local variety hall. The name given to touring troupes of sexualized performers was female minstrelsy, and these women did, in fact, present a hybrid entertainment that combined the first part of the minstrel show, the variety olio, and a burlesque afterpiece in the style of Lydia Thompson. The cancan and formation dancing was found either in the olio or in the afterpiece. Almost immediately after the economic crash, troupes such as the Rentz-Santley Female Minstrels began to tour, performing in small halls and theaters across the country. Within two or three years, newspaper reports noted opposition to this form from ministers in local communities, but because troupes did not remain in any one place for more than a week, it was hard to stop them.

By the late 1870s the cancan and sexualized performance were beginning to attract trouble wherever they were performed, particularly by resident theater companies. Touring female minstrel companies stirred opposition to the dance, and by the end of the 1870s an all-male and predominantly working-class audience was becoming less attractive to managers of respectable variety because the kind of entertainment they desired increasingly drew the ire of local authorities, regardless of whether the content of individual acts was obscene. Variety managers moved toward offering a show that attracted a "family" audience, which ideally included women, or women and children, at matinee performances. In large cities such as New York and Chicago most variety halls sought to attract a family audience, and only a small number of venues continued to cater to men alone. The major problem for managers of family variety halls was to find a way to distinguish themselves from other less respectable theaters. During the mid-1870s terms such as "first-class" were used, but increasingly the term "vaudeville" came to distinguish family-style entertainment from the more rough-and-ready entertainment of sexualized variety.

During the early 1870s there was no consistent use of the term "vaudeville." It had been used earlier in the century to denote French-language theatrical presentations, particularly in New York City, but by the late 1860s it was also being used by legitimate English-language companies, most often in combination with the term "burlesque." These companies used this combination of terms to indicate that they presented sophisticated literary and comic drama that also included music. So, for example, in 1867 the Fifth Avenue Theatre presented a company of legitimate actors, including Lina Edwin, Mr. and Mrs. Leffingwell, Kate Howard, and Sol Smith, billing them as a Burlesque and Vaudeville Company. Three years later, Lina Edwin described her theater as the "Bijou theatre of America . . . in the front rank as a popular house for vaudeville and burlesque."[14] At the time her company was presenting *Black-Eyed Susan* and *Camille* and the following week presented an adaptation of Dickens's *Barnaby Rudge*. The repertoire, and the fact that Edwin charged $1 admission to her matinee and fifty cents for children, indicates that for her these terms carried respectable and literary associations.

The other New York theaters that used the term "vaudeville" early in the 1870s were those presenting sexualized variety, which were, for the most part, also those theaters operated by entrepreneurial rather than performing managers. The Globe Theatre, which opened in late September 1870 and was managed by John Stetson of Boston, is the first variety theater I have found using the term "vaudeville" in New York City.[15] The *New York Herald* noted that it was opening as a "grand Vaudeville and Novelty Theatre," and the first bill offered at the theater featured Lisa Weber's Burlesque Troupe and Signor Costa's Grand Ballet with fifty female dancers. Seasoned variety performers, including Sheridan and Mack, Charles Vivian, and Master Barney, were also on the opening bill, presumably in an olio between the burlesque and the ballet.[16] While the *Herald* referred to this theater as a variety theater in all subsequent reporting, the more proper *New York Times* continued to use the term "vaudeville," and when the Olympic Theater, which had been programming primarily opera bouffe, switched to variety in early 1874, both the theater and the *Times* used the term "vaudeville and novelty theatre" to describe the entertainment it offered.[17] In the following year, when Robinson Hall opened as the Parisian Varieties, the *Times* employed the same phrase to describe that venue. At least in the pages of this single newspaper, a distinction was drawn between vaudeville and variety. While the Olympic and the Parisian Varieties offered vaudeville, Tony Pastor's and Hitchcock's Third Avenue Theater, which were both run by performer-managers, offered variety.[18]

The Metropolitan Theatre, which also offered sexualized fare, began to advertise itself as "the People's Vaudeville Theatre" just weeks after the police raided it and while it was still exhibiting the cancan. This move may have been intended to cloak a potentially indecent performance in the respectability of a literary term, or it might have been a satirical move intended to point out the hypocrisy of polite society. The cancan had been respectable in the context of Offenbach's *La Vie Parisienne*, staged at the Theatre Français in New York in late March 1868, and it had not been raided when the piece was revived by Mlle. Aimée's troupe at the Lyceum in 1874 or burlesqued by the Viennoise Ballet Troupe at a performance at the Grand Opera House in 1870.[19] Clearly there was a double standard in play, and context was the determining factor when it came to decency—in the Grand Opera House or the Lyceum the dance was daring but not obscene, while at the Metropolitan and Robinson Hall it was outside the bounds of decency. Given that it was common for minstrel and variety companies to make fun of elite culture in burlesques of some of the most popular operas and plays of the day, perhaps we can also view this use of the word "vaudeville" as a form of burlesque.[20]

155

By the late 1870s the term "vaudeville" had largely lost its associations with the cancan and had come to be used interchangeably with the term "high-class variety," which was the term most often used by Tony Pastor, particularly outside New York City. And at the end of the decade the term "vaudeville" came to be more closely associated with managers who sought to attract a broader family audience, many of whom were entrepreneurial managers, while variety represented entertainment for men.

Within variety, there was also a divide between theaters that offered entertainment to an English-speaking audience and those that catered to immigrant populations, which, in the 1870s were most often German. Germans had long run beer gardens, not only in New York City but also in cities such as Milwaukee and Cincinnati, both of which had large German populations. German managers had also long sought to cater to a family audience that included men, women, and children, and this gave them a business advantage in the late 1870s and early 1880s as variety expanded its audience. A number of German managers, including Heuck in Cincinnati and also Klaw and Erlanger in Brooklyn, were highly successful in making the transition from a German-speaking audience to an English-speaking one.

Vaudeville was also a term more often used by the managers of touring first-class variety troupes, even in the early 1870s. These managers sought to distinguish themselves from the managers of local variety halls, and given that touring variety troupes most often booked into the legitimate theater or hall-for-hire in the town, they also needed to reassure their broader audience that they presented decent entertainment. For example, the following announcement for a touring combination appeared in the pages of the *Stevens Point (Wisc.) Journal* in 1874: "McCulloch's Hall—To night Hayden's Vaudeville and Comedy Combination make their debut before a Stevens Point audience, and from our exchanges we find this organization is composed of the leading members of the Theatrical Profession organized for a short season at the Opera House, St. Paul. They are now on their return trip to Chicago, stopping at a few places *en route*. Their performances have been attended by the 'caste' people of the larger cities and their entertainment is chaste and finished and being a novel one in this section of the country we can assure them a liberal patronage."[21] The concern over decency here is evident, as is the fact that variety entertainment was a relatively new phenomenon in rural Wisconsin and even St. Paul, Minnesota, in 1874.

The brief association of the term "vaudeville" with sexualized variety that occurred during the depths of a devastating economic depression and only within the confines of New York City seems to have escaped the notice of theater managers and audiences in the rest of the nation. But this second use of the term "vaudeville" within New York City may explain why it was slow to be adopted by first-class variety managers within that city. Indeed, Tony Pastor preferred the term "variety" even after the Boston manager B. F. Keith had brought the term "vaudeville" into widespread use in New York in the 1890s.

Noting the use of these two terms, variety and vaudeville, is important, however, because it illuminates the tensions between sexualized and respectable performance that were present within the form for its entire history. These tensions include those between performing and entrepreneurial managers; between traditionalists, who sought to keep their male audience happy, and innovators or pragmatists, who sought to expand their audience to include women and children and later ethnic populations; and finally between the older generation of managers, who had shaped the development of the genre in its first decades as an independent form, and younger, entrepreneurial managers, who entered the genre during the 1870s, 1880s, and later.

Second, the terminological question is important because it shows that the periphery of the theatrical world—in other words, everything outside New York City—did not necessarily follow the same practice as the center. New York was home to up to half a dozen major variety theaters during the 1870s, while most other cities, even large ones such as Chicago or Buffalo or Pittsburgh, hosted only one major variety hall as well as one or two minor venues that struggled to attract talent. In these cities, touring troupes posed serious competition for the local manager offering high-class variety, who also needed to distinguish his theater from the smaller venues offering disreputable acts. The economic crisis of the 1870s only heightened these stresses, and it was during this period that a number of innovative high-class variety managers changed their policies, disbanding their own companies and hosting touring troupes instead.

The sheer number of performing opportunities in multiple venues and the large potential audience in New York meant that the city had long been the center of theatrical activity for the nation, and neither economic downturns nor shifting business practices changed this. As a result older styles of management tended to last longer within that city than outside it. The fiercer competition outside New York also meant that regional managers, such as John Stetson, Col. Sinn, and later B. F. Keith, developed aggressive management styles that worked to their advantage within the more old-fashioned world of New York, where friendship and cooperation between competing managers was not uncommon. Actors and actresses were not the only ones who moved from the periphery to the center. Managers and management styles also took this route, and while New York moved more slowly, it did come to change and accommodate the developments in regional variety, and the periphery was instrumental in shaping variety entertainment at the center, New York.

Sex Rears Its
Ugly Head . . . Again
Female Minstrelsy

> May Fisk's Famous and Original Troupe of English Blondes. May
> Fisk, Manageress . . . "The Devil Fisheth best for the Souls of Men
> when his Hook is Baited with a Lovely Limb." Three Weeks at
> Tony Pastor's, Two Weeks in Philadelphia, Through the Heat of the
> Summer. The Only Blonde Troupe Now Existing, and The Only
> One That Has Not Succumbed. Keep Clear of Our Track. We Are
> Represented by Brains and Beauty.
>
> —Advertisement placed by May Fisk and addressing the variety
> profession, *Clipper*, August 24, 1878: 176

I n April 1878 the regional actress May Fisk formed her own
theatrical troupe and embarked on a summer tour of the Midwest. Fisk, who was 29, had been on the stage for seven or eight
years, and despite her not inconsiderable ambitions had been unable to rise
above supporting player in stock companies in Boston and Milwaukee.[1] During
1873 she had been part of the company at the Opera House in Milwaukee, and
while the audience loved her, the theater reviewer was less certain, finding her
"pleasing" but unsuited to the drama of the role.[2] By the following season she
had moved on to a smaller company and was finally able to take the leading
roles she desired. In February 1875 Fisk performed in her own play entitled
Pygmalian and Galatea in Janesville, Wisconsin, and by the following month
had assumed management of the Janesville Opera House.[3] As manager, she
took a company on the road, playing in smaller Wisconsin towns, including

Stevens Point.[4] Fisk then disappears from the record for a number of seasons and was most likely working in another regional stock company or in a relatively anonymous position in theater.

The troupe that Fisk assembled at the end of the 1877/78 season had little connection with her previous work in legitimate drama with regional theater companies. Fisk assembled a female minstrel company that included the variety performers Bessie and Dolly Warren, Dolly Byron, A. D. Weaver and his wife, Ida Siddons, the Arnold Brothers, and Louisa and Gracie Sherwood. Fisk advertised a show that included "the latest of sensational Extravaganzas, especially arranged and adapted for this company by May Fisk, entitled, A CELEBRATED BLONDE CASE; or, a Blue Bird of Paradise" and "the Arnold Brothers' Novelty Sextette, the six champion Clog Dancers of the world. Six End Men, six Song and Dance Artists, and a number of prominent performers."[5] The early reviews for this troupe, billed as the "English Blondes," were promising, and there was little to indicate that the entertainment offered was anything other than a standard variety show.

At the same time, Fisk ran into opposition almost as soon as her troupe went on the road. The *Chicago Inter-Ocean* ran a column describing the process of hiring extra dancers for Fisk's ballet, which carried the suggestion that most of the young women who applied did so because of dire financial need and were horrified by the immodest costumes required by the job.[6] In October the *Chicago Daily Tribune* noted that Fisk had been refused a license to perform in Keokuk, Iowa, and had initiated a lawsuit against the city to recover damages.[7] This was not the last lawsuit filed by Fisk against local authorities when bookings had to be canceled, and it explained the increasing bravado in the advertising Fisk placed in the *Clipper* during the late 1870s and early 1880s. Fisk's advertisements boasted of her success and her troupe's superior abilities, challenged her opposition, and dared both the authorities and others to try to stop her. All of the advertisements list May Fisk as manageress; occasionally the names of men associated with the troupe as performers or in supporting roles such as advance agent were noted, but these changed from year to year, and it is likely that she was the leading figure behind this venture for close to a decade, apparently working without financial support from any other variety managers.

Before the advent of Fisk's Troupe, there had been no successful female managers in variety, and very few women had ever attempted to manage either a theater or a troupe alone. I have found only two other women listed as the manager of a variety theater during the 1870s. Ninon Duclos managed the Folly Theater in Chicago for just a few months from February to May 1878, offering her customers a mixed fare of variety, ballet, and burlesque.[8] Duclos, whose real name was Bridget O'Neil, had been part of a troupe of tableaux vivant artists exhibited at the Parisian Varieties in New York in 1877 and had briefly managed a summer garden that presented similar fare in the same city.[9] Sometime during the following year Duclos and her husband, William O'Neil, moved to Chicago and assumed management of the Folly, with O'Neil acting as the theater's business manager.[10] Almost immediately, Duclos met opposition from local reformers, and editorials in the *Chicago Daily Tribune* both protested her presence and crowed about her impending failure. After leaving Chicago, Duclos largely disappears from the record, although she led a female minstrel company for a brief period during 1879 and also appeared as a performer with this troupe at Thomas Snelbaker's Vine Street Opera-House in Cincinnati.[11]

Annie Hindle also attempted to enter management, taking charge of the Grand Central Variety Hall in Cincinnati. Unfortunately she did so in 1874, which was a particularly difficult year for theater because of the financial panic of the previous year. The *Clipper* reported that the owner of the Grand Central was a woman from Cincinnati, and while I cannot link Hindle to her, this perhaps explains why she chose to manage that particular theater. The economic downturn most likely damned the venture to failure, but mismanagement by Charles Howard, Hindle's business manager, probably contributed to the theater's downfall because the *Clipper* had reported that the house was doing a good business.[12] Faye Dudden notes that female managers in legitimate theater found it difficult to break into the all-male network of the theater business,[13] and this was also the case in variety management. The difficulty faced by other women who took on the role of manager makes May Fisk's success in this field all the more remarkable.

From 1878 until the early 1890s May Fisk performed a delicate balancing act presenting sexualized variety entertainment for predominantly male audiences all over the United States, facing fierce opposition both from the communities in which she performed and from within the theatrical world. Fisk openly taunted her opponents in advertising placed in the *Clipper*, which addressed members of the theatrical profession rather than the wider public. In 1878 she claimed that hers was "the only blonde troupe now existing and the only one that has not succumbed," and she warned her competition to "keep clear of our track."[14] Over the years Fisk's advertising became more inflammatory as she defied her opposition within the theater world, and the defensive and escalating language of her advertising suggests its strength.[15] In the tighter economic climate of the 1870s, variety managers at times resorted to underhand business tactics—William Sinn blacklisted performers who played at competing theaters, for example—to gain an advantage, and while I have seen no sign of an active conspiracy against Fisk or any of the female managers, the presence of a female manager, particularly in the field of sexualized performance, may well have offended men in variety. One result of this opposition was that Fisk consistently played at second-class venues and also in smaller towns; she was largely locked out of the first-class halls and the major circuits.

The earliest reviews of Fisk's Troupe indicate that she ran a standard touring female minstrel combination that presented minstrelsy, burlesque, and variety together in a single evening. In September 1878 her troupe included the variety performers the Sanyeahs, Bobby and Alice Dailey, Harris and King, and Billy Wylie when it played at Indianapolis, and during that season the *New York Clipper* treated her with respect and reported on her activities in its "Variety Halls" column.[16] Fisk ran into trouble early in that season, however, and was banned from performing in Richmond, Indiana, in September 1878, from Keokuk, Iowa, in October 1878, and from Baltimore in March 1879.[17] The *Clipper* noted that she had opened at Nachman's Front Street Theatre in Baltimore on March 24, but that she had drawn only a small audience. On March 28 the manager of this theater was forced to cancel the rest of the run due to the obscene nature of the troupe's performance.[18] Fisk apparently used obscenity as a marketing tactic to increase her audience at the next town in which she was to play, but this came with distinct risks. First, Fisk was more likely to be arrested and fined as a result of perceived obscenity or to have performances preemptively canceled by city authorities who had the power to revoke theatrical licenses on such grounds. Fisk's response was to take her opposition to court and to sue them for lost income.[19] Second, once Fisk's Troupe had earned the reputation for presenting "blue" material, she was less likely to be able to find bookings in first-class halls or to attract the best variety performers, who had an interest in maintaining their reputations, to her company, and this also endangered the success of the troupe. While a reputation for sexually charged material attracted a male audience, it also drew the ire of local authorities and reformers, as the protests against Fisk attest.

The trope of the uncontained and uncontrolled burlesque actress running rampant through the American landscape was frequently invoked in relation to May Fisk's Troupe, but hers was not the first troupe described in these terms. The model was established in the late 1860s when the English dancer and burlesque actress Lydia Thompson and her British Blondes Troupe toured the United States in the 1868–70 seasons. They drew huge audiences and equally large opposition from those who felt the performance was indecent. Thompson performed English literary burlesques, some based on historical and mythological figures like *Ixion* and others based on literature like *Robinson Crusoe*. The scripts were written in rhyme and depended on puns and

162

wordplay. The members of the company, which was comprised primarily of women, inserted topical references and asides at will, disrupting the already fragile narrative of the form; there was just one man in the troupe, and he played comic female roles. The revealing costumes and fractured narrative of burlesque, with actresses playing both male and female roles, challenged middle-class ideas about what constituted decent entertainment. Ministers in Chicago preached against the threat posed by this troupe, but for many the opposition increased the appeal of the performances.

The newspaper reports of Lydia Thompson's tour established the model for offstage behavior for burlesque actresses. Even before she arrived in the United States, newspapers had included snippets of gossip about Thompson, commenting on her skills, her career to that point, and her appearance. While the initial reaction to performances given by Thompson's troupe was positive, newspaper coverage soured as the fad for burlesque grew. Six months after Thompson's arrival in New York, the *Times* theatrical column complained that "burlesque madness" had broken out across the city: "The distinguishing symptom of the epidemic is a singular and easily detected appearance of masses of light and golden hair on the stage of the afflicted theatre; after this symptom the spectator is appalled by observing a tendency in the patients to dispossess themselves of their clothing . . . then follows a series of piercing and incoherent ravings called puns, and finally, strong convulsions denominated breakdowns and walk-arounds. . . . Some dismal folk have predicted destruction to our community from the example of the burlesquers. It is feared that the light hair, the clotheless and the convulsive symptoms may spread to every home and carry desolation to every hearth. The true remedy . . . is quarantine! The infection comes through late importations from England." Despite the light tone and joking manner, the author of this column was serious about the threat of burlesque, expressing his true concern below this comic diatribe: "The burlesque is a species of entertainment to dramatic art, because it defies criticism."[20] The real appeal of this form, he continued, lay not in its literary or musical merits—both the province of the theater critic—but in the physical appeal of the women in the cast. The popularity of the form threatened theater because it left little room for serious drama with literary merit that required great acting.

Later in this season and during the next season the protests against the troupe increased in number, and even before leaving New York City they had been involved in a violent altercation. In late May 1869 Alexander Henderson, the manager of the troupe and Thompson's husband, had an altercation with George Butler, the theater reviewer for the *New York Herald* and *Wilkes' Spirit of the Times*. Butler had written reviews critical of the troupe for these newspapers, and Henderson took them personally. The feud between the men escalated and culminated in Butler and several friends confronting Henderson at Niblo's Theater after a performance and severely beating him. They also threatened to shoot anyone who tried to stop them. Charges were brought against Butler for assault and libel.[21] While the reporting was initially sympathetic to Henderson, it quickly turned negative when Lydia Thompson pleaded that personal attacks should come to an end. The *New York Times* accused Henderson of hiding "behind the skirts of a woman" and defended the legitimacy of the charges brought against him in reviews and commentary on the troupe.[22] While Thompson's troupe was still incredibly popular, the journalistic tide had turned and had formed the consensus that burlesque was a danger to American theater.

After leaving New York City, the British Blondes toured the rest of the country and quickly ran into more disputes with local newspapermen. In February 1870 they were once again involved in a physical altercation, but in this case they were the aggressors. Lydia Thompson and Alexander Henderson, along with the actress Pauline Markham, attacked the editor of the *Chicago Times*, Wilbur F. Storey, because they were upset at his negative coverage of their performances in that city. The two actresses and their manager were arrested and tried for assault and fined and then later sued by Storey in civil court. The events were covered with much amusement by newspapers all over the country, because the image of a woman attacking a man with a riding crop was compelling. Despite there being little sympathy for Storey, this event came to represent the multiple threats of burlesque and other popular theatrical forms that relied on the exhibition of scantily clad women in the popular imagination. The *New York Times* complained: "Since the horsewhipping exploit of Miss Lydia Thompson and her fair associates in Chicago, an unusual degree of belligerency has developed itself among their sisters throughout the land. Apparently, some such example was the one thing they needed to show them with what impunity the tyrant might be attacked with his own weapons, and so to urge them to a long-premeditated onset. To one who reads the newspapers it really seems as if the women of the country, animated by a common impulse, had all at once procured horsewhips, and were going around like roaring lionesses seeking whom they might chastise."[23]

The sense of panic at the women of the nation being out of control is palpable in this report, and it reflects the trope of the out-of-control horsewhipping actress—a woman who lacked modesty and restraint and was financially less dependent on men than most women—which was firmly cemented in the public imagination. The rate at which women attacked men with whips did not rise significantly in this period, but as the feminist cause revived after the end of the Civil War, anxiety over women's ambitions and desires to exceed their accepted social role increased, and Thompson's success only confirmed this.[24] Even though the majority of newspaper reports about horsewhippings during the 1870s involved two men, a significant number of prominent women were also accused of taking justice into their own hands. Less than a year after Thompson's fracas in Chicago, the *Georgia Weekly Telegraph* reported in snide tones that the abolitionist Anna Dickinson was contemplating horsewhipping a minister. The actress and onetime manager of the Folly Theater in Chicago, Ninon Duclos (Bridget O'Neil) was also accused of cowhiding a wool merchant in Providence, Rhode Island, who had cheated her of $27,000.[25]

The trope of the horsewhipping burlesque actress running rampant through the landscape reached new heights in the coverage of May Fisk's Troupe. Fisk was reported as seeking vengeance against men twice in a two-year span, during which time a number of newspapers also relished reporting on her many legal difficulties, license denials, and altercations with other members of the profession.[26] She was also frequently reported as having legal disputes with the members of her troupe, and the image of a coercive, manipulative, and exploitative manager emerges from these reports scattered in Midwestern and East Coast newspapers. At the same time, Fisk hired experienced performers and specifically advertised for variety veterans; during the late 1870s and 1880s her troupe included a good number of the leading performers of the early 1870s, including the Sanyeahs, A. D. Weaver, Ida Siddons, and even Annie Hindle. And, despite the large number of reports that excoriated Fisk for her obscene performances, the small number of newspapers that actually bothered to review the content of her show described a perfectly standard variety performance with a burlesque afterpiece. How are these two, very different pictures to be reconciled?

There is no one answer to this question, and the hostility to Fisk from city authorities needs to be differentiated from the hostility expressed from within the theatrical profession, although they are not completely unconnected. Male managers of female minstrel troupes, such as Michael Leavitt who managed the highly successful Rentz-Santley Troupe, also ran into opposition from civic authorities, but it tended to be less violent than that encountered by Fisk, and the Rentz-Santley combination was rarely denied licenses to perform. But it is notable that Leavitt escaped censure by other theater professionals.[27] Even though reviews suggest that there was little substantive difference between the performances staged by the two troupes, Fisk and her performers were treated as a threat to public morality and even public safety, not only by local newspapers, but also by the trade newspapers. The *Clipper*, which appears to have employed a policy similar to the old adage "if you can't say something nice, say nothing at all" was initially neutral about Fisk, reporting on her activities in a very matter-of-fact way. Eventually it stopped reviewing Fisk's Troupe, but continued to carry her advertising. The *New York Dramatic Mirror*, on the other hand, lambasted Fisk, calling her an "old harridan" and "that stench in the nostrils of the variety profession" and describing members of her troupe as a "collection of painted and scrawny 'dizzies.'"[28] Founded in 1879, the *Dramatic Mirror* was a newspaper dedicated to the support of high-class and moral variety, but I have seen no similar attacks in its pages of male managers who ran female minstrel troupes.

165

Fisk's crime, from the perspective of the variety world, appears to have been that she operated without the guidance of a male co-manager, unlike the Chicago theater manager Ninon Duclos who was in partnership with her husband, or under the patronage of a more powerful male variety manager such as Pastor or Stetson, or a minstrel manager such as Leavitt. The *Dramatic Mirror* depicted her as an actress of insufficient skills, whose beauty was long faded. The description echoes language used a decade earlier by the feminist actress Olive Logan in her attack on the sexualized literary burlesque of Lydia Thompson's Troupe.[29] Fisk's presence in the theater world was viewed as threatening the well-being of the wider profession because of the hostility and opposition she elicited from nonprofessionals. Fisk is described as though she is a madam presiding over a brothel full of unattractive women who lacked the sense to know any better. Just as Logan felt she needed to distance her profession from the taint of prostitution, so too did the *Dramatic Mirror*.

There was little about the composition of Fisk's Troupe or the entertainment she staged to distinguish her troupe from other female minstrel companies managed by male managers. Fisk did, however, provide employment for a significant number of actresses and dancers during the decade or more in which she was active. It is unclear if the terms of employment she offered were substantially different from those offered by male managers, but it is evident that she was willing to employ older women whose careers were declining and whose attractiveness to male managers might have waned. And despite reports of contract and payment disputes with members of her troupe, there is also evidence that her performers were intensely loyal to her. A report in the *Chicago Daily Tribune* in October 1878 described Fisk physically attacking two Chicago managers to force them to pay the full wages of local ballet girls who were hired to supplement her company while performing in that city.[30] The wages of the additional ballet dancers were divided between Fisk and the managers of the Metropolitan Theatre, and the dispute arose from their insistence that the money be deducted from Fisk's share of the income earned from the show, which was also divided between the house and the troupe. The loyalty of Fisk's performers is clear in this report, which depicts them rushing to her aid in her physical attack on the Chicago managers.

Despite the outraged tone of the report, which noted that the house staged immoral performances, it celebrates Fisk in a backhanded way. The column commented that her troupe's performance at the Metropolitan Theatre was less than a full success because "the show was not particularly immoral, and the display of female charms not above the average."[31] Unintentionally, this newspaper agrees with the many reviews of Fisk's performances that appeared in the *St. Louis Globe-Democrat*, a newspaper that carried extensive theatrical coverage and whose reviewers were intimately familiar with the theatrical world. In September 1878 the *Globe-Democrat* described Fisk's original troupe members as "the most perfect in form and beautiful in feature of any troupe that has appeared here. They are excellent artists, besides, and some of them are superb vocalists."[32] The last comment probably refers to Grace Sherwood, who went on to perform in burlesques and operettas in the 1880s. The *Globe-Democrat* consistently treated Fisk's Troupe as a regular variety combination and praised the performances she presented, as did other newspapers with similarly comprehensive theatrical coverage.

The civic authorities in smaller cities and towns were opposed not only to Fisk, but to most burlesque and variety combinations and the venues that hosted them. This opposition was driven, in part, by antitheatrical prejudice that still ran strong in smaller towns and cities. Theaters in such towns had been able to survive only by arguing for the educational or morally uplifting power of drama. This was not an argument that had any traction where burlesque and even respectable variety was concerned, and so managers hosting these entertainments almost inevitably faced some opposition. The association of variety with alcohol and with working-class men also posed a problem. While New York, Philadelphia, and other large cities were home to multiple theaters, smaller towns and cities had just one hall, which hosted a range of touring dramatic troupes—from opera and spoken drama to minstrelsy and variety. If there was a permanent variety hall in the city, it was most often associated with a local tavern or bar and was not patronized by women or most respectable townspeople.

During the depression of the 1870s, small variety halls increasingly relied on touring troupes that provided a higher quality entertainment than local managers could muster on their stages, and these were the kinds of venues in which May Fisk's Troupe played, while respectable variety troupes performed in the respectable theater. As was the case with respectable variety, the business model in sexualized variety had shifted from permanent stock companies based in a single theater and supplemented by star performers, to one in which the local manager provided a licensed hall with a stage and some drops and the touring manager provided everything else. In the early 1890s the struggle to maintain a large traveling female minstrel company drove May Fisk from the business, and she returned to the stage as an actress, taking character roles in musical comedies. Sexualized variety was consolidated under the control of a number of enterprising male managers such as Michael Leavitt and Sam T. Jack, who both operated burlesque theaters in Chicago and also controlled multiple touring road troupes. Female minstrelsy thrived under the guidance of these and other businessmen, who formed circuits and organizations that paralleled the developments in respectable variety as it was transformed into vaudeville.

Moral Reform
in Regional Variety
The Fight to Preserve
Community Standards

Vine Street Opera-House. Only "Sensational Show" on Earth! "In Limme" Pleasure Begins.... First time of a Gorgeous First Part Setting. Scenic Effects from the Studio of O. J. Kover and the NATURAL EFFECTS in the SHAPE OF SHAPES from all parts of the Universe where FEMALE BEAUTY is to be found. Grand Matinee To-Day (Sunday), at 2:15 P.M. Extra Matinee Christmas Day!
—*Cincinnati Commercial*, December 21, 1879: 9

The economic collapse of the mid-1870s saw a renewed emphasis on moral reform all over the nation, and local authorities once again focused on variety as they passed ordinances to bring renewed order to their towns. These included new laws restricting itinerants and vagrants, including men who found themselves out of work, as well as laws governing service industries that were seen as contributing to moral disorder. During the 1870s conflicts over variety halls and the decency of variety performance appeared in a number of cities in the Midwest, often triggered by touring female minstrel troupes. The *Clipper* noted the passage of antivariety ordinances in small cities in Pennsylvania and also in Cincinnati, which had been a town in which variety had found a home since the 1860s. In Cincinnati the conflict arose from the same social tensions that had driven the passage of the Anti–Concert Saloon Bill in New York in the early 1860s—the debate over who controlled public space in the city and conflicting views of what constituted decency or worth in commercial entertainment. The conflict over variety in Cincinnati not only reflects shifting power in city politics, but also the increasing importance of ethnic populations and the commercial entertainment that catered to them in the world of variety.

169

At the mid-nineteenth century, the population of Cincinnati was divided into a number of groups, including "Buckeyes," locally born Ohioans or young men who had moved to the city from the South or neighboring states and had adopted the customs of the locals; Yankees, who were transplants from the Northeastern states and comprised the social, intellectual, and artistic elite of the city; and immigrants, who were primarily German or from England, Ireland, or Scotland. Buckeyes, who preferred simpler and more convivial entertainment to the Yankees, comprised the largest proportion of the population, followed by the Germans, British immigrants, and then the Yankees.[1] Apart from these major resident populations, Cincinnati was also home, at least temporarily, to a population of transient workers engaged in the city's river trade and also to workingmen employed by the city's manufacturing industries. These men tended to live in boarding houses located on the west side of the city.

Theatrical bills from the two major theaters operating in Cincinnati during the 1840s reflect this social makeup. Of the major north-south thoroughfares, Broadway and Sycamore Streets were the city's main streets and home to businesses patronized by respectable citizens—both Buckeyes and Yankees. Vine and Race Streets, north-south streets three or four blocks to the west, were associated with businesses catering to the town's workingmen. These included saloons, boarding houses, beer halls, billiard halls, bowling halls, shooting galleries, and other forms of inexpensive amusements.[2] The National Theatre, which opened in 1837, was located on Sycamore near Fourth Street and catered to the Yankees, who lived primarily on Fourth Street, as well as to Buckeyes, who lived east of Broadway. This theater had a stock company and presented a range of dramas from serious plays that would more likely to have appealed to the Yankees in the audience to melodramas, farces, and burlesques that would have been more to the taste of the Buckeyes. Touring stars played at the National, supported by its stock company, and in the summer it hosted touring troupes of performers. The location of the city on the Ohio River made it easily accessible by river from Pittsburgh and downriver from St. Louis and ultimately New Orleans, and the city maintained its theatrical links with these cities into the late nineteenth century.

During the mid-1840s a number of theaters competed with the National, the first of which was the People's Theatre, located on Third and Vine Streets.

The manager of this theater, William Shires, had begun his career as a saloon owner who also began to offer entertainment to his patrons. The People's opened in 1845 and offered entertainment ranging from melodramas of the more sensational kind to novelty acts such as circus-style acts, magicians, ventriloquists, and other variety acts.[3] This fare was intended to attract the city's workingmen and the transient population of laborers to this theater. In contrast to the National, touring combinations played at the People's only occasionally, and in the summer, the People's moved its entertainment outdoors, offering equestrian shows and fireworks along with variety.[4] The People's Theatre was short-lived, closing in 1846, but Rockwell's Amphitheatre on Sixth and Vine soon took its place.

In the summer months, the differences between these theaters was less evident as the National hosted touring minstrel companies. During the heat of the summer, those residents who could leave the city did so. Located in the Ohio River valley and surrounded by steep hills, summer in Cincinnati was often hot and humid, and the city also suffered periodically from outbreaks of yellow fever. Hillside summer resorts opened in the surrounding countryside to offer members of Cincinnati society who abandoned the city respite from the heat. For those remaining in the city, other outdoor amusements were often more attractive, and theaters adapted their bills or scaled back the entertainment offered during the hottest months of the summer. When the National shifted to more popular fare during the summer, it threatened competing theaters in the city, but every fall at the beginning of the new theatrical season, the National was also quick to reassure its traditional patrons of its respectability. As James Dunlap notes: "Two statements appear often in newspaper bills for all theatres throughout the period, and particularly at the beginning of the season. They are significant. The first: 'A strong and efficient police will be in attendance.' The second: 'No female will be admitted unless accompanied by a gentleman.' Behind these statements lay two conditions which made theatre attendance a dubious practice for those of a refined nature. The pit of the theatre was a favorite gathering place for the rowdies; the third tier (in the case of the National, specifically) was a popular resort for the city's prostitutes."[5] After summer seasons in which the city's "rowdy" elements ruled the National Theatre, it was important to reassure the respectable audience that the theater was once again safe.

The theater scene in Cincinnati in the 1840s–1860s was similar in many ways to those in New York City or other large East Coast cities at the beginning of the nineteenth century. With a population of around 150,000 at midcentury,[6] Cincinnati was not yet large enough to support a wide range of professional theatrical entertainments segmented by social class. As a result, the most successful Cincinnati theaters needed to cater to a broad cross-section of Cincinnati residents if they were to remain in business. By the 1870s, however, the situation had changed considerably, as had the social dynamics of the city. Beginning in the 1850s the growth in the immigrant and working-class population began to shift the balance of power from the Whigs, who represented the city's traditional leaders, who were from the Buckeye and Yankee portion of the population, to the Democrats, whose power base lay among the working class and the Germans. By the 1870s the divisions between these populations had widened, and the number of theaters catering to the city's working-class and immigrant residents had also increased. Not surprisingly, those calling for the moral reform of the city came from the middle and upper classes. Reformers in Cincinnati sought primarily to cleanse public spaces to make them safe for respectable citizens, which meant among other things closing the many popular theaters on Vine Street that offered both wine and female performers to their patrons seven days a week.[7]

Despite the odd early protest about theater in the late 1850s, no action was taken until the end of the 1870s. The Civil War slowed theatrical life in the city, but also encouraged the growth of variety halls. These continued to operate sporadically during the depression years of the mid-1870s, but the recovery at the end of the decade allowed variety halls to flourish, and their resurgence drew the attention of moral-reform forces in the city. A fierce battle was waged over theater in Cincinnati between 1878 and 1881, and the business practice most opposed by reformers was the staging of Sunday performances, which were a standard part of Cincinnati life in the post–Civil War period due to the large German population of the city. Reformers also protested against the kinds of acts presented in variety theaters and focused in particular on acts that featured women, such as the cancan. The cancan was a feature of Cincinnati theater life from the beginning of the 1870s and was particularly associated with variety. One early variety hall, the Race Street Varieties, had regularly offered the cancan, exhibitions of tableaux vivants, and a resident female minstrel company as part of its bill between 1870 and 1872, and the cancan was regularly presented in other theaters in the years after this venue failed, particularly during the summer months.[8]

During the mid-1870s, variety was most often staged at the respectable theaters in Cincinnati by touring combinations managed by East Coast managers such as Tony Pastor, and while variety-only halls also opened in this period, they invariably failed.[9] By 1878, however, fifteen full-time variety houses were operating in the city.[10] Many of these were located on Vine Street, and there were also several variety theaters located in the German section of the city north of the Miami Canal, which ran east-west to the west edge of the downtown area, where it turned north, among them Hubert Heuck's Opera House. The canal was rather satirically called the "Rhine" by Cincinnatians because it marked the divide between the Anglo and the German sections of the city. The German section was called "Over-the-Rhine," and the name survives to the present even though the German residents and the canal are long gone.[11] The Vine Street Opera-House, which stood on the corner of Vine Street and Canal Street at the north edge of downtown Cincinnati and just south of the Miami Canal, was the primary focus of the city's reform forces.

The Vine Street Opera-House was, in many ways, not unlike the old Race Street Varieties. First, it unabashedly appealed to the city's working-class men and made no attempts at politeness. Advertising placed in local newspapers by its manager, Thomas E. Snelbaker, tended to dwarf all of the other theatrical advertising, and even when he did not place oversized advertisements, the language used was brash and overblown. In October 1879, for example, Snelbaker proclaimed he offered "the only 'sensational show' on earth" and warned his prospective audience "never, no, never will you see the like again. Come early for we play to packed houses."[12] Snelbaker was also not above thumbing his nose at authority. In January 1881, as the new city ordinance on theater licensing was under discussion and a new Sunday law was being debated at the state level, Snelbaker ran an advertisement offering a "Clergymen's matinee, Sunday, 2:30 P.M. Any antiquated or 'bum' deacons who are not in Columbus engaged in lobbying or wearing stripes, are invited to our Temple of Pleasure."[13] Like the Race Street Varieties, the Vine Street Opera-House also regularly featured a cancan, tableaux vivants, and female minstrels, along with a number of variety performers who had found success in the late 1860s and early 1870s.[14]

Snelbaker's advertising also clearly shows that the manager considered the theater operated by Hubert Heuck further north on Vine Street in "Over-the-Rhine" to be his major competition. Snelbaker aggressively advertised to prevent his Anglo audience from crossing the canal for entertainment. In late December 1879 Snelbaker placed an advertisement for his performances on Christmas Day that appealed to nativist pride, parodying the tone of a sermon: "Friend! Brother! We reach our hands unto thee and offer that which will please, and pray that you may be spared the perils of a trip across that WEARY, WEARY, VINE STREET BRIDGE! And thus be forced to endure the NARCOTICAL SHOWS to the Northward of it."[15] Always an enterprising businessman, Heuck sought to extend his audience beyond the local German population, and his hall offered an English-speaking bill along with the beer and sausages preferred by his German clientele. Snelbaker took this challenge personally and aimed to divert as many English-speaking patrons as he could into his own theater, robbing Heuck of the business. He had no desire to attract Heuck's German patrons, however, and placed no advertising in Cincinnati's German-language newspapers.

Snelbaker's theater ran an old-fashioned variety show that catered to an all-male English-speaking audience. It followed the standard variety format, presenting a series of singing, dancing, and novelty acts followed by a short comic play or burlesque presented by his resident company. He maintained a ballet corps at his theater that appeared primarily in the cancan. While Heuck's theater generally offered a more respectable bill than Snelbaker, including brass bands and short plays in German, he took the competition with his neighbor to the south seriously. Heuck's theater had been open for at least two seasons when Snelbaker opened his Vine Street theater. At the beginning of the 1879 season Heuck sought to compete directly with Snelbaker, perhaps intending to force him out of business, by engaging May Fisk's Blondes to open his theater for the season. Heuck's gambit failed, but it did help raise a revolt by the city's moral reformers against variety and what these forces viewed as indecent performances.

The antitheatrical campaign in Cincinnati was waged sporadically for over a year, and it reveals the deep divisions within this city. The major reformers included Republican city council members and their middle- and upper-class constituents, as well as a number of Methodist ministers intent on closing all theaters or at the very least curtailing the Sunday performances given in the city.[16] No single group countered the antivariety commentary that ran regularly in the *Cincinnati Gazette*, but the moral reformers were opposed to some degree by most, but not all, Democratic councilmen, theater managers, the police, and the audiences who patronized the city's variety halls. Neither side of this argument, however, represented a united force. As was the case in New York licensing battles, groups on each side of the argument formed temporary alliances, which meant in this case that no one group was willing to apply ongoing pressure on the city authorities or the police or even to lobby at the state level to fully curtail the activities of variety theaters. As a result, the changes made to the Cincinnati ordinances in 1879 and 1881 did little to change the business practices of many of the city's variety halls.

The major complaint of the reformers was against Sunday performances staged at the variety halls, although reports in the city's newspapers also show a conflict between middle- and working-class values. A report in the *Gazette* on Monday, November 11, 1879, estimated that close to ten thousand city residents had been present at the city's major theaters on the previous evening. While the author's primary goal was to expose the lack of respect shown for the Sabbath, he also complained about a number of other features of the performances, including the youth of the audience—he frequently noted the presence of young men under the age of 25—and the easy mingling of young men and women in these venues. He also claimed that beer and liquor was sold at most theaters, that they allowed smoking in the auditorium, that the shows contained coarse language and lewd acts, and that prostitutes had been soliciting customers in the theaters.[17] This report launched a two-pronged attack by this newspaper that lasted for over a month. On one hand it called for action to change laws at the state level to forbid Sunday performances. On the other, it focused on the theaters in the city whose performances had most offended the sensibilities of the author of the original article—the variety halls.

174

As a result of these protests, the mayor revoked some licenses, and the council revised the ordinance that governed the licensing of variety halls. The council's target was, almost certainly, Thomas Snelbaker, but debate over the ordinance also revealed deep divisions within the city council. These did not merely run along class or ethnic lines or with political affiliation. Members of the German community were at pains to draw distinctions between "decent" and "indecent" houses and to invoke their cultural traditions of Sunday entertainment, but they also more closely adhered to middle-class standards of decency than did the Anglo workingmen of the city. A number of the city's other English-language newspapers also defended the rights of workingmen to leisure on their only day of rest and made the same distinction between "decent" and "indecent" theaters, but they were generally less concerned than the Germans that theaters provide entertainment suitable for a family audience. One council member who represented the city's elite population fought to exempt the venues patronized by his constituents from the more stringent licensing rules, but his objection was overridden because, as one council member noted, "he would rather sweep the hilltops than to leave an entering wedge to allow cancan shows and the like to slip in under that head should an exception be made in its favor."[18]

Snelbaker went to court to fight the passage of this ordinance and a subsequent revision made a year later, and while he was able to outwit local authorities in Cincinnati he lost ground in the wider world of variety because the business practices he employed were rapidly becoming old-fashioned. The Vine Street Opera-House continued to operate into the mid-1880s, but it foundered primarily because of changing business practices, including a shift away from sexualized performance and toward the kind of entertainment already staged by managers such as Hubert Heuck. Heuck's theater, on the other hand, flourished into the twentieth century. During the last decades of the nineteenth century, Heuck cemented his empire, buying interests in a number of other theaters in the city, and he became a leading figure in the theater scene in Cincinnati. While he had begun his career catering to a single ethnic group, Heuck succeeded in the long term because family-style entertainment that appealed to a range of classes and did not offend women and children was coming into vogue, and he had always catered to this kind of audience.

The licensing struggles in both New York and Cincinnati were initiated by middle- and upper-class reform forces who sought to regain control over their city's streets and entertainments venues. In New York, lobbying to control concert saloons began when the city recovered from an economic downturn that had shut a number of concert saloons. As concert saloons reestablished themselves in once-fashionable areas of the city's major thoroughfares, reformers acted, citing the danger these establishments represented to the young, impressionable men mobilizing in the city for the Civil War. In Cincinnati the economic recovery of the late 1870s triggered a similar battle between entertainment catering to the city's laboring classes and reform forces. In neither case did the reformers win, and variety entertainment continued to flourish.

At the same time, variety was shaped by efforts to impose middle-class values on working-class leisure. In New York, the licensing process had imposed a sense of order on variety, mostly through the creation of an auditorium that was free of alcohol. This change had far-reaching effects that shifted the emphasis of this entertainment from conviviality to theatrical, not only in New York but eventually also at the national level. It also established a performance context that seems to have been preferred by the performers themselves. Managers, threatened with legal intervention and unable to rely solely on meeting the needs of their traditional audience of drinking men, now sought to broaden their audience to include women and children. It was this fact, rather than the intervention of moral reformers in Cincinnati, that eventually brought about the demise of the more bawdy performances catering to an all-male audience in that city. It should not be imagined, however, that moral reformers had no effect on Cincinnati variety. The constant attention brought to Vine Street amusements raised the issue of what constituted suitable entertainment for the whole city, and ongoing police actions and legal battles undoubtedly encouraged a number of variety managers to preemptively modify their business practices to avoid becoming the victims of similar police raids and legal battles.

This combination of internal reform, brought about by the desire of performers and managers for more conducive performance space and external pressure from moral reformers determined to eliminate immoral entertainments, shaped variety as it expanded across the United States. But this process did not happen in a uniform way at one time, but rather gradually as the country expanded. Variety retained its rough-and-ready quality and catered primarily or exclusively to men in frontier regions and in towns whose major industries relied on unskilled and seasonal laborers until late in the nineteenth century. As towns grew and became more established, the leading residents became less and less tolerant of frontier behaviors and entertainments and services that catered to the poorest residents. Anxieties triggered by economic downturns and the Civil War only heightened these tensions. Managers increasingly adapted their business practices to shape the entertainment they presented to conform to what they imagined would avoid middle-class moral-reform objections and changes to local laws and statutes.

One real consequence of the ongoing conflicts between variety and moral-reform forces was that both managers and performers began to preemptively adopt middle-class values as central to their business practices and performance aesthetic or, at the very least, be more aware of the line between the decent and indecent defined by those values. The influx of entrepreneurial managers who had been previously engaged in nontheatrical business ventures further encouraged this move. But variety also inevitably modified middle-class values, shaping and adapting them to conform to working-class aesthetics. So, for example, no one active in theater accepted the view that the presence of women on the stage or in the audience made the entertainment inherently indecent. Neither did they accept that the easy fraternization between young men and young women in theater audiences was a bad thing. Instead women without male escorts were not allowed admission, except during matinee performances that were aimed at women and children. Nor did theater managers inquire into the relationship between young women and the men who brought them to the theater during evening performances. Similarly, while variety managers could not claim that the shows they presented were educational or morally uplifting, they could claim popularity and argue that surely no indecent performance could attract such a large and fashionable crowd. Popular appeal became the primary marketing ploy in New York City in the wake of the passage of the Anti–Concert Saloon Bill, and it was also widely employed by variety managers across the country.

The self-imposition of middle-class values had a real effect on the contents of acts in the long term. If the focus during the 1860s in New York was on removing alcohol from the auditorium to force halls to adopt a decent performance space, by the 1870s the focus had shifted to what happened on the stage. The presentation of cancan and performances featuring large numbers of female dancers left theaters vulnerable to legal action by city authorities, including license revocation and police raids, and these actions almost inevitably led to difficulty with license renewals in subsequent years. As a result, it was in the best interests of local managers who sought to operate for the long term to pay greater attention to what was happening on their stage and to reprimand actors who stepped out of the bounds of decency, at least as interpreted by the theater manager and his staff. B. F. Keith's prominent advertising that boasted of the decency of his theaters as compared to other vaudeville houses should be seen in light of this development. Once managers began to take an active interest in the content of acts they could claim decency as well as popularity, which might prove to be an added attraction in a competitive entertainment market.

There were managers who did not fully comprehend these developments and continued to cater to their traditional constituency of white working-men, and these theaters rapidly lost status during the 1880s and 1890s. These "low-class" variety houses provided employment for older performers who were unable to meet the new standards of decency imposed by the shift to polite variety. This shift occurred slowly and was not always clear, except in retrospect. Increasingly, bookings in first-class theaters relied on the performer already having secured bookings in these theaters. In this context, reviews in the *Clipper* and other trade newspapers became crucial to a performer's success, as did the representation of a good agent who could offer management reassurance about their clients.

In industrial cities of the Northeast and Midwest, the managers of prominent variety halls located on the major shopping and commercial streets of the city were under the greatest pressure to adapt to the changing standards of decency because neighboring businesses complained if they viewed the theater and its customers as threatening their well-being. This pattern can be seen in New York and also in Chicago, where audiences were forbidden from congregating on the sidewalk before and after the performance—in these cases managers became responsible not only for the acts on their stage, but also for the behavior of audience members as they left the premises. This changed the relationship between the audience and variety managers. No longer could variety managers cater exclusively to the audience they attracted to their theaters; they also needed to cater to a theoretical audience that included women and children—an audience that adhered more closely to middle-class values. But they also could not do this in ways that alienated their steady customers. This tension came increasingly to bear on variety managers in the later nineteenth century, and it also began to be felt by performers by the end of the century.

Frontier Revelry
vs. Respectable Variety

Industry, Audiences, and Sustainable Leisure in Economically Difficult Times

> The main streets of the town were rendered indescribably gay and
> fantastic by the fighting woodsmen, the lives of law-abiding citizens
> often being jeopardized by their murderous outbreaks. . . . The truth
> was, the tradesmen were "out" to get the woodsmen's coin, and
> the rough element got most of it, from Warren Bordwell's show
> house, on Washington Street, to the ever open row of resorts on
> Franklin Street.
>
> —James Cooke Mills, *History of Saginaw County Michigan*
>   (Saginaw, Mich.: Seeman & Peters, 1918), 408

In early spring 1882 May Fisk's Female Minstrels traveled north
into Michigan to perform at the Bordwell Opera House in East
Saginaw, Michigan.[1] A decade earlier, this hall had hosted the
leading variety performers of the 1870s, including both Annie Hindle and Ella
Wesner in a period when these women were commanding $150 a week. But
the economic collapse had taken its toll on East Saginaw, a town that relied
primarily on logging for its income, and William Smith, the manager who
had run the Opera House in the early 1870s, abandoned the city and eventually sold the property to the theatrical manager Warren Bordwell. Under
Bordwell's management, the Opera House became a notorious blight on the

city's landscape as a center for crime, drunkenness, and prostitution. The skills of the performers in Bordwell's shows declined precipitously, and Fisk's visit, during which the featured burlesque was entitled *Blondes on a Lark; or, Little Sins and Pretty Sinners,* represented a welcome rise in quality rather than a descent into obscenity.

The rapid decline of the Opera House in East Saginaw raises important questions about the kinds of contexts in which variety theaters could and did thrive in the second half of the nineteenth century. Variety flourished in New York and large East Coast cities such as Philadelphia and Baltimore and also in industrial and trading centers such as Troy, Pittsburgh, Cleveland, and Cincinnati and other river cities such as St. Louis and Memphis, but not all industrial cities were welcoming to variety. Boston, for example, did not have a full-time variety hall until the 1870s, despite its large population. The factory towns in New England also hosted variety only in the summer months when touring troupes passed through this region. Clearly the size of the city and its proximity to transportation routes were not the only determining factors, and in the case of Boston, a local preference for minstrelsy and pantomime appears to have shut variety out of the city.

179

An important factor that determined the success of a local variety hall, and whether it presented sexualized or respectable performance, was the presence of a large working-class population with defined work hours and a certain amount of disposable income. Farming communities in which the work schedule and availability of ready cash were governed by seasonal change were never successful in hosting a variety theater and were only infrequently visited by touring troupes. Cities along the Mississippi, Ohio, and other river and lake trading routes tended to have at least one and often more variety halls because the docks supplied a large number of jobs for laborers, and there were also transient workers from boats or barges to augment the audience. But theaters that relied on transient labor rather than workers who lived in the city, and may also have had extended family there, were also more likely to offer sexualized fare and draw the ire of local authorities.

The divide between respectable and sexualized variety that had existed from the outset of the form in New York was also found away from the East Coast. In most large cities outside New York there was only one hall hosting respectable variety, but there were also often one or two smaller halls where less respectable variety could be found. Sometimes the smaller halls fostered local talent, performers who had not found success at the national level, but they hosted touring female minstrel shows that catered to an audience of men, and they were sometimes associated with prostitution and other criminal enterprises. It is difficult, however, to know what proportion of the many complaints of illegal activity reported in local newspapers was due to hostility fostered by local moral-reform forces and how many were legitimate. Regardless of the truth of the charges brought against small, low-class variety halls, their presence was seen as threatening the larger, first-class halls offering respectable variety, who feared being tarred with the same brush, and tensions between respectable and sexualized strands of variety became evident from as early as the mid-1870s.

At first glance, East Saginaw would appear to have been a town perfectly suited to hosting variety entertainment, and this assumption would seem to be supported by the early success of the city's halls in the late 1860s and early 1870s. But this view is belied by the sudden collapse of the variety scene in the face of the 1870s depression and the subsequent rise of sexualized variety in the town. A more detailed history of the variety theater in East Saginaw is needed to provide insight into the kinds of conditions in which variety flourished and the conditions that resulted in a shift from one strand of variety to the other. What, for example, caused the shift from respectable to sexualized variety in this city? Did the variety hall merely fall victim to a prolonged economic depression, or were other factors at work in this city? And, given that sexualized variety flourished as the economy improved, why did respectable variety not return to this Michigan lumber town?

Three businessmen, Norman Little, James Hoyt, and his son Jesse Hoyt, established the city of East Saginaw on the east bank of the Saginaw River in 1848. Development of the east side of the river was a risky proposition because the land was low and swampy and subject to flooding. But Little and the Hoyts were fortuitous in deciding to establish their new city at about the same time that lumbermen were moving into the region to exploit the forests of central-lower Michigan. Little built the town's first mill to produce wood for the new plank roads for his city. The town, known as East Saginaw, was surveyed and platted in 1850; by the middle of the 1850s East Saginaw was as large as Saginaw City on the opposite bank of the river; and by the end of the 1850s the population was almost double that of Saginaw.[2]

The lumber mills and other wood-related industries brought great wealth to East Saginaw. By the early 1870s Saginaw Valley was home to more than three hundred sawmills, although other manufacturing industries, such as shipbuilding, barrel making, and furniture and box making, also provided employment for a small percentage of the laborers in this area.[3] Local saltworks, which were attached to lumber mills and used the excess steam produced in the milling process to evaporate brine pumped from wells, also employed around six hundred people in Saginaw County.[4] The vast majority of laborers, however, were employed cutting trees in the winter months, in the booming industry that ran logs downstream to the mills, or in the mills cutting wood in the spring and summer months.

The spring thaw brought literally thousands of unruly workers into the town at the end of logging season. These men, with their pockets stuffed with winter pay, spent their first weeks in East Saginaw and other towns along the Saginaw River avidly pursuing leisure before securing a mill job or a job with a booming company. Those who found work in the mills continued to fuel the local economy, spending money on lodging, food, and entertainment. Workers who could not find jobs in these sectors dispersed into the countryside to take seasonal agricultural work in surrounding farming communities. For these men, entertainment was only a marginal part of their summer months because of the long hours of farmwork and the distance to town. But at the end of the summer, they returned to these cities for one last riotous spree before heading into the relative isolation of the forests for the winter months.

The influx of workers into East Saginaw fostered a number of service industries that catered primarily to itinerant laborers. These included boarding houses, hotels, dry goods merchants, and commercial entertainment. These businesses were often known for their unscrupulous business practices, but workers, who were not year-round town residents and had few community ties, found little sympathy from town residents and had little recourse against merchants and proprietors who cheated them. The preferred forms of entertainment for loggers at the end of a season in the forest were alcohol, prostitution, and theater, and by the end of the 1860s East Saginaw provided an ample choice for loggers on a spree. In the early 1870s East Saginaw had close to two hundred saloons, numerous brothels, and a number of theaters offering everything from touring dramatic combinations and minstrelsy to variety, female minstrelsy, and burlesque. Other public halls hosted dance parties and masquerades, and a huge ice-skating rink, with galleries seating 1,600, could also be used as a public hall. In the summer months East Saginaw hosted touring circuses, and the town racetrack also drew crowds.[5]

There were two major theaters in East Saginaw by the late 1860s, the Opera House and Jackson Hall. While most of the venues that catered to loggers were clustered on Water Street, along the river, and close to the railroad station on Potter Street, the Opera House, which was managed by William B. Smith, stood on Washington Street, one of the city's major thoroughfares. Jackson Hall was located several blocks to the north of the Opera House, and in 1873 its manager, Samuel Clay, gave up his lease on that hall and opened the Academy of Music, directly across the street from the Opera House. A number of smaller variety halls, all short-lived, also operated in East Saginaw from the late 1860s into the early 1870s.

The Opera House and Jackson Hall, and later the Academy of Music, were operated on two very different business models. Smith ran a traditional variety hall, employing a stock company and hiring individual acts to fill out his bill. Despite East Saginaw being a small city and only on a small branch rail line, Smith managed to attract some of the highest paid and most skillful variety performers of the period to his house.[6] Bookings at the theater lasted one to two weeks on average, and actors performed on a variety bill of a dozen or so acts and then took part in the short burlesque or comic play presented by the stock company that concluded the performance, usually improvising their roles. Smith's operating costs were covered in part by the fifteen cents admission he charged his patrons, but were also heavily subsidized by alcohol sales. Smith maintained a wine room, in which waitresses and actresses from his stock company plied patrons with alcohol.[7] Given the size of the Opera House—the hall seated fewer than seven hundred in this period—the sale of alcohol most likely provided the greatest proportion of Smith's income. Samuel Clay, on the other hand, booked touring dramatic troupes to play at his theater. His theater was well maintained and most likely had a supply of generic drops, as well as employees able to provide technical assistance. It is also likely that Clay was able to hire local musicians when needed, but he did not maintain a stock company, nor did he maintain a barroom in his theater.

During the late 1860s and early 1870s Clay and Smith also catered to very different segments of the town's population. Smith's audience was comprised primarily of men, and his financial livelihood was dependent on his ability to draw workingmen into his theater. Smith's reliance on the workers who flocked to East Saginaw in the spring and worked in the mills over the summer months is reflected in the season maintained by his hall. While the national theatrical season for variety halls began in September or October and ended in March, the season at Smith's was tied to the logging season that ruled the lives of the majority of his patrons. The season at the Opera House ran from September until Christmas. Men employed as loggers in the Michigan forests left town during November as the ground froze, enabling men to move the felled logs through the forests to the rivers, where they were stored on the ice. Because the beginning of the season was dependent on the weather, Smith could rely on a depleted audience into December, and some loggers returned from the forests to town for the holiday period. In January, when the loggers returned to the forests until the spring thaw, the theater closed. In March or April, when the rivers thawed, loggers ran the logs down local rivers to mills. Smith reopened the Opera House and ran a second season until the end of July or early August, when he shut for two or three weeks before reopening in September.

Unlike Smith, Clay was allied with reform elements that sought to cleanse the town of the fistfights and disorder associated with loggers on their annual sprees.[8] Clay was also determined to bring high-class drama to East Saginaw even if he had to do so at a financial loss.[9] He kept his theater open for the entire year and offered a broad range of entertainment to his audience, varying from companies offering dramas or English operas to touring minstrel or variety troupes. During the winter months he most often hosted legitimate drama and speakers on educational or moral subjects; a number of the troupes hosted by Clay appear to have been local or regional companies, but he also managed to book companies with nationally recognized actors.[10] This fare was more suitable for a mixed audience including women and children than the entertainment offered by Smith, and Clay attracted an audience of more respectable year-round town residents. Clay also kept his theater open during the winter months but ran a reduced program. This is further indication that his primary patrons were resident in the city, although in East Saginaw even a legitimate theater could not rely entirely on the townsfolk for its income. In the summer months, when the town's residents abandoned the theater for cooler outdoor amusements, Clay hosted touring minstrel and variety troupes for short stays, drawing workingmen away from Smith. On these occasions, the men were apparently willing to sacrifice their ability to drink during the performance for a single evening at Clay's hall.

While variety theaters played to capacity houses in good economic times, their audiences were significantly affected by economic downturns. When national lumber sales dropped in the wake of the financial crash in the mid-1870s, mills in town were idled, and unemployed loggers moved elsewhere to look for alternate employment. The local lumber barons, on the other hand, fell back on salt production to make up their lost income. This meant that service industries catering to town residents did not suffer as badly as those catering to a reduced seasonal labor force. Despite the depression, legitimate theater flourished in East Saginaw, and Samuel Clay opened the Academy of Music, across the street from the Opera House in 1873. The Opera House was hit hard by the depression, and Smith closed his theater in early July 1874, cutting the summer season short. The following September Smith announced his retirement and moved across the state to Grand Rapids.

During the mid-1870s the Opera House was rented by a succession of managers, each of whom failed to make a success of the building despite hiring nationally known performers for their bills. By 1878 Smith was the manager of a successful variety hall in Grand Rapids and wanted to dispose of his East Saginaw property. He finally sold the property to Warren Bordwell, who had managed a number of theatrical touring companies during his career.

Bordwell's early advertising in the *East Saginaw Republican* as well as the *New York Clipper* suggested that he intended to run the Opera House as a first-class variety house. Many of the big-name national acts that were advertised did not appear, however, and in his first week Bordwell changed the program midweek. In a business in which bookings were made a week at a time, a midweek change suggests that the acts he had hired did not please his audience. Soon after this Bordwell began to present an odd assortment of entertainment that included short melodramas, burlesques, and female minstrels, as well as specialty acts. Unlike Smith, Bordwell never attracted the best variety performers, and most of the people who appeared at his theater were most likely local performers of doubtful abilities.

Bordwell employed female minstrels at his theater from as early as 1879, and his company was composed of young women from the local region in their mid- to late teens. The major form of employment for such women was as domestic servants. Bordwell paid them $8 dollars a week for their services, which was less than they would have earned at a first-class variety theater, but considerably more than they would have earned in domestic service. They could also supplement their wages with tips earned working in the wine room after the performance. Girls were expected to drink with male customers, encouraging the men to buy alcohol and also to treat them to drinks. Bordwell had constructed small stalls in the wine room, and these and the boxes in the gallery were used by men who purchased sexual favors from the young women. Local prostitutes also frequented the wine rooms looking for customers, but Bordwell did not allow them to use the boxes or stalls, which were reserved for the use of his own girls.[11] Bordwell often advertised in the *Clipper* seeking female performers, but this newspaper never reviewed his theater.[12]

William Smith's move to Grand Rapids was both well timed and prudent. In October 1875 Smith opened Ball's Adelphia Theater on Waterloo Street in Grand Rapids as a variety theater. Like East Saginaw, Grand Rapids had strong ties to the lumber industry, but its industrial base was more diverse than that of East Saginaw. Grand Rapids was home to a range of other industries, including furniture making, machine shops, ironworks, gypsum quarries, and mills. The diverse industrial base of Grand Rapids provided Smith with an audience that was composed primarily of laborers and skilled workers from local mills and factories, although it was most likely supplemented by loggers in the spring and summer months. The town's economy was also diverse enough that a slump in any one industry could be offset by other town businesses, and, because most industry ran year-round in the city, there was no sharp division between seasonal labor and town residents. Smith operated his variety theater in Grand Rapids on a similar business model to his old theater in East Saginaw, providing theatrical entertainment and alcohol to his audience.

With a steady audience that could not engage in the kinds of wild drunken sprees that marked East Saginaw without endangering their jobs, and with no other competition, Smith was able to build a hugely successful theater. At the end of the 1870s, as patterns of booking variety changed, Smith dispensed with his stock company and brought touring variety and theatrical troupes to his theater. In 1885 Smith opened a new theater that was better able to accommodate a broad range of theatrical presentations. His new theater had a capacity of around 1,300 and was described as being "of a pleasing style of architecture, and . . . among the handsomest in the country."[13]

While the economic depression of the 1870s contributed to the decline of variety in East Saginaw, the town's reliance on a single industry and the theater's reliance on its workers for an audience played a more significant role in this process. The seasonal nature of the lumber industry did not allow variety managers to consistently present high-class variety shows that catered to towns' residents and itinerant workers, particularly in the slow winter months when the theatrical season was at its peak in other parts of the country. The other problem that faced variety managers in East Saginaw was the desire of itinerant loggers for a riotous release after months spent in isolated forests. The loggers' desires for alcohol and sex needed to be met in order to ensure business success. These needs ran counter to variety's move toward respectability in the 1870s and 1880s and resulted in the steady decline in the quality of entertainment in East Saginaw's Opera House. Bordwell's lack of success in attracting even minor figures in the national variety scene indicates a number of things about this manager and his theater. It seems likely that from the beginning of his tenure at the theater he was unable to provide performers with a venue that met their standards, and this was compounded by his lack of personal contacts with variety performers. Smith, on the other hand, had built those personal relationships during the late 1860s and early 1870s and was astute enough to also be able to change with the times and adopt a new business model in the 1880s. Newspaper reports and legal depositions also show that Warren Bordwell felt little loyalty to his patrons. As a manager, he was notorious for shortchanging his customers and for myriad other schemes to rob them of their money. His relationship with the young women who formed his stock company was equally exploitative. But he was a determined businessman and fought the city's attempts to close his theater through the 1880s and 1890s, donating money and holding benefits for city charities to win the public's goodwill and support in his ongoing disputes with civic authority.

As a result, the city did not manage to shut his theater until the mid-1890s, and he was still engaged in a legal battle with the council when he died.

The battle between Thomas Snelbaker and Herbert Heuck in Cincinnati can also be understood in terms of the divide between respectable and sexualized variety, as well as between a traditionalist and innovative management style. In the late 1870s neither Snelbaker nor Heuck offered an entirely decent show, but Snelbaker was a manager who identified closely with the traditional variety audience, while Heuck was an innovator who catered to women and families. In the midst of the licensing battles in Cincinnati, the *Daily Gazette* ran a long article describing the many Sunday performances staged in that city, protesting not only the desecration of the Sabbath but also the immoral nature of the performances staged and the behavior of the attending audiences. This report includes over a dozen venues, many of which were so small that they placed no advertising in the city's newspapers, but it also includes descriptions of the major venues, including Heuck's Opera House, which is described as "one of the over the Rhine places of entertainment which makes pretensions to something like respectability, and it measurably justifies its claims."[14]

Heuck's Opera House had a seating capacity of approximately 2,000, but it was described as being crowded beyond capacity, and the writer estimated that more than 2,500 people had squeezed into the auditorium. No complaints were made about the bill, which was varied and mixed elements of variety, spectacular and topical and character sketches. The audience "seemed to be made up almost wholly of the people of the social rank of mechanics . . . a very large percentage, half if not more, were either Germans or of German parentage, and the majority was made up of young men and women; hundreds were boys and girls between thirteen and nineteen years of age. Occasionally could be seen a pater familias with wife and children, but such groups were rare. The amount of beer drank [sic] was prodigious, but the best of decorum was preserved in the mode of its delivery."[15] Compared to the other halls described, Heuck's had the potential to become a truly respectable venue, particularly with the removal of beer from the auditorium, the cessation of Sunday performances, and the more stringent control of the easy mingling between the young men and women in the audience.

Thomas Snelbaker had not yet taken on the management of the Vine Street Opera-House when this report appeared. The theater was known as Grieff's Opera House, and it presented a bill consisting of dramas and farces with a brief variety olio between them. Patrons could smoke and drink in the auditorium, and waiters served "cigars, pretzels, mineral water, and beer, the latter being mostly called for."[16] The audience was small, comprising about one hundred

186

people, including families. While the manager of the house aimed to run it as a respectable theater, the venture didn't pay, and the quality of the show declined and the theater closed by the end of the year.[17] Thomas Snelbaker took over management in January 1879 and quickly found a business formula that worked. Snelbaker hired more female than male acts for his theater, relying on old-time variety performers like Jennie Engel and Minnie Hall and dancers such as Lizzie Derious and Minnie Wesner. He also employed a cancan line, which was a nightly feature of this house, and periodically presented tableaux vivants. Snelbaker did not seek to attract women or families to his hall, programming a bill designed to be attractive to the many young men of all classes who flocked to Vine Street in search of entertainment. Snelbaker was a traditionalist manager, and there was no way to reform his bill without correcting its gender balance and eliminating the ballet corps altogether; but this reform would have put him out of business because he would have had to compete even more directly with Heuck for an audience. Even without the harassment of the local authorities, Snelbaker was fighting a losing battle against changing public tastes, and his theater was bound to fail.

Clearly economic conditions were crucial in shaping the development of variety, and sexualized variety flourished in both large and small cities in economically difficult times as traditionalist managers sought to maximize their income. Lea's theaters had survived the brief economic downturn of 1857 because of their appeal to a broad range of men. The resurgence of theaters offering the cancan and female minstrelsy during the prolonged depression of the 1870s reflects the tendency of traditionalist managers to cater to their most loyal customers—unmarried, working-class men. At the same time, financially difficult times also increased the pressure on these establishments from outside forces, particularly moral reformers and the law. The various campaigns against sexualized variety inevitably affected high-class variety too and further increased the tension between these two strands of the profession. While Tony Pastor could maintain a business connection with a cancan troupe early in the 1870s, by the end of that decade these connections were less and less possible.

The passage of restrictive ordinances and laws and the threat of action by civil authority were clearly not enough to eradicate this strand of variety, and a small number of managers and theaters offering sexualized variety operated for decades. The audience may well have been attracted by the illicitness these threats brought, and given that police never arrested the audience when they raided the theater, they may even have desired to push performers into transgressing the law in order to watch the fun of a raid. For most managers of sexualized variety, this risk was also worth taking, and when doing business became too difficult they left town, closing the theater and moving elsewhere.

For managers such as Bordwell and Snelbaker, sexualized variety was merely business, and when it was no longer profitable they were quick to innovate to maximize their incomes. If innovation occurred at the expense of performers, this was of concern only if they met resistance from performers. And in the financially difficult 1870s, as theaters were failing across the nation, managers could always find performers who would accept their terms. The desire to maximize profit and the lack of close personal connection to performers were things these managers shared with entrepreneurial managers in respectable variety, but, unlike these men, managers of sexualized variety cared more about meeting the desires of their audience than pleasing the broader community in which the theater was located. Also, while the entrepreneurial managers of respectable variety tied their business success to imposing their best interpretations of middle-class values on the acts on their stages, sexualized variety's success relied on promising more than they delivered. It was not in their best interests to routinely transgress decency as defined by the local community and city ordinances, but managers routinely allowed, and indeed encouraged, performers to present material that pushed decency to its limits, and they also pushed their interpretation of theater law to the limits.

It is also clear that theaters consistently offering respectable variety were most likely to be found in cities with a diversified economy with multiple industries with defined work hours. The economy of East Saginaw, which was dominated by a single seasonal industry, proved to be unsuitable for respectable variety; variety could not aim to provide riotous release for its audience if it was to operate successfully and attract both the most skilled performers and a steady audience, especially when the peculiar needs of the woodsmen in East Saginaw placed a premium on riotous leisure. This continued to be the case in the twentieth century as new vaudeville halls opened across the United States. In 1928 the Keith organization opened the Palace Theater in Marion, Ohio. Located in north-central Ohio at a rail hub, Marion was home to numerous manufacturers by the early twentieth century. While the busy manufacturing and trading port of Cleveland, located to the north of Marion, had long had variety theaters, Marion's vaudeville theater did not open until the town emerged as a vibrant regional trade and manufacturing center. Two large factories, the Marion Steam Shovel Company and Huber Manufacturing, employed large numbers of local men, and smaller manufacturing companies, including a number that employed skilled workers, were also located in the city. This provided the same kind of diverse economic base that Grand Rapids, Michigan, had provided Smith's variety hall in the 1870s and 1880s.[18]

Ironically questions of decency and middle-class values came to dominate both strands of variety by the end of the nineteenth century, but in very different ways, and as these strands moved in opposite directions the tensions between the extremes dissipated. While respectable variety managers of the 1870s and 1880s sought to distance themselves from female minstrelsy and the theaters that staged burlesque performances, by the early twentieth century B. F. Keith ignored burlesque altogether and sought only to distance himself from old-style variety, which lay in the hazy ground in between these two forms. This area between the extremes, which was designated "small-time" in the early twentieth century, is also where the greatest interaction between the polite and impolite, the apparently decent and indecent, most likely occurred, and it was also, ironically, the only training ground left for young vaudevillians who lacked the skills and experience to break into the big-time vaudeville circuit.

Conclusion
Entertainment as Industry

Variety entertainment, as it developed in the mid- to late nineteenth century, parallels the shifts in the work lives and identities of the people it entertained during the same period in a number of ways. Variety both reflected the changing composition of the working class in the United States as well as changes in the structures that governed the American workplace. During the second half of the nineteenth century, manufacturing shifted from artisanal production, in which skills were systematically passed to apprentices who also had the opportunity to rise within the business, becoming first a skilled journeyman and then master, to mass production, in which any given worker knew only a fraction of the entire process and there was little opportunity to move up. Variety, as it developed during the last decades of the nineteenth century, also provided amusement that fit increasingly well with the rhythms of the industrial workplace and also flourished best where a diversified economy meant that booms and busts in specific industries did not adversely affect all of the members of the audience. The consolidation of the bill into a shorter performance (approximately two rather than four hours) by the end of the nineteenth century further reflects this shift, which had begun at midcentury with the removal of alcohol from the auditorium.

This change in work practices is also reflected within the world of variety. When stock companies and ballet corps were disbanded during the 1870s as a result of economic pressure, a valuable training ground for young performers disappeared along with a steady source of employment for seasoned performers. Younger performers of the 1880s and later had no systematic way in which to acquire performing skills. They could gain entry to vaudeville through amateur nights—performances in which nonprofessionals had a chance to perform on the stage for a prize—but they could not easily learn the wide range of skills needed by earlier variety performers unless they were born into families already active in the genre. In many ways variety performers and their audiences can be seen as sharing similarly changing and uncertain work conditions in which the skills required for work became less certain and less valued and jobs depended less on knowing a wide range of skills that enabled one to understand the entire production process than on mastering a narrow range of skills that suited the worker to a particular niche in the manufacturing process or entertainment world.

Vaudeville, under the auspices of B. F. Keith, firmly cemented this process with the introduction of the continuous show in which performances were presented for twelve hours with no break between shows. This format was adapted from earlier traditions in which variety managers had staged shows every two hours on holidays when workingmen had a day free from work. On July 4, 1854, George Lea staged performances every two hours during the day, beginning at 9 A.M. His last performance for that day was scheduled for 9 P.M. at the conclusion of the fireworks.[1] This practice was not peculiar to New York, and I have found theaters in Boston offering similar performances during the 1860s.[2] Keith normalized a common but infrequent holiday practice as standard operating procedure, which fundamentally changed the structures and relationships within variety. Not only did this practice impose a hierarchy in which the highest paid performers also appeared only twice a day, while lesser performers appeared between three and five times a day, but it radically altered the structure of the vaudeville bill. The variety show had consisted of two parts, the variety olio and the comic afterpiece. Vaudeville maintained the two-part structure but dispensed with the afterpiece and in the first decades of the twentieth century consolidated the bill to approximately nine acts with an intermission between the two halves.[3] Keith's centralized booking system and weekly reports from managers in theaters affiliated with his organization resulted in a further standardization of acts—a process that had already started in the late 1870s and early 1880s due to the proliferation of touring combinations that played short bookings—and also provided a disincentive for acts to innovate. While variety had valued individual performers for their specific skills and their ability to fit flexibly into multiple places on the bill and to assist in a range of sketches and dramatic pieces with little notice, vaudeville treated each act as a product to be slotted into one specific position on the bill in order to build the anticipation for the featured stars or to manipulate audience reaction.[4]

This move toward a hierarchy within the profession was one that had occurred within other forms of legitimate theater several decades earlier as theater shifted from stock companies to companies headed by prominent stars with a supporting cast, and it should, perhaps, be seen as reflecting a sense of growing professionalism from individual variety performers, each of whom hoped to reach star status. The increasing specialization by performers and the narrowing of skills that occurred in variety may have been peculiar to that genre and due largely to the abandonment of improvisation and comic afterpieces that pressed most performers into service. The hierarchical bill of vaudeville in which star players—often drawn from legitimate theatrical genres—were distinguished from the many ordinary players who filled out the continuous bill was just one sign of this change. The other was in the stricter structures of vaudeville. While vaudeville continued to present a series of acts unconnected by narrative, in the earlier twentieth century there was a greater emphasis on pace and on building anticipation for the star acts. No longer did performers appear multiple times but instead were in competition against each other for the smaller numbers of spots on the bill, each act hoping to appear in one of the better positions during the evening, just as semiskilled workers were in competition with each other for manufacturing jobs.

Much of the history of variety centers on economic downturns, such as the panic of 1857 or the long depression of the 1870s. During the former, variety, which was still in its infancy as an independent form, was dealt a hard blow, and many of the halls that had opened in New York City and Philadelphia failed during financially uncertain times. This first economic downturn reinforced the importance of close relationships between managers and performers, and the managers who prevailed in this difficult period were, to a large extent, those who also performed. The situation during the depression of the 1870s was very different, and it demonstrates the growing importance of business acumen in the entertainment world. While variety in the 1850s had been small-scale and informal, in the 1870s it involved larger numbers of performers and managers, as well as a support infrastructure comprising agents, advance men, songwriters, and others. In this environment, the entrepreneurial mangers who could cut costs most effectively survived—and these were likely to be managers who did not feel a sense of obligation or have close personal ties to the performers, whose wages were cut or whose jobs were eliminated; these managers continued to shape business practices into the early twentieth century.

While external economic forces drove internal reform in variety, they also drove the opposition to the form. Because variety entertainment operated within a broader social context that conflated personal morals and the well-being of the nation, when the nation was threatened—with economic depression or Civil War, for example—the genre came under attack from moral reformers who viewed theater, alcohol, and women in public as corrupting forces. Moral-reform movements also affected other theatrical genres, but variety was most likely to be targeted because it catered to a working-class audience and thus could be viewed as victimizing its patrons, whose lack of financial wealth also indicated their lack of restraint and work ethic. That variety theaters, like saloons, were able to sustain themselves in the face of opposition fueled by such circular logic is testament to the ingenuity of their managers. With each change in the law or outside attack, these managers subtly shifted their business strategies to continue to appeal to their audience, while also staying within the bounds of what was legal.

Variety managers reacted to the external pressures in one of two ways. On one side innovative managers sought to avoid opposition by dispensing with the features most likely to elicit opposition, such as alcohol and women in sexualized performances or service positions. These managers can be viewed as embracing middle-class values, at least to some extent, which also allowed them to expand their audience to include women and children. This further protected them from attack and also compensated for any loss of male audience members to more sexualized performance. On the other side of the divide, traditionalist managers sought to retain as much of their audience of working-men as they could without eliciting a reaction from reform forces. This strategy worked most effectively in smaller towns, where a frontier mentality prevailed, or in cities in which reform forces were relatively disorganized and theater managers did not try to operate in areas patronized by the city's premier districts. Ironically, middle-class reform forces and the traditionalists within variety were motivated by similar fears, namely the loss of status quo and change. Clearly neither approach to staging variety was a losing strategy given that both vaudeville and modern burlesque survived into the twentieth century, but the managers who sought solely to cater to the traditional audience of workingmen faced more opposition at the local level and may also have found sustaining their business over the long term more difficult.

Variety also reflects the changing composition of the working class in the United States during the second half of the nineteenth century. Variety acts and the repertoires of singers expose the subtly shifting ethnic and class identifications of the performers and audience. The numbers of ethnic Americans among both the audience and the performers on stage increased, and the acts of variety performers reflect this changing composition; indeed the acts performed within variety and later vaudeville helped to construct the social category "white" that came to include many of these immigrant groups. Songs presented by variety performers show that the depiction of immigrants was increasingly complex, and over time depictions moved from two-dimensional parodies to more sympathetic portrayals that showed immigrants as being essentially not unlike the native-born working class. The initial depiction of any immigrant man, whether Irish or German or later Jewish or Italian, was negative and depended greatly on stereotypes already established in the context of minstrelsy. Immigrants were depicted merely as foolish or funny and incapable of a range of experiences and emotions. In the case of Germans, the depiction fairly quickly deepened. The Irish followed, albeit at a slower pace, and it may have been Irish participation in the Civil War as regular soldiers that aided in this transition, although prevailing anti-Catholic bias sustained negative characterizations. The acceptance of any given immigrant group did not eliminate the negative stereotypes that circulated in variety, but they began to be balanced with a more complex depiction that worked against the original view.

An examination of who was active on the variety stage, and the kinds of acts they performed, also shows that some ethnic groups were limited to nonsinging roles. These included Arabs and other Middle Easterners, Japanese and Chinese, Spanish and Hispanics, and other non-English-speaking performers, who were all largely confined to acrobatic and other circus-style acts. These people were not placed in the position where they were the butt of a joke, but neither could they take an active role in complicating the stereotypes attached to them, and as a result they were largely confined to roles that inspired awe and wonder and stayed well within Orientalist tropes. This suggests that these ethnic groups were peripheral to both the world of variety performers and the variety audience, and when small numbers of Asian American performers entered vaudeville in the early twentieth century as singers and dancers, they drew on the stereotypes established for African Americans, because there were no existing Asian stereotypes that allowed for singing or speaking roles.[5] The variety audience went to the variety hall to see themselves represented, and while they were happy to see others on the stage, those depictions were bound to remain narrow as long as members of that group were not present in the audience. This also suggests that despite variety being no longer an informal barroom entertainment, it maintained its roots in working-class convivial traditions that united those present into a temporarily cohesive group.

The roles accorded to both African Americans and women in variety confirm this interpretation. There is no evidence of the presence of African Americans on the variety stage before about 1900, and after that date only a relatively small number of black performers were ever active in variety; there is also little evidence of African Americans in the variety audience.[6] The depiction of African Americans in variety remained fairly two-dimensional during this period and was closely related to stereotypes found in minstrelsy. Evidence from the early twentieth century shows that the vaudeville audience did not desire to see more complex depictions of African Americans. Managers' reports from the Keith circuit reveal that while male African American comedic song-and-dance teams were routinely well received, solo black acts, and particularly acts that did not present stereotypical coon songs, did not fare so well, particularly in smaller cities and away from the East Coast. So, for example, the classically trained soprano, Rosa Lee Tyler, who was billed as "The Creole Nightingale," was well received in Keith's Boston Theater in January 1904 despite the fact that her trunks had not arrived and she was forced to perform in street clothing. The manager noted: "She is a very good singer, and went well with the audience." Just one week earlier in Providence, however, the manager's report had noted: "Like most of these people when they attempt classical singing, she falls decidedly short. Seems beyond the Negro Race to do this. Her voice is metallic and screechy."[7] The difference in these reports was more likely to lie in the perceptions of the manager and his ideas about what constituted a suitable act, than in a radical change in this singer's voice. The comedian and coon singer Harry Brown, who worked solo, received a similarly mixed reception even though his act came closer to what was expected from a black performer; in Philadelphia Brown made a hit with the audience, while a week later in Pittsburgh the audience preferred a blackface comic duo over Brown's performance.[8]

195

While blackface acts were a persistent part of variety, even in the 1850s and 1860s, these performers did not dominate the stage. The two-dimensional stereotype of the minstrel figure remained shallow due to both the segregated nature of variety and vaudeville and the prevailing racism of the working class, who comprised the audience for these theatrical genres. This stereotype did deepen slightly in the contexts of other entertainment forms, particularly in all-black minstrelsy and other kinds of musical theater that emerged late in the nineteenth century and catered to a higher class of patrons. It is also highly likely that similar stereotypical characters formed the core of variety entertainment staged by black performers for an audience of their peers—evidence of this can certainly be found in the skits and routines that survive in "Chittlin' Circuit" movies that were shown in segregated movie houses and accounts of black vaudeville performances on the TOBA circuit.[9] Considerable work is needed on informal variety entertainments staged for an African American audience in the nineteenth century. The major problem in conducting this research will, no doubt, be the scarcity of sources that document it. The sources for variety are fragmentary and incomplete, and this is even more the case for African American entertainments. But despite the lack of evidence, we should not assume they did not exist, particularly in saloons and other venues catering to this segment of the population.

The case of women's representation on the stage is more complex, but also reinforces the idea that the variety audience came to the theater primarily to view people like themselves on the stage. While it is difficult to know what proportion of the variety audience was comprised of women at any given period, it is highly likely that the audience was largely male into the 1880s and later. Police reports from the 1870s and 1880s note the presence of women in some New York City variety theaters, but they do not convey the sense that these women comprised a large part of the audience. Greater numbers of women attended German venues that catered to families, but variety audiences were mostly or exclusively male, especially in regional theaters where managers catered to laborers. The 1870s saw the introduction of matinee performances for women and children in regional variety, and the success of these performances is indicated by the fact that they became a standard part of the variety business—given that managers could not afford to stage performances for an empty house, they must have drawn enough income to make the venture worthwhile—but it was not until closer to the end of the century, when entrepreneurial German managers found a place in variety, that more women attended the theater.

The role of female performers echoes this incremental increase in female audience during the same period. In the 1850s very few women performed in free and easies, and those who did tended to be singers and dancers who were often related to the proprietor. Here the young women fulfilled the function of being pretty and tuneful, but were also free from the taint of prostitution and protected from audience harassment through family ties to the owner of the establishment. When variety moved into concert saloons and larger-scale entertainment was staged, the solo female singer remained, but there was also an influx of ballet dancers onto the variety stage, as well as female acrobats who performed with family circus troupes. Again, these women functioned primarily as a pleasing visual diversion, who rarely spoke on the stage. Female seriocomics did not appear in any number in variety until the later 1860s and 1870s, as the presence of women in the variety audience increased with the introduction of the matinee.[10]

Surviving repertoire also reflects this change, as does the growing complexity in the depiction of women. The earliest surviving repertoire in both sheet music and songsters is associated with male performers, and repertoire associated with a small number of female singers was not included in songsters until the late 1860s. The number of songs associated with female performers grew during the 1870s, and songs sung by the Richmond Sisters, the Foy Sisters, Jennie Engel, Jennie Hughes, and the male impersonators Ella Wesner, Blanche Selwyn, and Alecia Jourdan can be found in a number of songsters from this decade. The presence of these women, most of whom represented a complex view of working-class femininity, did not eclipse the popularity of women in more sexualized acts. Ballet dancers continued to be a popular feature of variety into the 1870s, and the rise of female minstrelsy in the mid-1870s also increased sexualized performance by dancers on the stage, specifically in the form of the cancan, Amazon chorus, Zouave drills, and other kinds of formation dancing performed by groups of largely anonymous women.

The latter view of women can also be found in the elaborate lithographs on songster covers from this decade. What is most interesting about these songsters was that they primarily contained songs associated with male variety or minstrel performers, the texts of which rarely focused on women. The suggestive picture on the cover was an effective marketing ploy to tempt young men to purchase the songsters, and this echoes the approach taken by managers of sexualized variety in the same period. Cigarette manufacturers used the same ploy in the 1890s when they included photographs of scantily dressed burlesque actresses in their packaging to promote sales. The lithographs featuring women included on the covers of the *National Police Gazette* and also at about page three (this picture almost always featured a burlesque actress in costume) played a similar role, and this has continued into the present so that we are now almost unconscious of the vast numbers of actresses' images used to promote various products. Ironically, manufacturers of retail goods for an expanding middle-class consumer base used similar imagery to market their wares in advertising placed in magazines and newspapers, which only increased the tensions between sexualized "male" culture and mainstream and respectable American culture—the more that images of women were used to market respectable products, the more they needed to be guaranteed to be free of the taint of indecency. By the end of the century, attention had come to focus increasingly on the offstage lives of actresses, opening the "domestic" sphere to public scrutiny to reassure consumers of the decency of this class of "public" women.

As with immigrants, the greater the number of women active in variety—both as performers and audience members—the more complex was the picture that songs painted of women's experiences. But songs also clearly mark differences between men's and women's experiences of the world. While the definition of appropriate female behavior varied greatly from that of the middle class, women's songs were focused on personal relationships, including love and marriage, and on sentiment, while men were more concerned with professional standing, status, and making a mark in the world. Men's songs tended to view women either as part of urban leisure or as potential spouses. The anxiety expressed over courtship and marriage in men's songs is interesting, particularly given the lack of anxiety in this area in women's repertoire, and it suggests that for young men marriage not only meant settling down and curtailing leisure activities, but it also meant entering the women's realm of the home and a loss of control in one aspect of their lives. Courtship was the young man's first experience of this loss of control.

198

It is not enough to note the increasing numbers of Irish, Germans, Italians, Jews, and others on the variety and later vaudeville stage or the numbers of songs representing these characters. To fully understand the contestation of class, ethnic identity, and gender in these performances, we need to note the date at which the depictions of ethnic characters became more three-dimensional and allowed for sympathetic understandings of these people. Knowing who performed individual songs and taking into consideration the performance skills that particular performers brought to the song adds another layer of meaning. The discussion here suggests that performers who felt a personal connection to the characters they portrayed were more likely to feel the need to deepen and soften their representations, avoiding derogatory humor as much as possible. Other forms of popular culture such as scripts for sketches and comic afterpieces would also reflect this process, but, as with songs, work on the performance skills brought to these sketches is also needed. It is never safe to assume that songs or sketches were performed as written.

Another question raised by the entrance of ethnic women into variety is the degree to which Anglo-American women, or women who did not identify with any particular immigrant group, chose to enter other forms of theater rather than vaudeville in the 1880s, 1890s, and later. There were certainly connections between variety and other forms of theater such as minstrelsy, circus, and pantomime. But the extent of these is, as yet, unclear, as are later connections between vaudeville and musical farce or musical comedy. To more fully explore these, it will be necessary to follow specific performers in and out of various productions. I have found a number of occasions in which variety performers sought to tour musical comedies, and these were met with mixed success. Lillian Russell is probably the best-known performer of the 1870s who made the transition from variety to operetta and other forms of musical theater, but as the case of Gus Williams shows, there may well be others, just as there were later vaudevillians who crossed into other forms of musical theater and into films.

Like Gus Williams, the male impersonator Ella Wesner made two attempts to take musical comedies on the road during the 1870s and 1880s. The first, *Mixed*, was a piece written specifically to show off her skills as a male impersonator, supported by a stock company as she performed songs and dances in male character, although the details of the plot are unclear from reviews that appeared in the *Clipper*. Beginning in mid-November 1874 Wesner toured the piece through a number of Midwest cities, including Chicago, Buffalo, and Detroit. By the end of December she had abandoned the venture and returned to variety. The reviewer in Buffalo noted that Wesner was a good specialty artist, but needed more "practice in dramatic reading and action to enable her to appear to better advantage."[11] A decade later Wesner made a second attempt to break into musical comedy with a piece entitled *Captain of the Queen's Own*. Advertising in the *Clipper* announced that she had arranged all of the music for the piece and had engaged her cousin Mamie Bernard as the soubrette. The reviews for this production were positive, but unfortunately after less than three months on the road the company collapsed due to internal conflict, and Wesner returned once again to variety performance.

Wesner's experience provides some insight into the difficulty of securing and touring a successful show. First, the variety performer needed to have the acting skills to sustain a performance of several hours in the central role; the ability to perform in specialties was not enough. Wesner had earlier experience working as part of a dramatic stock company in Galveston, Texas, and she had also taken part in dramatic afterpieces in variety. Even so, her acting skills were found wanting, which was also the case for Gus Williams when he moved into musical comedy. While Wesner's second attempt to move into musical comedy was more successful from the perspective of both the piece and her performance, she could not manage the internal conflict in her company, and the tour failed. If Wesner had been working with the support of a powerful manager active in musical comedy or, perhaps with a powerful male actor, this might not have happened. But because she took the leading male role, she was expected to fulfill the leadership role of the male star both on and off the stage. In addition, reviews show that the essential elements of Wesner's act had become fixed after more than a decade performing male characters in variety. She relied on a relatively narrow range of sketches and characters—a drunk captain falling asleep in a barber's chair had become her major character by this point—and this likely ill suited her to narrative drama suitable for a middle-class audience including women.

The other option available to variety performers was to enter musical comedy as a novelty act. This was, however, more common for comic male singers as well as young female dancers, who found a role in musical comedy performing specialty dances; the skirt dancer Loie Fuller, who had worked in a range of theatrical contexts including variety, appeared in *A Trip to Chinatown*, for example. Young women who might once have sought employment in variety ballet corps may also have joined the choruses of pretty girls that were a feature of many musical comedies. Dancers almost certainly also moved into full-length burlesques that followed in the style established by Lydia Thompson's Troupe. A great deal more work is needed to determine the training and performing skills of the many young women active in burlesque and musical theater in the last decades of the nineteenth century, and following their career paths would certainly illuminate connections between the myriad forms of musical theater that existed in this period.

The complexity of the world of variety, and indeed the entire theatrical world in this same period, calls into question our understanding of the flowering of commercial entertainment and public leisure at the beginning of the twentieth century. Given the many different kinds of entertainment present in the American urban landscape that catered to a range of audiences, from all-male to mixed gender, from working class to middle class and higher, and from small towns to large cities, is it still safe to consider the early twentieth century as a period that is significantly different from earlier decades? Might it be more productive to view the expansion of public life and commercial leisure in the first decades of the twentieth century as continuing a trend that had begun in the nineteenth century when the cohesive mixed-class audience of the theater first fractured and split?

A more complex historical narrative of nineteenth-century theater would also call into question who was active in this growth of public amusement. The flowering of new forms of musical theater certainly represents the growth of entertainments catering to a middle-class audience, but so too do the growing number of middlebrow forms that emerged from before the 1880s. It is true that, during the nineteenth century, portions of the middle class, particularly those with firm religious beliefs who viewed theatrical entertainment as a corrupting force, had been loathe to participate in public amusements, except perhaps those with educational value such as public lectures and demonstrations. But the middle class—like the United States as a whole—was not a stable entity and was constantly expanding and changing. I would argue that the children and grandchildren of working-class variety audiences of the 1860s and 1870s were among the middle-class audience for public amusements in the period around the turn of the century. As variety and early vaudeville came increasingly to represent a diverse range of ethnic groups, who also made up its audience, the white native-born no longer identified as working class. Abandoning variety and vaudeville, they sought new forms of entertainment that maintained some of the fun and novelty of variety, but that shared characteristics—such as narrative—with older legitimate genres.[12]

This fracturing of culture along class lines had begun before the Civil War, and it continued into the early twentieth century. As twentieth-century vaudeville increasingly sought middle-class respectability, other forms such as small-time vaudeville, the nickelodeon and burlesque show, the dime museum show, and the seaside carnival among others, emerged to cater to working-class audiences and those who wanted less respectable amusements. Some of these, such as the dime museum show, are at least as old as variety and may indeed be where old-fashioned variety found a home after the emergence of vaudeville. In addition, the middle class was also considerably less cohesive than it had been a half-century earlier, and the array of entertainments aimed at this class were no less numerous and ranged from Chautauqua lectures and rational amusements that included religion, education, high art, and music to Ziegfeld's and Schubert's revues.

As Martin J. Burke shows, Americans have long found ways to delineate class distinctions while also maintaining that they are committed to a classless society.[13] One of the difficulties in discussing social class in the United States is its extremely fluid nature. Commercial entertainment forms can give some insight into this fluidity, and considerably more work is needed—particularly on middlebrow forms—in order to fully understand the ways that class and other kinds of identity are forged through public discourse and debate that occurs in the context of theatrical and other performance. In many cases we have lost most other kinds of records such as personal papers and writings that would provide insight into this, but a careful reading of surviving scripts, songs, newspaper reviews, and commentary against a thick description of the cultural context for these performances may provide us insight into this process.

This narrative represents only a partial view of a history of nineteenth-century theatrical entertainment that may never be fully written because of the fragmentary and incomplete nature of the evidence from this period. At the same time, I firmly believe that it is possible to construct partial narratives for a range of interconnected music theatrical genres and that the picture that emerges will not only complicate our assumptions about the nineteenth century, but also our beliefs about popular culture as it continued to develop into the twentieth century. Despite the initial foreignness of these lost theatrical worlds, the continuities into the present are compelling and need to be examined because in many ways the needs of the variety audience—to see themselves represented on the stage—continue to be our own.

Notes

Introduction

1. See *New York Herald*, May 9, 10, 11, and 12, 1849.
2. *New York Herald*, May 10, 1849: 2.
3. Levine, *Highbrow/Lowbrow*.
4. *New York Herald*, May 10, 1849: 2.
5. Snyder, *Voice of the City*; Nasaw, *Going Out*.

Chapter 1: The Singing Saloonkeeper

1. Between 1855 and 1865, census takers noted that the number of men in New York City who gave their profession as barkeepers more than doubled from 987 to 1,984, while the number working as saloonkeepers more than tripled from 871 to 3,925. *Census for the State of New York, 1865*, lxxv–lxxvi.

2. Rosenzweig, *Eight Hours for What We Will*, 37.

3. Ibid., 35–49. For a longer discussion of the effects of legislation relating to all kinds of leisure activities on working-class Americans, and the increasing alliance between private moral-reform efforts and government regulation, see Montgomery, *Citizen Worker*, 52–114.

4. Ibid., 36–40.

5. Powers, *Faces along the Bar*, 17–18. Powers notes that breweries underwrote the cost of saloon refurbishment to help boost sales of their product.

6. Ibid., 180–206.

7. Ibid., 199.

8. The advertisements for Hitchcock's free and easy in the *New York Herald* on August 13, 1856: 7, notes: "This evening an extra amount of talent. Hitchcock always at home, and James Fraser, the wonderful comic singer, in the chair at 8 o'clock."

9. "Amusements" [Advertising], *New York Herald*, August 11, 1856: 3; and August 26, 1856: 7.

10. McConachie, *Melodramatic Formations*, 16, 19–22. For a description of the audience of the Bowery Theater in 1847, see 122. By this time the theater had been abandoned by the elite audience and catered to a working-class and male audience.

11. This tactic was also employed in the later nineteenth century in pantomime performance, which was a staple of the English Christmas season. As pantomimes grew larger and the stage machinery more elaborate, managers employed music hall performers as part of their casts, and leading English male impersonators such as Vesta Tilley and Hetty King took leading roles as the principal boy in these productions. When machinery jammed, these and other music hall performers could appear in front of the drop curtain to entertain the audience while repairs were made.

12. Bills listed in the *New Orleans Daily Delta*, for example, included the note "(with songs)" after the actress's name in plays that had music, although they never noted if any male characters sang during the performance. See, for example, the advertisement for the St. Charles Theatre, placed on November 22, 1845: 2, col. 1. The bill that evening featured the husband-and-wife team of Mr. and Mrs. Skerrett, who were featured in the comedy *She Stoops to Conquer* and the farce *The Loan of a Lover*. In the latter Mrs. Skerrett appeared as Gertrude, a role that called on her to sing.

13. Needham, *I See America Dancing*, 135, 138. Needham notes that American-trained dancers were largely relegated to working in the ballet corps during the nineteenth century, and foreign-born dancers, first French and then Italian, took lead roles in ballet.

Chapter 2: Girls! Girls! Girls!

1. "A Born Speculator Dead," *New York Times*, August 21, 1902: 9.

2. "Letters from J. F. Schinotti to Ludlow and Smith," in *Sol Smith and Theatre Folk, 1836–65*, ed. Stella M. Drumm, Glimpses of the Past 5.7–9 (July–September 1938) (St. Louis: Missouri Historical Society, Jefferson Memorial).

3. Odell, *Annals of the New York Stage*, 4:89. Originally this small venue had a capacity of only around 600, but after it was damaged by fire in the mid-1840s, it was most likely renovated and enlarged. Handcock advertised it had a capacity of 1,600 (see Odell, *Annals of the New York Stage*, 5:401).

4. Costonis, "Personification of Desire."

5. *Chicago Inter-Ocean*, February 27, 1877: 4.

6. The tradition of tableaux as part of operatic performances held on into the mid-nineteenth century or later in some traditions. The French Opera troupe in New Orleans often specified how many tableaux would be staged during each evening's performance in their announcements in the city's newspapers; see *Daily Delta*, Febru-

ary 9, 1846: 2, col. 5. The advertisement for Meyerbeer's *Robert L'Diable* notes that the work has five acts and seven tableaux.

7. Altick notes the scientific, moral, or artistic associations invoked by the exhibitors of anatomical waxworks and also tableaux vivants, but also comments on the hypocrisy inherent in their claims by the 1850s (Altick, *Shows of London*, 342).

8. Ibid., 336.

9. These were museums in which wax models of human, and particularly female, bodies were exhibited. In anatomical museums, the bodies could be disassembled to show the inner workings of the anatomy. The idea is not so very different from contemporary exhibitions such as "Bodyworlds," which stresses science in its marketing, while much of the appeal of the show lies in the fact that real human bodies are on display. In the case of nineteenth-century anatomical museums, the bodies were wax reproductions, and the thrill lay in viewing the naked female form—almost all exhibited female models, using the title Venus. Disease museums exhibited models of diseased bodies, showing the effects of diseases like cholera or tuberculosis on the body. Other variations included the display of "Other" kinds of human, such as Moors or Aztecs. These exhibitions were all marketed with the caution that they were for men only. See Altick, *Shows of London*, 338–42. While Altick's discussion is confined to England, there are many advertisements for similar shows in the *New York Herald* and other newspapers, and these exhibitions can be seen to be related to the exhibition of freaks and oddities such as those on display in Barnum's Museum. The major difference, however, was the stress on the female body and the admission of men alone. It should also be noted that there were legitimate scientific exhibits in the same period and that the smaller venues mimicked these but also placed a greater emphasis on novelty and sex.

10. *New Orleans Crescent*, March 7, 1848: 2.

11. *New Orleans Crescent*, March 22, 1848: 2.

12. *New Orleans Crescent*, March 25, 1848: 3.

13. Tait, *Circus Bodies*, 16–18, 20–21.

14. See "Amusements" [advertising], *New York Herald*, August 25, 1856: 3.

15. "A Born Speculator Dead," *New York Times*, August 21, 1902: 9. While I have not found a single full-page advertisement, Lea did place a full page of advertising for the Melodeon in the *New York Herald* on November 16, 1861, the period in which Annetta Galletti was performing in his theater.

16. "Amusements," *New York Herald*, August 20, 1853: 7.

17. *New York Times*, October 20, 1856: 8.

Chapter 3: *Performers Take Charge*

1. *New York Herald*, December 17, 1849: 3.

2. Wilentz, *Chants Democratic*, 309–10. Tony Pastor also had engagement with temperance venues as a child performer and was likewise influenced by their concern for reform.

3. *New York Herald*, April 20, 1857: 7.

4. See *New York Times*, September 12, 1861: 2; and September 13, 1861: 3.

5. *New York Herald*, October 6, 1861: 7. This notice is found at the bottom of col. 3, and the advertisement higher in the same column also taunts the American, although at no point does Lea ever refer to White, Butler, or the theater personally. These notes mean very little without the additional information about the lawsuit that appeared in another daily newspaper.

6. Advertisements placed by Lea for the Melodeon continued to make snide references to the American Concert Hall at 444 Broadway and to the Broadway Music Hall at 483 and 485 Broadway. Butler was the proprietor of both halls and managed the Broadway Music Hall, while White took care of the house at the American. On November 16, 1861, Lea's advertisement derided the minstrel troupe that Butler had assembled at his house as inferior, while touting the superiority of Sam Sharpley's Minstrel Troupe that was then playing at the Melodeon (see *Herald*, November 16, 1861: 9).

Chapter 4: *Novelty Acts in Concert Saloons*

1. This description is based on reviews of Zanfretta's act published during her career in circus and variety, as well as on the lithograph of her performing as an olio act at the Boston Theater in 1861.

2. Ireland, *Records of the New York Stage*, 2:12–15.

3. Odell, *Annals of the New York Stage*, 7: facing 252. A photograph of Ella Zoyara (Omar Kingsley) is on the same page.

4. *Leavenworth (Kans.) Daily Times*, June 18, 1860: 3.

5. During the winter months a small number of circuses took up residence in the South and, before the Civil War, particularly in New Orleans, which was one of the few large Southern cities and a major port for Caribbean trade. But even in the southernmost parts of the United States, the weather could be too inclement for performances. This pattern continued to be the case into the early twentieth century, and an itinerary from 1903, reprinted in Lewis, *From Traveling Show to Vaudeville*, 141–47, shows a route in which the circus begins in the Mid-Atlantic region in April, moves north into New England and Canada during June and July, back into the Mid-Atlantic before heading into the Midwest in August and September, and then slowly moves through the South, ending in New Orleans in mid-November.

6. See Slout's entry for Pastor in his *Olympians of the Sawdust Circle*.

7. The fragmentary nature of the biographical information available for any of the thousands of performers active in circus and variety means that this conclusion is, at best, speculative. Slout's online encyclopedia, *Olympians of the Sawdust Circle*, is the best source of information on most circus performers, and his brief biographies bear out my observation that speaking roles in the circus were disproportionately taken by English and American performers.

8. See Slout, *Olympians of the Sawdust Circle*, for a brief biography of both Yamadiva and Sarbro, who were both also active in the circus world. Odell lists a number of

Japanese troupes in his *Annals of the New York Stage*, including Maguire and Risley's, Marshall and Doyle's, and the Hah-Yah-Ta-Kee Companies—all active between 1865 and 1870. The sudden popularity of Japanese acrobats in this period resulted in parodies by minstrel companies. During the 1870s the major troupes were the Royal Yeddo Troupe and Satsuma's Troupe, both of which appeared in variety.

9. See Slout, *Olympians of the Sawdust Circle*.

10. Cook, *Arts of Deception*, 1–29. Cook further explores Barnum's approach to humbug in the first three chapters of the book, which focus on the automaton chess player, the marketing of the feejee mermaid, and the creation and marketing of other oddities, such as the "What Is It?" before turning to staged magic acts and illusion in his final chapters.

11. Nadis, *Wonder Shows*.

12. Slout, *Olympians of the Sawdust Circle*.

13. Ibid. Upon reading Slout's encyclopedia, it is also evident that very many performers in acrobatic specialties died as a result of injuries sustained during performance before they were forced to confront the effects of aging on their careers. A number of French, German, or Italian families returned to Europe, and Slout includes no record of the end of their lives, but overall Japanese and Arabic performers appear to have had more limited career possibilities than their American and European counterparts.

14. During the 1845/46 season Stickney's top-billed horse was Cincinnatus, although the mare Black Bess was also mentioned in the billing for the drama *Dick Turpin*. Stickney was not alone in giving his horses individual billing. In December 1845 the New York Circus and Amphitheatre was performing under canvas in New Orleans, and their top-billed horse was Alexander. See advertising in the New Orleans newspapers *Bee* and *Daily Delta*.

15. *New Orleans Daily Delta*, March 3, 1846: 1.

16. *New York Times*, September 25, 1875: 2.

17. See Slout, *Olympians of the Sawdust Circle*. Tait offers an extended discussion of cross-dressing in the context of circus in her book *Circus Bodies*.

18. Senelick, *Changing Room*, 296–97.

19. Tait, *Circus Bodies*, 16–18, 20–21.

20. Snyder, *Voice of the City*, 142–43.

21. See Slout, *Olympians of the Sawdust Circle*, for brief biographical sketches of all of these performers. Slout's encyclopedia confirms the international nature of circus and the fact that many of the families engaged in circus were interconnected not only through business ties, but through intermarriage.

Chapter 5: Tripping the Light Fantastic

1. This attitude is evident in Olive Logan's *Apropos of Women and Theatres* and also Smith's *Sunlight and Shadow* and other guide books to New York City. Odell echoes the bias against dancers in variety in his *Annals of the New York Stage*, and because most of these women worked anonymously it is difficult to contradict this view.

2. See entry for Dick Sands in Slout, *Olympians of the Sawdust Circle*. Jig and clog dancing, along with singing Irish songs, were a popular part of circus performances until at least the last third of the nineteenth century.

3. Needham, *I See America Dancing*, 135, 138.

4. In *Actors and American Culture*, 23, McArthur notes that in the 1860s leading players in New York stock companies earned $50 to $100 a week, supporting players $15 to $40 a week, and general utility players, supers, and ballet girls $3 to $10 a week. This estimate is echoed in contemporary sources such as Burns's essay "The Ballet Girl" in his *Female Life in New York City*, 37–38, which cites the average for ballet dancers as $6 per week; and Hankins, *Women of New York*, 153–60, which gives the entering wage for ballerinas as $3 per week.

5. Odell, *Annals of the New York Stage*, 7:198 and 10:539.

6. *National Intelligencer*, October 10, 1860, shows Augusta Walby as one of the dancers in the Percival's Pagoda Company, a variety troupe that performed at the Odd Fellows Hall in that city. A review of the *Black Crook* can be found in the *Cleveland Herald*, March 7, 1868: 4.

7. For example, see Odell, *Annals of the New York Stage*, 7:2–3 and 8:359. Odell notes the activities of these sisters in the New York area between 1857 and about 1870.

8. Augusta Lamoureaux was in the Percival's Pagoda Company at the same time as Augusta Walby. See note 7.

9. The 1860 census for Philadelphia gives the names and ages of the Wesners as Charles, 48; Eveline [Emmeline], 40; Mary Yeager, 21; Ellen [Ella], 19; Sarah [Sally], 17; Elizabeth [Lizzie], 15; Margaret [Maggie], 11; Charles, 7; Sarah E. Yeager, 6; and Williminia, 4. Sarah and Williminia Yeager were Mary's children and Charles and Emmeline's granddaughters.

10. Wesner's obituary noted that she had begun her career at the Continental Theater in Philadelphia at the age of 9, which suggests that the family had arrived in the city only recently at the time the census was taken. "Obituary," *Variety*, November 16, 1917: 11.

11. *Philadelphia North American and United States Gazette*, January 20, 1851: 2, cols. 2 and 4. A news item containing essentially the same information also ran in the *Boston Atlas*, January 21, 1851: 1, col. 6.

12. "Notes about Town," *Philadelphia North American and United States Gazette*, March 11, 1878. Counterfeiting was a common crime in the mid-nineteenth century, and Charles Wesner was most likely driven by a sense that the rich amassed their wealth through unfair means. The most thorough discussion I have found of counterfeiting and capitalism in the nineteenth century is Mihm, *Nation of Counterfeiters*.

13. Information about the Wesner family can be found in the census records for Philadelphia as well as in city directories for the period 1850–70. For a more complete history of Ella Wesner and her family, see Rodger, "Male Impersonation."

14. "Amusements" [Advertising], *New York Herald*, April 3, 1869: 12.

15. Charles had been arrested in 1873 after being caught passing counterfeit money and then attempting to bribe the arresting officer to be let go. I have found no record

of his sentencing, but there is every chance that he was sent to prison on this offense. Emma may have listed herself as his widow to explain why he was no longer living with her and possibly also to make it easier to acquire a liquor license.

16. The last record of Charles being arrested was in 1883, when he was part of a scheme to fraudulently receive a Civil War widow's pension. See *Philadelphia North American and United States Gazette,* August 1, 1883: 1; and August 24, 1883: 1.

17. Odell, *Annals of the New York Stage,* 7:286.

18. Ibid., 7:521 and 7:562. While there is no list of the ballet for *Bel Demonio,* the New York Public Library Dance Collection holds a photograph of Ella Wesner and two other dancers who were part of the corps for this piece.

19. "Amusements: Dramatic Notes," *St. Louis Daily Globe-Democrat,* November 27, 1881: 16. This report gives her age as 27, but the 1860 census gives her age as 15. Given that the ages of the other children listed in the census appear to be correct, I suspect that she claimed to be younger than she really was in order to continue to work. Both youth and beauty were important assets for ballet dancers of the period. There is also a chance that this Lizzie Wesner was actually Ella's niece, Sarah E. Yeager, who would have been 27 in 1881.

20. Ella died in 1917, at the age of 76. She had worked well into her 60s in small dime museums and venues at Coney Island. It is not clear when Mary left the stage, but she died in 1924, aged 85. The *New York Times* ran notices of Ella's death and a short obituary for her. See "Ella Wesner, Aged Actress, Dead," November 12, 1917: 13; and "Ella Wesner Lies in Man's Garb," November 14, 1917: 15. Notices of Mary's death ran in the *Times* on March 30, 1924: S8.

21. "A Mock 'Can-Can': The Disreputables upon the Stage Neatly 'Pulled' by Captain Buckley," *Chicago Inter-Ocean,* December 23, 1880: 3.

22. This was a period in which each bank issued its own currency and there was no centralized banking system or uniform currency. This situation made it relatively easy for counterfeiters to operate; that Charles Wesner was caught passing counterfeit bills suggests that he was trying to pass very low-quality forgeries.

23. Ella debuted as a male impersonator in 1871 and very quickly became one of the leading performers of her day. She was able to garner $200 a week during her tour of California in 1872. During the prolonged economic downturn of the mid-1870s, Wesner left the United States and worked for four years in English music halls, where wages were considerably lower. When she returned to the United States in 1881, she was still considered a leading performer, and she maintained this position until at least 1885. Her career began its slow decline in the late 1880s, and by the late 1890s she was struggling to maintain herself and her sister Mary, who continued to rely on her income. She retired in 1903 and was supported until the end of her life by the Actors' Charitable Fund.

24. Ella Wesner was certainly an ambitious woman, and evidence shows that she had little or no desire to marry and raise a family. During the early 1870s she was paid considerably more than the average variety wage, and she managed to work steadily until at least 1890. Despite this, Wesner died in poverty. Annie Hindle, who was Wesner's

contemporary on the stage, supported her mother until her death in the mid-1880s, but after that had no family obligations. Unlike Wesner, Hindle was able to survive forced retirement from the stage in 1886 due to a scandal and appears to have returned to performance in the early 1890s because of the death of her wife (see Rodger, "Male Impersonation," for a longer discussion of Hindle's marriage and the resulting scandal).

Chapter 6: Legal Intervention

1. This account is based on reports carried in the *New York Herald, New York Tribune,* and *New York Times* on April 25, 1862.

2. Leavitt notes the concern of legitimate managers who felt that their livelihood was threatened by concert halls in *Fifty Years in Theatrical Management,* 81.

3. Rosenzweig, *Eight Hours for What We Will.* Baldwin also charts a similar process in his study of conflicts over the use of public space and over urban planning in Hartford, Connecticut, in *Domesticating the Street.* In this work he shows that reform forces used city planning for two ends: to dismantle the poorest neighborhoods and the institutions that served their populations and to maintain green spaces such as city parks as a buffer between poor and middle-class neighborhoods.

4. See, for example, *Ordinances of the City of Grand Rapids* (1883), 199; and *Charter and Ordinances,* 333.

5. New Orleans theaters also paid individual policemen to be present at performances. Records of the officers assigned to duty at theaters and various ballrooms around the city are noted in "New Orleans, Office of the Mayor—Oaths of Office for Aldermen, Recorders and Other City Officials, 1832–1863" 9mf#89-117, held in the Louisiana Collection of the New York Public Library. Ordinance #306 CS, passed on May 26, 1883, continues to require police presence at theaters, shows, balls, and exhibitions in this city. New Orleans city ordinances are also part of the microfilm collection at main branch of the New Orleans Public Library.

6. Smith, *Sunlight and Shadow,* 123.

7. Ibid., 186, 190.

8. *New York Times,* December 12, 1861: 4.

9. See Rodger, "Legislating Amusements," for a more detailed discussion of the genesis of theater law in New York.

10. *Statutes at Large of the State of New York,* 3:323–25.

11. "Descent upon a Broadway Concert Saloon—Arrest of the Proprietor and Sixty Others," *New York Times,* January 28, 1867: 8.

12. "Canterbury Hall," *Washington National Intelligencer,* January 18, 1864: 1.

13. "A Born Speculator Dead," *New York Times,* August 21, 1902: 9. For advertising for Lea's various businesses in Port Jervis, see *Port Jervis (N.J.) Gazette,* May 6, 1879: 1.

14. It should not be imagined that variety halls became completely dry as a result of this bill. The bill did impede the audience's ability to drink freely in the auditorium. Theater patrons desiring alcohol had to leave the theater and exit to the street before

they could enter the bar, which the theater managers walled off from the theater. The license for the bar was usually held by a relative or business partner, while the theatrical license was held by the theater manager, thus circumventing the law.

15. The Society for the Reform of Juvenile Delinquents had been established in 1824 after New York residents had petitioned the state legislature. In 1829 the state legislature appropriated funds from New York City Commission of Health to help maintain this society. A yearly sum of $8,000 was to be paid from the monies collected to maintain the Mariner's Hospital in New York. This 1829 act also required theater licensing and determined that a proportion of those fees also go to the society. In 1831 the state further modified the act by requiring an additional $4,000 from liquor licenses and excise taxes to be paid to the society, and in 1839 it was further amended to link the three sources of funding—harbor taxes, liquor licensing and excise, and theatrical licensing—and the fines for operating a theater without a license were substantially increased at the same time. The 1862 act builds on this web of legislation and, as far as theater law goes in New York, was remarkable for being the first law not to amend the original 1829 act. However, the 1862 act provided that fees and fines benefit the Society for the Reform of Juvenile Delinquents.

16. Robert A. Gunn was the first president for the Society for the Enforcement of the Criminal Law, which was established around 1888. This society took on much of the work that had previously been undertaken by the Society for the Reform of Juvenile Delinquents.

17. In my research in the New York City mayoral records I have not found any complaints brought against "legitimate" theaters that catered to a middle- and upper-class audience and presented spoken drama, opera, operetta, or other forms of narrative musical theater. All complaints seem to have been brought against theaters catering to a working-class audience and against variety halls. Note too that not all variety theaters catered to working-class audiences. A hall such as Koster and Bial's Music Hall, on 23rd Street, offered variety entertainment but was also well known for "its 'cork room,' a place where callow youth and men old enough to know better might assemble after performances and purchase wine for the obstinately gay women who made the bill" (*New York Morning Telegraph*, July 23, 1901, clipping found in Locke Envelope #1065, Billy Rose Theater Collection, New York Public Library).

18. New York City Municipal Archives, the mayoral records of Hugh J. Grant, Box 1421 Folder 360: Police Dept. of—Licensing of Theatres, 1890, July–Aug.

19. Ibid.

20. The term "mechanic[k]s" was used to denote skilled tradesmen rather than unskilled laborers, who in this report are denoted as workingmen.

21. New York City Municipal Archives, the mayoral records of Hugh J. Grant, Box 1421 Folder 360: Police Dept. of—Licensing of Theatres, 1890, July–Aug.

22. For example, on February 26, 1891, Henry C. Miner, proprietor of a number of variety/vaudeville theaters in lower Manhattan and a major power in theatrical management in the city, wrote to Hugh J. Grant, the mayor of New York, complaining about the proprietor of Howard House and opposing the granting of a concert license to

this establishment (New York City Municipal Archives, the mayoral records of Hugh J. Grant, Box 1422 Folder 362: Police Dept. of—Licensing of Theatres, 1891, Jan.–May). He notes that the saloon is a neighbor of his People's Theater, which meant that a concert license would have enabled the manager to compete for Miner's customers. But he also expresses concern about the kinds of customers attracted to Howard House. In this complaint Miner seems more worried about Howard's customers driving away his respectable patrons than any direct competition; this was the same complaint that the proprietors of Wallack's, Niblo's, and Laura Keene's had expressed some thirty years earlier. It is also important to note that as a manager of a variety theater, albeit a large and respectable one, Miner needed to work harder to establish his respectability in the eyes of the city's moral reformers than many other theater managers, and this protest may well have been designed to do just that.

23. Walters, *American Reformers*, 8.

24. New York City Municipal Archives, the mayoral records of Hugh J. Grant, Box 1421 Folder 354: Police Dept. of—Licensing of Theatres, 1889, Jan.–Apr.

25. So, for example, Louis Stajer, the proprietor of 255 Bowery, was refused a license in 1892 because he tolerated prostitutes soliciting on his premises. While this was the primary reason given for the refusal of the license, the police report also noted that he had been charged for keeping a disorderly house (New York City Municipal Archives, the mayoral records of Hugh J. Grant, Box 1421 Folder 363: Police Dept. of—Licensing of Theatres, 1891–92, June–Feb.).

Chapter 7: *Variety in Times of National Conflict and Economic Turmoil*

1. The first record of variety in the *Clipper* appeared in the "City Summary" column that reported on theatrical activity in New York City on May 2, 1857. The author noted that "there is a place in the Bowery, between Stanton and Houston streets, where 'Miscellaneous Amusements' are on the board for six cents admission money. Must we put this on our list?"

2. It is possible that Philadelphia was the home of early variety, as it emerged in the period after the Civil War. Scattered advertising in the *New York Herald*, along with a report on December 10, 1859, in the *Clipper* that notes the presence of seven concert saloons in that city (270), suggests that this city was a major center for early variety. A week earlier the *Clipper* had reported only five concert saloons in New York, although it ignored at least two of the prominent New York venues—the American Concert Hall at 444 Broadway and the Canterbury. This suggests a lively and highly developed variety scene in Philadelphia that rivals that of New York in many ways. A Philadelphia-based theatrical newspaper, the *City Item*, also includes variety advertising and sporadic variety reviews from the late 1850s, but it largely ignores these venues before 1858.

3. The *Richmond Examiner*, December 3, 1864, includes a report of a performance

in the newly opened Richmond Varieties theater by Charles O. White's Iron-Clad Burlesque Co., which staged a combined minstrel and variety show. Charles O. White was a Southern minstrel performer who was loyal to the Confederates during the Civil War and should not be confused with the New York minstrel and variety manager Charley White. Charles O. White performed in Richmond and Savannah during the war and later moved into regional variety, working as a stage manager at the Academy of Music in New Orleans in 1868 and as the manager of the Greenlaw Opera House in Memphis in 1873. He died in Detroit, where he had managed the Detroit Theater for thirteen years, in January 1889, at the age of 56 (see *Saginaw Evening News*, January 4, 1889: 6).

4. See "City Summary," *Clipper*, December 16, 1871; and "Local News in Brief: New York," *New York Times*, December 8, 1871: 8.

5. "Amusements," *Clipper*, February 7, 1874.

6. "Letters from J. F. Schinotti to Ludlow and Smith," in *Sol Smith and Theatre Folk, 1836–65*, ed. Stella M. Drumm, Glimpses of the Past 5.7–9 (July–September 1938) (St. Louis: Missouri Historical Society, Jefferson Memorial). This letter was written from Providence, Rhode Island, and was dated July, 10, 1836.

7. Determining the wages paid to performers in variety is highly problematic through most of its history, and we are forced to rely on claims made by individual performers during specific periods. In 1872, for example, Ella Wesner's manager claimed that she was being paid $200 per week to perform in California. This is only slightly higher than Zellers's estimates (in *Tony Pastor*) of the highest wages paid in this period, so it is most likely accurate. On the other hand, Wesner was among the most sought after performers of this period, and her performing schedule was booked for two or more years in advance. The only indication of the amounts paid to bit-players in variety stock companies or to lesser-known performers can be found in Tony Pastor's account books for the mid- to late 1880s held by the Harry Ransom Center at the University of Texas. Pastor was known to be a generous employer, and his account books show him barely breaking even in this period. Zellers's estimates are also based on these accounts so, until other evidence emerges, they are all we have to go on. Account books for a number of the Keith small-time vaudeville houses in New England survive, but these are written in code. Librarians at the University of Iowa, which holds Keith-Albee materials, made a point of asking me if I had the information to crack this code when I worked in the collection and were disappointed when I could not help them. In order to do so, one would need to know how much a number of these little-known small-time performers were paid—the code uses letters of the alphabet to apparently indicate a range of salaries (such as M = $200–$250 per week).

8. Following the performance schedules of male impersonators in the 1870s, I have found that individual performers fostered personal relationships with variety managers, including some in relatively small cities, and returned to their theaters at least annually, if not more often. For example, Annie Hindle and Ella Wesner both performed regularly at Smith's Opera House in East Saginaw, Michigan. When Smith moved

across the state from East Saginaw to Grand Rapids, both of these women booked into his new theater and neither returned to the East Saginaw Opera House under its new management.

9. "Amusements" [advertising], *Clipper*, July 10, 1875.

10. Leavitt, *Fifty Years in Theatrical Management*, 270.

11. "Amusements" [advertising], *Clipper*, December 26, 1874.

12. In the 1870s Brown published a book entitled *The Showman's Guide* that was designed to aid theatrical managers of all kinds. Advertisements for this volume, which cost $5, can be found in the *Clipper*; see "Amusements" [advertising], *Clipper*, October 31, 1874.

13. Here I am distinguishing between tours organized by a performing manager and the kind of reciprocal arrangement between two theaters in different cities controlled by a single manager, such as Frank Rivers's Melodeon in both New York and Philadelphia. In the case of a tour, the touring manager operated like a middle-manager, negotiating with other theater managers from whom he rented halls, while performers had no relationship at all with the theater manager and relied entirely on the touring manager for their income and traveling expenses.

14. See *Boston Post*, July 6, 1863: 3; July 11, 1864: 3; and July 11, 1865: 3 for announcements of the respective tours. Subsequent issues give reviews and announce closings.

15. In a review of close to fifty years of Boston newspapers I have found only a few attempts to open a variety hall in that city in the period before 1870. In each case managers abandoned a variety-only format within weeks and turned to offering pantomimes and sensational drama with a variety olio. See, for example, the advertising placed for the Theatre Comique in Boston in the *Boston Post*, October 3, 1865: 3. This theater opened by offering variety acts in the first half, followed by a pantomime, but the *Post* notes on October 17, 1865: 3 that it had moved to three-part bills consisting of a sensational drama, a short variety olio, and concluding with a pantomime. By November 1865 it no longer even advertised the olio and seems to have become a theater dedicated primarily to pantomime.

16. Pastor's 1882 account book notes that the Providence Opera House "has orchestra which we could have used free" (May 5, 1882), and he also notes the cost of hiring two extra musicians for the performance on May 6 at the same theater. This strongly suggests that he traveled with his own musicians but supplemented them with locals when needed, particularly for performances at the end of the week, which drew a larger crowd (Pastor Account Books, Touring Troupe 1882; Harry Ransom Center, University of Texas, Austin).

17. Ibid.

18. Ibid. In this case the salaries for the week amounted to $836.

19. Ibid. See the accounts for week six at the Grand Opera House in New York. Pastor paid $16.20 to Michigan job printing in that week.

20. See, for example, week one of his 1886 tour, which was spent in Boston. Charges for printing, entered as "Boston," were $132.55. The following week was spent in Wil-

liamsburgh, New York, and the charges for printing (now entered under Boston Job) were $59.83 (Pastor Account Books, Touring Troupe 1886; Harry Ransom Center, University of Texas, Austin).

21. Advertising, *Clipper*, April 17, 1880.

22. *Clipper*, May 1, 1886: 103.

23. "City Summary," *Clipper*, July 29, 1876: 142.

24. Advertising, *Clipper*, July 10, 1875.

Chapter 8: *Just to Please the Boys*

1. Engel began her career singing in concert saloons in 1860 or 1861 and also appeared with her sister as part of Laura Keene's production of the spectacular play *The Seven Sisters* and was billed as a sentimental vocalist. Her sisters appeared as "Kentucky" and "Virginia" in the tableaux of "The Thirty Four States," which was added in the middle of the run and lasted a full season (Odell, *Annals of the New York Stage*, 7:312). A biographical sketch, "Miss Jennie Engel," in *Jennie Engel's Bouquet of Melodies Songster* (New York: R. M. De Witt, 1873), 3, claims she was part of the production although Odell does not include her among the performers who took part in it, while he does note that her sisters appeared. This further suggests that she appeared as an olio act rather than as part of the cast.

2. Saloons in the nineteenth century offered a separate entrance to a backroom of the saloon, where women could drink, but the saloon was almost exclusively male space. Powers discusses the gender relations of the barroom in *Faces along the Bar*, 26–35. This gender segregation of the barroom disappeared in much of the United States in the twentieth century, although it may still be maintained in small neighborhood bars in working-class neighborhoods. This arrangement, including the separate entrance leading to the "Ladies Lounge," was maintained in my native Australia into the late 1980s, along with the assumption that any unchaperoned woman in the all-male barroom was a "loose" woman or a wife who had violated the segregated space to drag her husband out and escort him home. This latter event caused great amusement among the victim's friends and caused him temporary loss of face.

3. *Washington National Intelligencer*, March 14, 1864: 1; and March 21, 1864: 1.

4. See "West Point Cadet" (G. D. Russell & Co., 1874), which was published as part of the collection *Miss Jennie Engel's Favorite Songs*. This song is held by the Lester Levy Sheet Music Collection at Johns Hopkins University and is also available as part of Music of the Nation: American Sheet Music 1820–1860 & 1870–1885, which can be found at the Library of Congress: American Memory Collection (http://memory .loc.gov/ammem/browse/ListSome.php?category=Performing%20Arts,%20Music).

5. That Engel's sisters were ballet dancers makes it likely that she was part of a family of dancers similar to the Wesners. The biographical sketch in her songster includes no details about her early life beyond the fact that she was born in New York of German and English parentage.

6. "Biographical Notice of Miss Jennie Hughes," in *Jennie Hughes' Rose of Erin*

Songster (New York: R. M. De Witt, 1874), 6. While there are exaggerations in this sketch, Hughes's work history is supported by both newspaper evidence and Odell's *Annals of the New York Stage.*

7. During late 1870s Hughes toured in *The French Spy*, a piece made famous by the scandalous actress Adah Isaacs Menken. See, for example, *Philadelphia North American*, July 25, 1876; *Boston Daily Advertiser*, April 17, 1877; *St. Louis Globe-Democrat*, February 2, 1879: 3; and *Chicago Inter-Ocean*, May 3, 1879: 6.

8. *Morning Oregonian*, December 10, 1899: 17.

9. Apart form the De Witt songster, which includes forty songs, thirty-four of them sung by Engel, I have found six songsters, nine individually printed songs, and two song sheets associated with Engel. The earliest of these are the undated song sheets "I'm the Merriest Girl Out," published by J. H. Johnson in Philadelphia, and "You'll Soon Forget Kathleen," published by H. De Marsan in the early 1860s (it notes that she performed the song at the American Theatre, 444 Broadway, which makes it possible to date more precisely). In 1868 the St. Louis publisher Compton & Doan published a series of *Jennie Engel's Songs* that included at least five songs. I have found the song "A Motto for Every Man," which was written by the English performer Harry Clifton; all of the other titles referenced on the cover of this song are English. The same publisher published the song "I'll Ask My Mother and Let You Know Next Sunday Afternoon" (lyrics by Tom Boursley, music by George Ernshaw) also in 1868. In 1870 G. D. Russell also published a series entitled *Jennie Engel's Songs*, which included the songs "I Should Like to Be a Fairy" and "Popsy Wopsy." Again, these songs were all written for Engel by other songwriters. The songsters were published by a number of New York publishers. These include *Jennie Engel's Burlesque Songster* (Fisher and Denison, 1870); *Jennie Engel's "Up to the Mark" Songster* (Ornum, 187?); *Jennie Engel's "Courting in the Rain" Songster* (R. M. De Witt, 1872); *Jennie Engel's "Upon the Grand Parade" Songster* (Fisher and Denison, 1872); *Jennie Engel's "Little Jack Sheppard" Songster* (R. M. De Witt, 1873); and *Jennie Engel's Serio Comic Songster* (Fisher and Denison, 1873).

10. *Our Girls Songster* (New York: Ornum & Co., 1876), *Black Crook Belle Songster* (New York: Ornum & Co., 1866), and *The Bewitching Girl Songster* (Ornum & Co., 1870) all feature lithographs of beautiful women on their covers, the latter two in brief stage costumes with short skirts. All are held by the Hay Special Collections in Brown University Library.

11. The burlesque leader Lydia Thompson, on the other hand, had multiple songsters dedicated to the repertoire of her troupe. These were designed to capitalize on her popularity.

12. Hughes's songsters are *Jennie Hughes' "I Should Like To" Songster* (R. M. De Witt, 1872), *Jennie Hughes Serio Comic Songster* (R. M. De Witt, 1872), and *Jennie Hughes' Rose of Erin Songster* (R. M. De Witt, 1874).

13. "You'll Soon Forget Kathleen" was published by H. De Marsan, most likely in the early 1860s. Jennie Engel and her sister Hattie were part of the company at the American Theatre during 1861 and 1862. The song sheet is held by the Library of Congress: America Singing Nineteenth-Century Songsheets Collection.

14. In *Jennie Hughes' Rose of Erin Songster* (New York: R. M. De Witt, 1874). This songster is held by the Hay Special Collections in Brown University Library.

15. Powers notes that sentimental songs were the favored repertoire of working-class men who sang in saloons in this period; see *Faces along the Bar*, 199. Unlike saloons, the variety hall was more likely to bring different populations together, so the sentimental song became an even more crucial unifying force among groups of men who may well have had little in common.

16. "*The West Point Cadet*" (words by Jennie Engel, music by M. de Donato) was published by G. D. Russell & Co., Boston, in 1874, as part of a series entitled "Miss Jennie Engel's Favorite Songs, arranged by Ned Florence." The sheet music is held by the Library of Congress: Music for the Nation Collection.

17. "Marching with the Band" (words by Jennie Engel, music by H. Wannemacher) is part of the same series as the song above and was published by G. D. Russell and Co. in 1874. It is also held by the Library of Congress.

18. This song was published by White & Goullaud in Boston in 1872 as part of a series entitled "Miss Emma Alford's Songs." Louis P. Goullaud also published it as part of a series of songs associated with the leading variety of the day, with a cover that listed the full catalog. The White and Goullaud version is held by the Library of Congress: Music for the Nation Collection, while the other is held in the Lester Levy Collection at Johns Hopkins University (http://levysheetmusic.mse.jhu.edu/). Neither edition gives the name of a composer or lyricist. The Library of Congress incorrectly gives the composer's name as W. F. Walker, which is the signature of the engraver given on the cover of "Miss Emma Alford's Songs."

Chapter 9: Dutch, Irish, Minstrels, and Other Characters

The sheet music for the epigraph is held by the Library of Congress: Music for the Nation Collection (http://memory.loc.gov/ammem/mussmhtml/mussmhome.html).

1. *New Orleans Daily Picayune*, January 11, 1891: 8. It is entirely possible that Phil Gannon served during the Civil War and died in action. At the time of the conflict he was only 30 years old and still young enough to be drafted. I can find no record of his performing in New York City after November 1860.

2. The only source of biographical information on Gannon is a brief sketch, "Autobiography of Phil. J. Gannon," that appears at the front of *Phil. J. Gannon's Original Irish Songster* (Philadelphia: Barclay & Co., 1859), which is held by the Harris Collection of American Poetry and Plays in the Special Collections in the John Hay Library at Brown University.

3. My dating of these sheets in the period from 1860 to 1862 is based primarily on the fact that this is the period in which Harry Fox was most active in minstrelsy and variety, as well as on the date at which the publisher, H. De Marsan, began producing song sheets. Fox does not appear in Odell's index before 1858, when he appeared as a guitarist performing in olio acts. By 1860 Fox had moved into minstrelsy, and a number of songsters containing his songs survive from this period, including *The Concert*

Room Comic Songster Containing Yankee, English, Irish and Dutch Songs (Philadelphia: A. Winch, 1860) and *Vaughn and Fox's Banjo Songster; or, Minstrel Time Melodist* (New York: A. Winch, 1860). As well as performing in blackface as a minstrel singer and banjo performer, the *Concert Room Songster* suggests that Fox apparently also portrayed Irish characters in variety. The song sheet for "Paddy McFadden" indicates that Fox had sung it at Hitchcock's National Concert Hall. Fox was appearing at this hall in 1861 and 1862 during the period of the passage of the Anti–Concert Saloon Bill (Odell, *Annals of the New York Stage*, 7:439), and after the passage of this bill Hitchcock's changed its name to the National Theatre. Nothing is known about the second Irish character singer, M. Cox. These song sheets are held by the Library of Congress: America Singing Nineteenth-Century Songsheets Collection (http://memory.loc.gov/ammem/amsshtml/amsshome.html).

4. "I Spy Your Little Game" was printed by H. De Marsan and sung by J. P. Johnson at the American Theatre, 444 Broadway. "The Suit of Corduroys" was also published by H. De Marsan, and both sheets date from the 1860s and are held by the Library of Congress: America Singing Nineteenth-Century Songsheets Collection (http://memory.loc.gov/ammem/amsshtml/amsshome.html).

5. I had not thought about the power of nonsense syllables as a bonding moment in group singing until I heard a BBC report in July 2008 about a recently released recording of sea shanties that involved celebrities and pop singers such as Bono from U2 and the actor Tim Robbins. A sound clip from this project was aired, and the excitement and energy in the voices of the singers as they moved from the verse to a chorus of nonsense syllables was remarkable. One participant in this project also described these songs as being like rock and roll. This story, with the title "Johnny Depp's Sea Shanties on Stage," can be found on the BBC website at http://news.bbc.co.uk/today/hi/today/newsid_7521000/7521051.stm (accessed 10/9/2008 at 2:41 P.M.).

6. "Clear the Way! (Parade Song)" (words and music by Joseph P. Skelly) was published as a song sheet with melody but not harmony by E. H. Harding in 1877. It is held by the Library of Congress: Music for the Nation Collection (http://memory.loc.gov/ammem/mussmhtml/mussmhome.html).

7. Odell lists a minstrel named White performing with the circus at Bowery Amphitheater in January 1841. No first name is given, but Williams and Whitlock were also in the group (*Annals of the New York Stage*, 4:511). Odell's next record of White was performing as part of a troupe that included Williams and Whitlock, as well as Dan Gardner and others, at Castle Garden in September 1844, and he maintained his association with these performers through at least that season (see *Annals of the New York Stage*, 5:160–63).

8. Ibid., 5:308.

9. *Daily Picayune*, January 11, 1891: 8. This report notes that White caught cold after standing outside in the chill watching as his old friend Henry C. Miner's Fifth Avenue Theater burned on January 3, 1891. He continued to perform, even though he was obviously ill and in distress, and he died less than a week after the fire.

10. "Kitty Kimo" was "composed by Charley White and sung nightly by Old Dan

Emmit, with thunders of Applause. If you want to spend a pleasant evening and enjoy a hearty laugh, go to White's Melodeon, 53 Bowery" (New York: H. De Marsan, n.d.). While this sheet is not dated, it was probably published between 1850 and 1852, which is when White's Melodeon was operating at 53 Bowery. The song is held by the Library of Congress: American Memory Collection.

11. The Keith vaudeville managers' report books, held by the University of Iowa, include a number of African American performers active in Keith small-time during the period 1902–22. These reports contradict the perception that there were no black single acts in vaudeville. The performers mentioned include the DeWolf Sisters, singers; Cole & Johnson, comedians; and the Two Alexanders, a man and woman, performing in Keith's Boston and Philadelphia theaters in 1902. Rosa Lee Tyler, a soprano, appeared on the Keith circuit in 1903, and both Burt Grant and Harry Brown won success as solo comedians in 1904. Harry Brown appeared in Keith's theaters over a number of seasons with great success, although, upon reading the reviews of his performances, as well as those of other African Americans in vaudeville, it is clear that they were seen as succeeding despite their color, but failing because of it.

12. The Arcade Concert Saloon operated in the basement of 127 Grand Street, under the Franklin Museum, from December 1856 to the summer of 1858, when it closed. The rooms were either empty or operating as a saloon alone until late April 1859, when the Broadway Varieties opened at this address. It has been noted that Merrifield was one of a number of early performers from Philadelphia. I am not certain who Sanford was; the first advertised bill for the Arcade Concert Saloon advertised "Sanford, baritone" (Odell, *Annals of the New York Stage*, 6:590), and Odell later lists several performers with the last name Sanford active in variety. There were also Sanfords associated with minstrelsy. Odell includes no references to Rochez.

13. The Hungarian-born actor S. Z. "Cuddles" Sakall is probably most associated with this role and often played the slightly befuddled German in films such as *Tea for Two* and *Lullaby of Broadway*, both starring Doris Day and released in the early 1950s.

14. Graham, *Histrionic Montreal*, 250. Finson notes that Williams was born in 1848 and died in 1915 in his *Voices That Are Gone*, 300.

15. *Chicago Inter-Ocean*, August 18, 1877: 3. This article concentrates primarily on the wages earned by legitimate actors and actresses, but it also includes Williams along with the minstrel Cool Burgess.

16. Finson offers a discussion of the different ethnic types in variety in *Voices That Are Gone*, 292–307, and also notes the more gentle portrayal of the Germans, especially when compared to the Irish in the 1870s and to the Jews and Italians later in the century. He also notes the German lack of longing for a lost homeland (301). Perhaps the German stereotype lasted as long as it did because the population was slow to assimilate, maintaining separate newspapers, churches, school, theaters, and cultural organizations into the early twentieth century and not abandoning the German language until the national anti-German sentiment in response to World War I.

17. "The Finest Police in the World!," words and music by Joseph P. Skelly (New York: E. H. Harding, 1875). This sheet music is held by the Library of Congress: Music

for the Nation Collection (http://memory.loc.gov/ammem/mussmhtml/mussmhome
.html).

18. While Stetson is generally credited as a variety pioneer in Boston, all of his
early attempts, and efforts by other variety managers such as Josh Hart, to open a
variety-only theater failed. Newspapers in Boston document a number of attempts
to open variety halls in the 1860s, but these quickly fell back on pantomime. In 1868
Rich and Trowbridge opened the Howard as a variety hall with the veteran Josh Hart
as stage manager (see *Boston Post*, August 11, 1868: 3 [Advertising]). Pantomimes and
ballet performances began to dominate the bills at this theater by mid-November, and
variety was limited to the olio. Stetson later went into business with Trowbridge and
Rich, and despite several subsequent attempts to stage a variety-only program at this
theater, pantomime and burlesque continued to dominate through the 1870s.

19. *Boston Daily Advertiser*, February 19, 1878.

20. "M'Vicker's," *Chicago Inter-Ocean*, February 3, 1880: 4.

Chapter 10: *Just Ordinary Workingmen*

The songster from which the epigraph is taken is held in the Harris Collection
of American Poetry and Plays in the Special Collections in the John Hay Library at
Brown University.

1. Horton, *About Stage Folks*, 9. The best and most comprehensive biography of
Pastor is Zellers, *Tony Pastor*; and this brief sketch of Pastor's career does not attempt
to approach the scope or thoroughness of Zellers's work.

2. "Tony Pastor and His Sixty Years on the Stage," *New York Times*, August 16, 1980:
SM3.

3. Sanjek, *American Popular Music*, vol. 2: *From 1790–1909*.

4. For example, a much reused tune was the song "Bow, Wow, Wow." Songs set to
this tune included "Joseph Tuck" (New York: H. De Marsan, n.d.), "The Great Know
Nothing Song, 'I Don't Know,'" by Francis Eastlack (Philadelphia: H. J. Kehr, n.d.), and
a song celebrating the end of the Mexican-American War, "The War Is Over Now," by
Eugene T. Johnston (New York: D. De Marsan, n.d.). All of these songs are held by the
Library of Congress: American Memory Collection. I have found the text of another
early song sheet with the title "Bow, Wow, Wow," but have found no melody for this
song. This may be a song from an English ballad opera "Love in Camp; or, Patrick in
Prussia," with music by William Shield, that was published in the mid-1780s.

5. Manifold, *Penguin Australian Songbook*, 8–9. I first came across this song in the
mid-1990s and as I hummed through the melody was surprised to find a song with
which I was familiar, having frequently sung it in class during my elementary school
years in Australia. At that point I knew that the chorus was identical to the version I
had sung, which was presented to us as an Australian folk song, but was surprised at
how closely Vivian's version corresponded to the song when I found it in a published
anthology. It appears that he barely altered it for his American audience. While one
would expect that the English public knew the history of the penal colony in Australia,

the popularity of this song in America—suggested both by its frequent performance by Vivian and later by the male impersonator Ella Wesner and the publication of the song by a number of music publishers—suggests that the American audience of the 1870s also had some understanding of this history and an empathy for the song's central character.

6. I have found a small number of full-score songs in handwritten manuscripts held by the Library of Congress: Music for the Nation Collection, and advertising placed in the *Clipper* during the 1870s advertised songs for professionals, sometimes at no charge. In contrast to this, songs associated with members of the Lydia Thompson Burlesque Troupe indicated that orchestral parts could be obtained from the publisher of the song. This suggests that publishers expected a larger market for these songs, which also included other performers. I have not found the same indication on any songs associated with variety.

7. Sanjek notes that music publishers in the very early nineteenth century sold songs associated with a performing songwriter at a higher price (*American Popular Music*, 62), and, given the large proportion of sheet music that noted the performer's name on the cover during the rest of the century, there is no reason to think that this situation changed. Even when the songwriter was not a performer, the association with a variety performer made the song more valuable, which is, no doubt, why songwriters supplied music to the profession at low and sometimes even no cost.

8. Spitzer, "'Oh Susanna.'"

9. These are held in the Harry Ransom Center at the University of Texas at Austin. A finding aid for this extensive collection of scripts for sketches, financial records, and other materials associated with Pastor can be found at http://research.hrc.utexas.edu:8080/hrcxtf/view?docId=ead/00106.xml&query=tony%20pastor&query-join=and (accessed 4/23/2009 at 6:50 P.M.). The song books and scores I examined were for "Tony Pastor's Comic Songs" and "102 Songs," Ser. II Box b18.5–b20.2.

10. Because the history of these books is not clear, I cannot tell when these insertions occurred. It is entirely possible that they result from new songs having been copied onto the back of existing scores, as suggested by the crossed-through arrangements.

11. There is the possibility that some of the titles given in this book were actually the words of the first line of the chorus, which makes locating them in the Library of Congress catalog impossible. Only twenty-six of the songs were found in archival sources in the United States, and in some cases I am not certain that the song I found is identical to that in the Pastor books or merely shares the same title. Thirty-nine of the songs were held by English archival collections at Oxford or Cambridge University (or both), and the majority of these were apparently not published in the United States.

12. This source contains more than 116 songs. Those up to #116 are in a relatively neat hand, and all but five have titles. At this point the writing in the books becomes increasingly messy and titles are omitted. For this reason I am considering only the first 116 songs. I found only 12 of these in other archival sources.

13. I have found a small number of songs sung by English performers, including "New Policeman," sung by the male impersonator Vesta Tilley; "Water Cresses" and

"Dark Girl Dress'd in Blue," sung by Harry Clifton; and "Organ Grinder," sung by Arthur Lloyd. The traditional songs such as "Yankee Doodle Dandy" and "Garry Owen" were clearly also not exclusively sung by Pastor.

14. This song is available online at the Library of Congress: American Memory Collection (http://memory.loc.gov/ammem/award97/ncdhtml/hasmhome.html) and is held as part of the Historic American Sheet Music, 1850–1920 Collection at Duke University (Music B-1063, Duke University Rare Book, Manuscript, and Special Collections Library).

15. The small number of datable items in Pastor's personal repertoire make this assessment necessarily tentative.

16. Even though we have little or no evidence for how many of these songs were performed, I do not believe that speculating on performance style is a futile act. I have had the occasion to test these speculations in live performance in a 2005 concert given by the Milwaukee Choral Artists, which presented English and American songs from the 1870s–1900s. On this occasion I worked with the singers to help them understand the cultural context for each of the songs presented, as well as the character type presented in the song. Where possible this was augmented with recordings of English music hall performers and also old film of English and American performers active in early-twentieth-century music halls. The result was a hugely successful performance that went well beyond presenting songs as museum pieces and actively engaged the audience.

17. A report of a performance at Tony Pastor's Opera House in the Bowery appeared in the *New York Times* in 1875, and this is the only explicit reference I have found to audience singing (see "A Saturday Night Scene in the Bowery," *New York Times*, January 31, 1875: 2). In this case, Pastor invited the audience to join in the chorus of a familiar favorite song, and the column notes that the young boys who sat in the gallery sang along, at first tentatively and then with more enthusiasm after further encouragement by Pastor.

18. "The Roman Fall," music by Alfred Lee, lyrics by Geo. T. Evans, was published in San Francisco by M. Gray in 1872 and was also sung by the male singer J. H. Milburn. The song is held by the Library of Congress: American Memory Collection.

19. Vivian's second wife documents his performance as the Admiral in *H.M.S. Pinnafore* and the Judge in *Trial By Jury* with James Duff's Company, first in Chicago and then in St. Louis (Vivian, *Biographical Sketch*, 67, 73–75). This biography also confirms that Vivian's singing voice was central to his act. When he was ill and his voice affected, he canceled his performance at Wood's Comique (81). Reviews of Ella Wesner's performances from as early as the 1870s note the hoarse and rough quality of her voice, but they also praise her act—clearly, here beautiful singing was a secondary consideration.

20. Vivian, *Biographical Sketch*, 11. Most of the biographical material available for Charles Vivian relies on this slim volume written by Vivian's wife and published well after his death. Most of the book deals with their life together as itinerant performers in California and the West. Beyond a brief mention of Vivian's arrival in the United

States and his entry into variety performance, which appear to be factually correct, there is no record of his early career before he met and married Imogen Holbrook. The *Clipper* did not note Vivian's arrival in the United States, but it carried a record of his first performance at Butler's American Theatre on November 30, 1867. It also periodically carried reports of his performances, particularly after his marriage to the English male impersonator Annie Hindle on September 16, 1868, in Philadelphia (see "Music Halls" *Clipper*, September 26, 1868). This first marriage was never formally ended, and it is possible that Vivian's second wife did not know about the existence of the first because he had relocated to the West Coast. Vivian was a founder of the Benevolent and Protective Order of Elks, and there is some interest in his life from members of this organization. The Elk historians with whom I have had contact are ambivalent, at best, about the information I have to offer on Vivian—all indications are that he was an unpleasant and violent man—and as yet I have seen no indication that the official Elk history recognizes the existence of his first marriage.

21. For a discussion of "lions comiques" active in English music halls, see Bailey, *Music Hall*, 49–69.

22. It should also be noted that while English music hall songs continued to represent types based on class and regional differences into the early twentieth century, the Americans treated all white native-born men as equal, regardless of regional origin, and by the 1870s even the Yankee had become less common.

23. Advertisements for songs in newspapers made much of the number of leading variety singers who performed the song already, indicating that in the American context the appeal lay more in the skills and character of the specific performer than in the repertoire per se.

24. Ella Wesner debuted in 1871 as a male impersonator singing a repertoire that consisted largely of songs sung by Vivian in the late 1860s. I suspect Wesner acquired these songs from Annie Hindle, who had been married to Vivian during 1868 and sang a similar kind of repertoire, when she was working as Hindle's dresser and learning this performance genre. By 1871 Vivian had been resident on the West Coast for two to three years, and while it is possible that Wesner had seen him perform before he left, it is unlikely that she remembered that repertoire, which was then published by a San Francisco publisher.

25. Harry Vandemark may have been an English performer or perhaps a singer active outside New York; I have found no record of him in Odell's *Annals of the New York Stage*. This song was originally an English song and was published in New York by E. H. Harding in 1872. It is held by the Library of Congress: Music for the Nation Collection.

26. J. P. Skelly's song "Get Your Head above the Crowd" encouraged daring ambition and upward aspiration. The song sheet for this song, published in 1875 by E. H. Harding, is held by the Library of Congress: American Memory Collection.

27. "Where There's a Will There's a Way" was sung in America by Charles Vivian in 1868, but was originally an English music hall song sung by Harry Clifton and published by William Pond. "I Will Stand by My Friend," words by Bedford Reute and

arranged by George T. Evans, was part of Charles Vivian's repertoire and was published by M. Gray in San Francisco in 1873. All of these pieces are held by the Library of Congress: Music for the Nation Collection.

28. Bailey, *Music Hall*.

29. Oliver Ditson also published this song in Boston in 1868, which is held by Dartmouth University Library's Collection, while the song sheet, published by H. De Marsan, is held by the Library of Congress. This song was not sung widely in the United States. I have found it sung by Vivian and briefly also by Annie Hindle, who most likely acquired it from Vivian when she was married to him.

30. This song sheet is held by the Library of Congress: American Memory Collection.

31. Both "Isabella with the Gingham Umbrella" and "The Sewing Machine" are held by the Library of Congress: Music for the Nation Collection.

Chapter 11: Champagne Charlie

The songster from which the epigraph is taken is held in the Harris Collection of American Poetry and Plays in the Special Collections in the John Hay Library at Brown University.

1. Advertising, *Clipper*, October 24, 1868.

2. The most complete published biography of Hindle is less than a page in length and found in Graham, *Histrionic Montreal*, 214–15. This account relies, in part, on a newspaper article published in the *New York Sun*, December 27, 1891: 13. This article includes an interview with Hindle, who was then around 50 and mourning the loss of her wife, Annie Ryan. Graham's account goes further than the *Sun* article in supplying details of Hindle's career and is largely accurate. A lengthier biography of Hindle can be found in my dissertation ("Male Impersonation"), although I have found additional information about this remarkable woman's career in the decade or more since it was completed.

3. *New York Sun*, December 27, 1891: 13. Imogen Holbrook Vivian's biography of her husband speaks of him only in glowing terms, but even so it is evident that he spent a great deal of his time off the stage drinking with fellow actors and friends. Imogen was not part of these social evenings, which were loud and raucous affairs, and early in their marriage he sedated her with a homemade cold remedy so that he could join an evening of drinking. This is referred to as a practical joke (Vivian, *Biographical Sketch*, 27).

4. *New York Sun*, December 27, 1891: 13. The *Clipper* noted the appearance of Hindle and Vivian on the same bill at the Theatre Comique in New York City in the "Variety Halls" column under the heading "Gags" on February 2, 1878: 359. This report signals that the profession remembered the events that had led to Vivian relocating to the West Coast and, given that he had married for a second time, that possibly they expected some conflict between Hindle and Vivian and/or his new wife.

5. *New York Sun*, December 27, 1891: 13. This newspaper claims that Wesner was

a "factotum" of Hindle and that she worked as her dresser. But this claim was made in a paragraph noting Hindle's later marriage to her dresser Annie Ryan and before a longer discussion of Wesner's elopement with Josie Mansfield, who is noted as the "only romance of her life." I don't doubt that there was a connection between the two women—they had certainly worked together at least once—but there were few occasions on which they had the opportunity to meet, even in the late 1860s.

6. Bailey, *Music Hall*, 54–55. Bailey identifies the three types of swell in English drama, and also in popular music hall songs, as the "languid upper-class swell" or the fop or dandy; the man-about-town who enjoyed boisterous fun, drinking, and leisure; and the counterfeit, who aped the manners and behavior of his social superiors. All of these types also appear in American popular song, although they take on different meanings in the new context.

7. "Champagne Charlie," words by George Leybourne and music by Alfred Lee, was published in London by Alfred Sheard & Co. in 1867. Lee and Walker published it in Philadelphia in the same year, and it almost immediately appeared in versions associated with particular singers or groups. William Hall & Sons published the San Francisco Minstrels' version in 1868, and it also appeared in arrangement for piano. The Lester Levy Sheet Music Collection at Johns Hopkins University holds eight copies of this song by various publishers, as well as a number of gallops, polkas, and waltzes based on the melody.

8. John Stanton suggests that these initials stood for "Private rooms for gentlemen." See Bailey, *Popular Culture*, 231n30.

9. "Moët and Chandon," words by H. Hurrille and music by George Leybourne, was published in New York by William A. Pond & Co. This song comes from my collection and is undated, although was probably published around 1870, which was the year the song was first published in England. An undated song sheet with identical lyrics can be found in the Library of Congress: America Singing Nineteenth-Century Songsheets Collection, and a version of the song as sung by Gus Williams and published by White & Goullaud, Boston, in 1870 is held by the Library of Congress: Music for the Nation Collection. "I'm out for a Lark," words and music by Joseph P. Skelly, was published by E. H. Harding, New York, in 1877. This music is also held by the Library of Congress: Music for the Nation Collection.

10. Bailey, *Music Hall*, 54–55.

11. "Charley the Masher," words and music by Joseph P. Skelly, published by E. H. Harding, New York, in 1877, is held by the Library of Congress: Music for the Nation Collection.

12. "Hildebrandt Montrose," words and music by Edward Harrigan, published by E. H. Harding, New York, in 1875, is held by the Library of Congress: Music for the Nation Collection.

13. "Fifth Avenue George," words and music by Joseph P. Skelly, published by E. H. Harding, New York, in 1876, is held by the Library of Congress: Music for the Nation Collection.

14. The text to "I'm the Ladies' Beau Ideal" was published in *Ella Wesner's King of*

Trumps Songster by A. J. Fisher, New York, in 1875. This songster and a small number of pieces of published sheet music are an invaluable source of information on Ella Wesner's repertoire. The songster is held by Brown University Library, the sheet music for this song, with words by George Cooper and music by Richard Steirly, was published by E. H. Harding, New York, in 1871, and is held by the Library of Congress: Music for the Nation Collection. Unfortunately the same range of resources does not exist for Annie Hindle. In 1870 the New York publisher F. A. Brady published *The Annie Hindle Songster*, but unfortunately this volume does not appear to survive in any archival collection. It is listed in the *American Catalogue of Books, Published in the United States from Jan., 1866 to Jan., 1871*, vol. 2, compiled and arranged by James Kelly (New York: Wiley & Son, 1871), 18. Hindle's surviving repertory consists of just four published songs—one indicates she sang it on its cover, reviews indicate that she sang another, and two were dedicated to her by their composers, and while it is not clear that she performed them, they portray the right character type; advertising and reviews reference dozens of song titles that cannot be positively identified and probably did not survive.

15. "The City Beau," comic song as sung by Cool White, was printed by Andrews, 38 Chatham St., New York, most likely in the early 1870s, and is held by the Library of Congress: America Singing Nineteenth-Century Songsheets Collection.

16. Powers, *Faces along the Bar*, 90–91.

17. "I'm on the Teetotal" is found in *Ella Wesner's King of Trumps Songster* (New York: A. J. Fisher, 1875), 10–11. This songster is held by the Hay Special Collections in Brown University Library.

18. Both of these songs are found in *Ella Wesner's King of Trumps Songster* (New York: A. J. Fisher, 1875), 15, 24–25.

19. "Pretty Jemima Don't Say No," written by Frank Hall, arranged by Charles Belmont (Boston: Oliver Ditson & Co., 1868). This music is held in the Sheet Music Collection at Dartmouth College.

Both of these songs are found in *Ella Wesner's King of Trumps Songster* (New York: A. J. Fisher, 1875), 15, 24–25.

20. "The Gymnastic Wife" is found in *Ella Wesner's King of Trumps Songster* (New York: A. J. Fisher, 1875), 34–35. This songster is held by the Hay Special Collections in Brown University Library.

21. "Don't You Put Your Foot on a Man When He's Down," words by Charles Vivian, composed by G. Marsden and arranged by C. E. Pratt (Boston: Oliver Ditson & Co., 1868). This music is held by the Lester Levy Sheet Music Collection at Johns Hopkins University.

22. Noted in "Latest News by Telegraph to the Clipper," *Clipper*, September 8, 1883: 404.

23. The sheet music for this song was published by Chas. D. Blake & Co., Boston, Mass., in 1885. It is held in the Lester Levy Sheet Music Collection (Box 137, No. 38).

24. Rotundo, *American Manhood*, 271–72.

25. Chauncey, *Gay New York*, 33–34, 36–37.

26. Ibid., 36–37, 40.

27. Ibid., 80.

28. See Faderman's *To Believe in Women* for a full discussion of this anxiety, which came to revolve around the figure of the mannish woman, blue stocking, or lesbian in the twentieth century.

29. For a full discussion of the differences in style between American and English male impersonation, see Rodger "Male Impersonation."

30. See "City Summary," *Clipper*, December 16, 1871; and "Local News in Brief: New York," *New York Times*, December 8, 1871: 8.

31. "Variety Halls," *Clipper*, May 17, 1873.

32. "Fact and Fancy Focused," *Clipper*, September 28, 1878: 214; and August 23, 1879: 174. W. W. Long was, at that point considerably older than Annie Hindle. He had been among the early concert saloon managers in Philadelphia in the 1850s, and my suspicion is that he married Hindle to give her the status she needed in some kind of financial or business transaction.

33. This marriage is on the public record in Grand Rapids, Michigan, and is indexed in the public library's Index of Marriages in the Genealogy Section of the main branch. I have a certified copy of the record of the marriage, which is #15174. Hindle gave her name as Chas. E. Hindle, her place of birth as England, her profession as actor, and her age as 31. At the time she was probably closer to 40 years old. Annie Ryan's age is given as 22 and her place of birth Wooden Cave, Canada. The record notes that Kerr B. Tupper, the pastor of the First Baptist Church, performed the ceremony, but all of the contemporary newspaper reports credit Brooks with marrying the pair.

34. *Grand Rapids Telegram-Herald*, June 7, 1886: 4. The article notes that "it was 3 o'clock this morning before Hindle would admit his sex to the reporter and acknowledge that he had been married to Annie Ryan." Reports of this marriage can also be found in the *Grand Rapids Daily Democrat*, June 8, 1886: 5; and *Grand Rapids Evening Leader*, June 7, 1886: 4, both of which ran considerably shorter stories.

35. *New York Clipper*, June 12, 1886: 198.

36. *New York Clipper*, June 19, 1886: 217.

37. "Stage Whispers," *National Police Gazette*, July 3, 1886: 2.

38. "Stage Whispers," *National Police Gazette*, August 21, 1886: 2.

39. The *Police Gazette* was particularly vicious in its attack on the soprano Christine Nilsson, who toured the United States in 1883. Calling her "the Swedish Sappho" and the "lyric Lesbian," the *Police Gazette* consistently depicted Nilsson as a woman who overwhelmed other women with her attentions and even dared to compete with men for women's affections. It also suggested that her affection for women was affecting her voice, stating "Christine Nilsson is developing such remarkable traits that no one would be astonished to find her bloom forth as a tenor soon" ("Stage Whispers," *National Police Gazette*, November 17, 1883: 3). The *Police Gazette's* use of the terms "sappho" and "lesbian" suggest that these terms were already becoming associated with what contemporary sexologists referred to as "sexual inversion."

40. See the report from Pittsburgh in "Variety Halls," *Clipper*, June 8, 1872. By late

June the correspondent from Louisville noted: "There was a rumor afloat that Josie Mansfield was in the city, and the hotel registers were besieged by an inquisitive mob from morning till night, but nothing definite was arrived at. There is a Josie Mansfield, a companion of Miss Wesner's, traveling with Pastor's company, but whether it is *the* Josie or not we are unable to state" (see "Variety Halls," *Clipper*, June 29, 1872).

41. "City Summary," *Clipper*, October 12, 1872.

42. "City Summary," *Clipper*, October 19, 1872.

43. "Amusements," *Clipper*, November 23, 1872.

44. Wesner featured prominently in Pastor's tour advertising from late November 1872 onward. Pastor did not usually announce the members of his touring company until after the New Year, but the 1873 summer tour was announced earlier than any of the tours before or after it. Pastor did not even have a complete company, and when the advertising first appeared it featured only an announcement of the tour and Wesner's name. Gradually, the names of performers were added under Wesner's, and on February 1, 1873, the full company was announced.

45. *Bangor Whig and Courier*, March 25, 1887.

Chapter 12: What's in a Name?

1. It should also be noted that female minstrel troupes were covered primarily in the variety column of the *New York Clipper* rather than in the minstrel column, which is one of a number of reasons for considering this kind of performance in a discussion of variety. A more pressing reason, however, is the link to earlier forms of sexualized variety such as those staged at the Franklin Museum, which had also used the term "Female Minstrels" to refer to its entertainment. This view departs from the narrative proposed by Allen in *Horrible Prettiness*, which credits Lydia Thompson's tour with introducing this style of performance.

2. An article in the *New York Times* that reported on a lawsuit brought against the proprietor of Robinson Hall notes that Tony Pastor had rented this hall to present the cancan on this occasion (see "Inconsistent Uses of Robinson Hall," *New York Times*, March 25, 1875: 2). Pastor seems to have been unwilling to offer this sexually suggestive dance at his own variety hall, perhaps understanding that the presentation of the dance would undercut his claims of running a family theater, but as a businessman he was quite willing to profit from the dance. I doubt that any of the managers, male or female, saw this dance as intrinsically obscene, but they did understand that others—particularly moral reformers—might not agree with them.

3. *New York Times*, August 16, 1874: 3.

4. "City Summary," *New York Clipper*, September 12, 1874.

5. Ibid.; and "The Metropolitan Theatre Company in Court," *New York Times*, September 2, 1874: 8.

6. "Amusements" [Advertising], *New York Clipper*, October 30, 1875.

7. "Amusements" [Advertising], *New York Clipper*, November 13, 1875 (emphasis original).

8. "Amusements" [Advertising], *New York Clipper*, June 17, 1876: 95; and May 6, 1876.

9. "The Sunday Police Courts," *New York Times*, January 4, 1876: 15. Montague assaulted Robinson with a wrench when Robinson refused to allow Montague to cut the most offensive verses rather than the entire song. Had the singer complied fully and cut the song he may well not have been fired, nor would he have ended up in court on assault charges.

10. "Variety Halls," *New York Clipper*, March 25, 1876. It is interesting to note that while the regular company was on the road, Robinson presented Ninon Duclos and her ballet troupe and a melodrama to his audience (see "Amusements," *New York Times*, March 26, 1876: 7).

11. The Globe was managed by Robert W. Butler, former manager of the American Concert Hall and a sometime variety performer, during 1872. The Theatre Comique was managed by Josh Hart, and Tony Pastor had always performed on his own stage. Of the theaters listed only the Olympic seems to have been managed by an entrepreneurial manager. This theater was among the earliest to use the term "vaudeville," and it also tended toward spectacular entertainment, but was never as blatantly sexual in its advertising as the Parisian Varieties.

12. *New York Times*, May 23, 1876: 8.

13. See reports of this event in the *New York Times*, October 15, 1876: 12; and October 16, 1876: 8. On October 15 the *Times* noted that, while held in jail, the actresses of the company disturbed the peace by shouting and "singing ribald songs."

14. *New York Times*, August 31, 1867: 7; and *New York Herald*, September 29, 1870: 6.

15. It is notable that a Boston and not a New York manager first employed this term in New York City. Given the use of the term "vaudeville" in regional theater to distinguish touring companies from variety presented at the local variety hall, this may be a case of regional practice being imposed on the nation's theatrical center. New York managers, on the other hand, continued to use the term "variety" until much later in the nineteenth century.

16. *New York Herald*, September 28, 1870: 6; and September 29, 1870: 6. It is also interesting to note that this bill differed from the standard variety bill of a long variety first part and a burlesque afterpiece. Stetson was from Boston, and this bill featuring a burlesque or extravaganza, an olio, and a ballet was much more typical of what was billed as variety in that city. Boston variety halls frequently featured one and even two pantomime performances with a variety olio. Perhaps the use of the term "vaudeville" to describe variety was also an innovation of Boston. I have found no evidence of this usage in that city yet, but given that B. F. Keith was raised in the city, it might explain his use of the term.

17. "Amusements" [Advertising], *New York Sun*, February 16, 1874; and *New York Times*, August 16, 1874: 3.

18. "Amusements This Evening," *New York Times*, December 9, 1875: 4.

19. *New York Times*, March 30, 1869: 4; March 25, 1874: 4; and August 2, 1870: 4.

20. While this kind of humor relying on language play and puns is now uncommon,

it can occasionally still be found. In Milwaukee, Wisconsin, a club featuring "adult" entertainment and including female dancers, called Art's Performing Center, is found just two blocks away from the city's premier performance venue, the Marcus Performing Arts Center, which is home to the city's symphony, ballet, and opera companies and patronized by elite audiences.

21. *Stevens Point (Wisc.) Journal*, February 7, 1874: 3.

Chapter 13: Sex Rears Its Ugly Head . . . Again

1. "Ages of Actresses," *San Francisco Bulletin*, February 28, 1878. This article also notes that Fisk was the cousin of Col. James Fisk, who had been murdered earlier in the 1870s, and that she was educated at a convent in Indiana.

2. *Milwaukee Sentinel*, December 31, 1873: 8.

3. *Janesville Gazette*, February 15, 1875: 4; February 27, 1875: 4; and March 11, 1875: 4.

4. *Stevens Point (Wisc.) Journal*, March 20, 1875: 3.

5. The members of Fisk's Troupe were listed among the arrivals at the Milwaukee Hotel, Newhall House, in the *Milwaukee Sentinel*, April 12, 1878: 3. Advertising appeared in the same newspaper on April 8, 1878: 8.

6. *Chicago Inter-Ocean*, July 27, 1878: 6. While this column, reprinted from the *New York World*, is snide about the kinds of performances required of these dancers, it is not openly hostile to Fisk. It also notes that the dancers hired were paid $6 to $10 per week, which was the standard rate for corps dancers in that period.

7. *Chicago Daily Tribune*, October 20, 1878: 11.

8. See *Chicago Daily Tribune*, February 3, 1878: 16, for an announcement of the opening of the Folly. Advertising ran sporadically during March and April, including a call for "fifty young ladies with good figures and voices" on April 28, 1878: 3. On May 7, 1878: 8, an article noted the indebtedness of the theater, and, according to an item that appeared on June 2, 1878: 8, it closed soon after this.

9. McCullough, *Living Pictures on the New York Stage*, 84.

10. "Ninon Duclos: How and Why She Horsewhipped a Bankrupt Merchant," *Chicago Daily Tribune*, March 19, 1879: 12.

11. "Out of Town Variety," *New York Dramatic Mirror*, April 19, 1879: 3; and *Cincinnati Commercial*, October 19, 1879: 4; and November 28, 1879: 4.

12. "Variety Halls," *Clipper*, October 16, 23, and 30, 1874.

13. Dudden, *Women in the American Theatre*.

14. Advertising, *New York Clipper*, August 24, 1878: 176. In claiming this, Fisk ignores the fact that Madame Rentz's Troupe, organized and managed by the minstrel manager M. B. Leavitt, was also operating in this period and was the leading female minstrel company until the turn of the twentieth century.

15. In an advertisement in the *Clipper* on August 30, 1879: 184, for example, Fisk bragged, "I snap my fingers at the Foeman's taunts." This kind of inflammatory language is typical of Fisk's advertising in this newspaper, but I have not seen the same bravado

from her in the daily newspapers of the cities and towns in which she played. In these the troupe is represented as a respectably performing combination.

16. "Variety Halls," *Clipper*, September 7, 1878: 191.

17. "Variety Halls," *Clipper*, September 14, 1878: 199; and April 5, 1879: 15; *Chicago Daily Tribune*, October 20, 1878: 11.

18. "Variety Halls," *Clipper*, April 5, 1879: 15.

19. See, for example, the *Chicago Daily Tribune*, October 20, 1878: 11; and October 22, 1878: 5.

20. *New York Times*, February 5, 1869: 5.

21. "A Theatrical Difficulty in New York," *Washington National Intelligencer*, June 3, 1869: 1.

22. "British Burlesque Again," *New York Times*, June 9, 1869: 4.

23. *New York Times*, September 28, 1870: 4.

24. The panic over women being out of control was also reflected in numerous images of young women from good families out in the city with no supervision that appeared in the *Police Gazette* during the 1870s. These images, with tongue-in-cheek captions that commented on the breeding and refinement of the young women, inevitably showed them smoking cigars, rowdily riding public transportation, or striding through the streets in a manner more associated with the upper-class man-about-town.

25. "Ninon Duclos, How and Why She Horsewhipped a Bankrupt Merchant," *Chicago Tribune*, March 19, 1879: 12.

26. The *Chicago Inter-Ocean*, October 6, 1878: 6, carried a report of a bill poster robbing Fisk of her cashbox and noted she had a gun and horsewhip and was searching for him. The following year the *Galveston News*, April 9, 1880: 1, noted that she had "cowhided the city editor of the Journal, on account of an article published against her company."

27. "Out of Town Varieties," *New York Dramatic Mirror*, June 28, 1879: 6.

28. *Dramatic Mirror*, March 29, 1879: 6.

29. Logan's best-known work on this topic is *Apropos of Women and Theatres*, but she also published elsewhere on the topic. I had long assumed that Logan's reason for wanting to distance herself from the branch of the theater that presented the "leg business" was her desire to protect the decent professional women in the theater from the indecent ones who catered only to men's basest needs. I have also wondered if Logan sought to justify the decency of her profession to the middle-class feminists whose cause she embraced. When looking at the cast list of Thompson's first company, however, I discovered that Olive Logan's younger sisters, Alice, Grace, and Kate, who were part of the stock company of Wood's Museum Theater, which is where Thompson played for the first part of her New York stay, were pushed into service to supplement the British troupe. In their opening performance of *Ixion*, Alice Logan played Juno and Grace Logan played Cupid, and both Alice and Kate were cast in the play that preceded the burlesque. See Odell, *Annals of the New York Stage*, 8:436–38. This raises the possibility that Olive Logan's outrage was at least partly on behalf of her sisters.

30. See *Chicago Daily Tribune*, October 22, 1878: 5; *Galveston Daily News*, April 9,

1880: 1; and "Belligerent Blondes," *Chicago Daily Tribune*, July 7, 1879: 5. In this latter article, which is a little over a single newspaper column in length, Fisk is shown defending the local women with the enthusiastic support of the members of her troupe. The author treats this as a comic event in which women ran amok, but also got the better of two of the city's least respectable theater managers.

31. "Belligerent Blondes," *Chicago Daily Tribune*, July 7, 1879: 5.

32. *St. Louis Globe-Democrat*, September 8, 1878: 3.

Chapter 14: Moral Reform in Regional Variety

1. Glazer, *Cincinnati in 1840*, 54–55.

2. It is interesting to note that Vine and Race Streets now mark the center of Cincinnati's downtown district and are the location of major hotels and the public library and are close to numerous entertainment venues and restaurants. Sycamore and Broadway mark the eastern edge of the area in which the headquarters of major businesses, such as Proctor and Gamble, are found, and also august cultural institutions that once catered to the elite of the city, such as the Taft Museum of Art and the Literary Club, both on East Fourth Street not far from Broadway. Today, both of these institutions lie in the shadow of I-71, the major north-south interstate highway.

3. Dunlap, "Queen City Stages," 30.

4. Ibid.

5. Ibid., 22.

6. The population of Cincinnati at midcentury was 115,436, and in 1861 it had grown to 161,000. Stevens categorizes the 1860 population of Cincinnati into 54% American, 30% German, 12% Irish, and 4% all other foreigners. By 1870 it had grown to more than 250,000 people. These figures are cited from George S. Stevens's *City of Cincinnati* by Grandstaff, "History of the Professional Theatre," 5, 7–8.

7. Baldwin notes a similar process in the development of urban planning in Hartford, Connecticut, in his *Domesticating the Street*, 39, 47–63. During the 1870s and 1880s Hartford had seen its immigrant population explode, and the 1890s–1910s saw a prolonged campaign by reform-minded middle-class women of the city for better housing to replace the overcrowded tenements that bordered the shopping district of the town, along with a campaign against the city's vice district and for clean and orderly streets free from refuse and billboards and other advertising.

8. The Race Street Varieties was announced in the "Music Halls" column of the *New York Clipper* on November 21, 1868, but I have found no evidence of the theater in Cincinnati until 1870, when advertising for the hall was placed in a number of the city's newspapers.

9. For a discussion of Annie Hindle's brief and unsuccessful management of a variety hall in Cincinnati during 1874, see chapter 13.

10. *Cincinnati Commercial*, September 1, 1878: 7, cited in Grandstaff, "History of the Professional Theatre."

11. The Miami Canal was drained in 1919, and during the 1920s the city began

work on a subway project that was abandoned by 1927 because of budget overruns. A broad street, Central Parkway, was built over the subway tunnels and follows the route of the old Miami Canal, running east-west across the city before turning abruptly north at Plum Street.

12. *Cincinnati Commercial*, October 4, 1879: 5.

13. *Cincinnati Times-Star*, January 22, 1881: 5.

14. These included the seriocomic Jennie Engel, who had frequently toured with Tony Pastor's summer troupe in the early and mid-1870s. Snelbaker also employed Minnie Wesner, the niece of the male impersonator Ella Wesner, as part of his ballet. All of the women in the Wesner family performed on the stage as dancers, and both Ella and her younger sister Maggie had success in solo song-and-dance acts. There is little doubt that Minnie Wesner was a highly skilled dancer who had received training from her older female relatives.

15. *Cincinnati Commercial*, December 21, 1879: 9 (capitalization original).

16. In January 1881, as the antitheatrical fight reached its peak, the *Cincinnati Times-Star* ran an article on its front page noting that the city's Methodist ministers were denouncing the Cincinnati College of Music because it had established an opera department to train singers. They viewed this as threatening the decency of all music offered at this institution, because the opera department placed it "at one end of a chain which is connected with the variety shows at the other end by a series of links comprised of theaters and operas of all descriptions" (*Times-Star*, January 24, 1881: 1). Clearly, the agenda of the Methodist ministers extended far beyond closing Sunday performances or "immoral" performances. This faction of Cincinnati's reform forces regarded all theater as intrinsically immoral.

17. *Cincinnati Daily Gazette*, November 11, 1879: 4. This unsigned article appeared on the editorial page and took the best part of four full columns of a six-column page. Invaluable for its description of the city's theaters and audiences, it was also clearly written by one of the city's middle-class residents who had no sympathy for the culture of the city's working classes.

18. "The Lewd Shows Must Go," *Daily Gazette*, December 19, 1879: 8.

Chapter 15: Frontier Revelry vs. Respectable Variety

1. Rydahl, "History of the Legitimate Theatre," 276–77.

2. Kilar, *Michigan's Lumbertowns*, 31–32.

3. Rydahl, "History of the Legitimate Theatre," 120.

4. Kilar, *Michigan's Lumbertowns*, 65–66.

5. Rydahl, "History of the Legitimate Theatre," 72, 119.

6. The male impersonator Ella Wesner played at the Opera House for two weeks in 1871, a period in which she was earning up to $200 per week. And Annie Hindle, who earned $150 per week, visited there twice, for a week in 1870 and again in 1873.

7. There is also some evidence that Smith tolerated, and perhaps provided, prostitutes operating in his theater. In his history of theater in Saginaw, Rydahl notes that a

brothel, called the Wigwam, was located next to Smith's Opera House, and he suggests a connection between the two venues ("History of the Legitimate Theatre," 135–36).

8. During the 1870/71 season, Clay had become involved in a dispute between Smith and the Hyam Sisters, an act booked by Smith for his theater. Clay supported the young women in their refusal to work in Smith's wine room and provided a benefit for the girls that was designed to win the sympathy of the town's most respectable citizens. The dispute was widely reported in one of the city's conservative newspapers, the *East Saginaw Courier*, and the coverage and the benefit provided good publicity for Clay (Rydahl, "History of the Legitimate Theatre," 70–71).

9. Ibid., 301.

10. Looking at the acts and plays noted in Rydahl's "History of the Legitimate Theatre," I have found a number of names I know from the *New York Clipper*, such as Lawrence Barrett, Olive Logan, Kate Randolph, and Emma Abbott and the Grand English Opera Company. Rydahl also notes that at times Clay hired local amateur actors to augment professional troupes from nearby cities such as Detroit and Cleveland, and he also regularly hosted local amateur performances of drama and music.

11. Howe, "Circuit Court Testimony," 5–6, 22. This document is a deposition taken from Frankie Howe, a young woman who had performed at Bordwell's and had been the manager's mistress for a number of years. Frankie Howe's personal history is harrowing, and the document graphically details the physical abuse meted out to her by Warren Bordwell. But it is also valuable in that it contains details of the day-to-day operations of the theater, of Bordwell's hiring practices, and of his expectations of the women who worked for him.

12. This is a similar situation to Harry Hill's dance hall, which is often counted among early variety venues. Hill advertised his hall weekly in the *Clipper* but was otherwise ignored by this newspaper.

13. Baxter, *History of the City of Grand Rapids*, 570.

14. *Cincinnati Daily Gazette*, November 11, 1878: 4.

15. Ibid.

16. Ibid.

17. Grandstaff, "History of the Professional Theatre," 57–58.

18. For a summary of the manufacturing and business activity in Marion, Ohio, during the period 1880–1907, see http://www.heritagepursuit.com/Marion/History1907/marhisc10.htm (accessed 4/10/2007 at 11:20 A.M.). This website provides the text of *The History of Marion County and Representative Citizens*, edited and complied by J. Wilbur Jacoby in 1907.

Chapter 16: Conclusion

1. *New York Herald*, July 3, 1854: 7.

2. *Boston Post*, July 4, 1865: 3.

3. It is not entirely clear from surviving evidence how the continuous show worked in practice. The format of two halves separated by an intermission was, I suspect, the

structure for the two shows each day that presented the full bill and included the "star" acts. The other performances that occurred around these two featured shows, which roughly correspond to a matinee and evening performance each day, were apparently presented without break. Given that the two main shows also often had overtures that marked, at the very least, the beginning of the performance, the role of an orchestra in these shows, and the rest of the continuous format, also needs to be investigated.

4. This is particularly true for those acts at the beginning and end of the bill. The first act was a "dumb" act that did not rely on dialog. This allowed stragglers to enter the auditorium during the performance. The acts on the bill that played the most frequently were also those that held the least appeal for the audience. These second-tier acts were designed to amuse, but not to encourage anyone to stay in the theater for too long. Given that the continuous performance did not conclude until the end of the evening performance, it was theoretically possible to buy a ticket and sit all day, but in practice this seems rarely to have happened. If the major names on the bill were seen as drawing in an audience, the secondary acts on the bill could be viewed as driving the audience out of the auditorium.

5. The documentary *Vaudeville* includes an act performed by the singing/tap-dancing team of Ming and Toy. This pair visually employed Asian-style dress and behavior, but when the music began they sang syncopated jazz-influenced popular song. Part of the appeal of the act was, I suspect, the disjuncture between their appearance and how they sounded.

6. The only indication I have found of African Americans in the variety audience was a report published in the *New York Times* that described a performance at Tony Pastor's theater in 1875 (January 31, 1875: 2). The writer notes African Americans among the boys sitting in the cheapest gallery seats: "There were Irish boys, with shock heads of red hair; American boys, who chewed tobacco and ate peanuts, colored boys who gathered in a corner by themselves, and Italian boys." Later he noted that an African American man had won one of the door prizes that evening. Descriptions of the variety audience are extremely rare, but I have found no other report of the presence of African Americans, and I suspect that while they may never have been formally excluded, African Americans were not welcome in less respectable New York theaters and in theaters away from the East Coast.

7. B. F. Keith Scrapbook No. 2 (MsC 356), 127 and 135. These scrapbooks are held as part of the Keith-Albee Collection at the University of Iowa Library Special Collections.

8. B. F. Keith Scrapbook No. 3 (MsC 356), 146 and 163. A number of other African American acts are reviewed in these scrapbooks, and those that came closest to the ideal established by minstrelsy fared best. So, for example, comic male duos in coon singing and grotesque dancing were highly preferred over all other male acts, while for women the ideal appears to have been a pair of light-skinned women in seriocomic songs (see, for example, a review of the Meredith Sisters in New York, in Scrapbook 3, 115).

9. TOBA, or the Theater Owners Booking Association, was a circuit of theaters operated by white owners that staged vaudeville for an African American audience. In

the Southern states, these were the only theaters that booked African American performers, and many star performers, including Ethel Waters, Gertrude "Ma" Rainey, Bessie Smith, Fletcher Henderson, Jackie "Moms" Mabley, Dewey "Pigmeat" Martin, and others, began their careers on this circuit.

10. There is evidence that Tony Pastor began working to attract women to his theater in this period, and this is also just before the introduction of the women's matinee performance.

11. "Amusements: Dramatic," *New York Clipper*, December 19, 1874.

12. The surviving promptbooks and scores of this kind of musical comedy that are preserved in the Tams-Witmark Collection at the University of Wisconsin–Madison reveal the fragmented narrative of these works. Promptbooks have numerous redundancies, and these, along with remaining markings on the scores, show that these shows could be remade numerous times from a single script. Reviews also confirm that specialty acts were frequently interpolated into the production, some taking speaking roles and others merely performing their acts. Each change of cast would also have radically altered the show and allowed the manager to rely on repeat visits from patrons during the run of the production.

13. Burke, *Conundrum of Class.*

Bibliography

Research and Public Library Collections

Bentley Historical Library and Serials Department, University of Michigan Library
Billy Rose Theater Collection, Performing Arts Library of New York Public Library
    at Lincoln Center
Boston Public Library Research Collection, Central Library, Boston, Massachusetts
Eddy Historical Collection, Hoyt Public Library, Saginaw, Michigan
Grand Rapids History and Special Collections Department, Main Branch, Grand
    Rapids Public Library, Grand Rapids, Michigan
Harold Washington Library Center, Chicago Public Library, Chicago, Illinois
Harris Collection of American Poetry and Plays, Brown University Library Special
    Collections
Jersey City Public Library, Reference Department
Keith-Albee Collection, Special Collections, University of Iowa Library
Milwaukee County Historical Society Research Library
Milwaukee Public Library, Central Library
Minstrel Collection, Harry Ransom Research Center, University of Texas at Austin
Museum of the City of New York, Theater Department
New York City Municipal Archives, Records of Mayoral Administrations
New York Public Library Research Collection, Main Branch
Pennsylvania Collection, Carnegie Library, Pittsburgh, Pennsylvania
Public Library of Cincinnati and Hamilton Country, Main Library
Science, Industry, and Business Library of New York Public Library
State Archives and Library, Ohio Historical Society, Columbus, Ohio

Toronto Reference Library, Toronto, Canada
University of Pittsburgh Library Serials Collection
University of Wisconsin–Madison, Serials Collection and Tams-Witmark Collection
University of Wisconsin–Milwaukee, Serials Collection
Wisconsin State Historical Society, Madison, Wisconsin

Newspapers

This listing includes only those newspapers that were read in runs of six or more months. Many other single issues of newspapers were consulted, most via online databases such as Proquest Historical Newspapers (*Chicago Tribune* and *New York Times*), Gale 19th-Century U.S. Newspapers, or Newspaper Archive Elite.

Boston Globe, 1872–1877
Boston Post, 1850–1883, 1892
Cincinnati Commercial Tribune, 1871–1880
Cincinnati Daily Gazette, 1858, 1872–1875, 1878–1881
Cincinnati Daily Times, 1861–1865
Cincinnati Daily Times–Star Times, 1866–1874, 1878–1881
Cincinnati Enquirer, 1863–1865, 1872, 1876–1881
Galveston Daily News, 1868–1869
London Era, 1875–1881
National Police Gazette, 1872–1890
New York Clipper, 1853–1860, 1867–1883, 1888–1895
New York Dramatic Mirror, 1879–1885
New York Herald, 1848–1860, 1862
New York Sun, 1862 and various issues
New York Times, 1862 and various issues
New York Times Theater Reviews, 1870–1885
Philadelphia City Item, 1855–1860
Saginaw Daily Courier, 1874–1879
Saginaw Daily Republican, 1869, 1874–1879 and various issues
Täglische Volksblatt, 1874–1881
Theatre Magazine, 1900–1931
Variety, 1901–1930

Secondary Sources

Adams, David K., and Cornelius A. van Minnen, eds. *Religious and Secular Reform in America: Idea, Beliefs, and Social Change.* New York: New York University Press, 1999.

Allen, Robert C. *Horrible Prettiness: Burlesque and American Culture.* Chapel Hill: University of North Carolina Press, 1991.

Altick, Richard D. *The Shows of London.* Cambridge: Belknap Press of Harvard University Press, 1978.

Anon. "About Woman: Her Rights, Wrongs, and Proper Sphere of Usefulness." *New York Clipper,* March 4, 1871.

Anon. "Actors Not Needed! Actresses Who Play Men's Parts So Well That It Is Solemnly Suggested We Might Get Along without Men on the Stage at All." *American-Journal-Examiner,* Great Britain, 1904. Found in Robinson Locke Collection (Box MWEZ+n.c. 26.791) at the New York Public Library at Lincoln Center.

Anon. "Man or Woman?" *Grand Rapids Evening Leader,* June 7, 1886: 4.

Anon. "Married as a Man." *Grand Rapids Daily Democrat,* June 8, 1886: 5.

Anon. "Married Her Maid: The Strange Story of Charles and Annie Hindle, a Man Masquerading as a Woman." *Grand Rapids Telegram-Herald,* June 7, 1886: 4.

Anon. "Musical and Dramatic Notes." *Sandusky Daily Register,* July 20, 1892: 4.

Anon. "Stage Arts Adamless Eden: Are Men Actors Really Needed? Countless Charming Substitutes Bravely Tackle Trousered Roles." *New York Herald Magazine,* July 10, 1904. Found in Robinson Locke Collection (Box MWEZ+n.c. 26.791) at the New York Public Library at Lincoln Center.

Anon. "Stranger Than Fiction: The True Story of Annie Hindle's Two Marriages." *New York Sun,* December 27, 1891: 13.

Anon. "Why an Actress Cannot Wear Trousers like a Man." *New York Journal,* February 13, 1898. Found in Robinson Locke Collection (Box MWEZ+n.c. 26.791) at the New York Public Library at Lincoln Center.

A.P. "Acting Helps a Woman to Live." *The Theatre* 20.161 (July 1914): 14, 42.

Ashby, LeRoy. *With Amusement for All: A History of American Popular Culture since 1830.* Lexington: University Press of Kentucky, 2006.

Bailey, Peter. *Popular Culture and Performance in the Victorian City.* Cambridge: Cambridge University Press, 1998.

Bailey, Peter, ed. *Music Hall: The Business of Pleasure.* Milton Keynes: Open University Press, 1986.

Baldwin, Peter C. *Domesticating the Street: The Reform of Public Space in Hartford, 1850–1930.* Columbus: University of Ohio Press, 1999.

Bank, Rosemarie K. *Theatre Culture in America, 1825–1860.* New York: Cambridge University Press, 1997.

Barth, Gunther. *City People: The Rise of Modern City Culture in Nineteenth-Century America.* Oxford: Oxford University Press, 1980.

Baxter, Albert. *History of the City of Grand Rapids, Michigan.* New York: Munsell, 1891.

Bell, Archie. "What Woman Has Done for the Stage." *The Theatre* 7.78 (August 1907): 216–17.

Blakeslee, Fred Gilbert. "Behind the Scenes in Vaudeville." *The Theatre* 9.96 (February 1909): 45–48.

Blodgett, Geoffrey. "A New Look at the Gilded Age: Politics in a Cultural Context." Pp. 95–108 in *Victorian America.* Edited by Daniel Walker Howe. Philadelphia: University of Pennsylvania Press, 1976.

Bloodgood, Clara. "The Stage as a Career for Young Women." *The Theatre* 4.46 (December 1904): 304.

Bogdan, Robert. *Freak Show: Presenting Human Oddities for Amusement and Profit.* Chicago: University of Chicago Press, 1988.

Booth, Michael R. *Theatre in the Victorian Age.* Cambridge/New York: Cambridge University Press, 1991.

———. *Victorian Spectacular Theatre, 1850–1910.* Boston: Routledge & Kegan Paul, 1981.

Bratton, J. S. "Beating the Bounds: Gender Play and Role Reversal in the Edwardian Music Hall." Pp. 86–110 in *The Edwardian Theatre: Essays on Performance and the Stage.* Edited by Michael R. Booth and Joel H. Kaplan. Cambridge: Cambridge University Press, 1996.

———. "Irrational Dress." Pp. 77–91 in *The New Woman and Her Sisters: Feminism and Theatre, 1850–1914.* Edited by Vivien Gardner and Susan Rutherford. Ann Arbor: University of Michigan Press, 1992.

———. "Jenny Hill: Sex and Sexism in Victorian Music Hall." Pp. 92–110 in *Music Hall: Performance and Style.* Edited by J. S. Bratton. Milton Keynes: Open University Press, 1986.

Bratton, J. S., ed. *Music Hall: Performance and Style.* Milton Keynes: Open University Press, 1986.

Breward, Christopher. *The Hidden Consumer: Masculinities, Fashion, and City Life, 1860–1914.* Manchester/New York: Manchester University Press, 1999.

Broadbent, R. J. *A History of Pantomime.* Reprint New York: B. Blom, 1964 (originally Simpkin, Marshall, Hamilton, Kent, 1901).

Brown, Henry Collins. *In the Golden Nineties.* Valentine's Manual 12. Reprint Freeport, N.Y.: Books for Libraries Press, 1970 (originally 1927).

Brown, Richard D. "Modernization: A Victorian Climax." Pp. 29–44 in *Victorian America.* Edited by Daniel Walker Howe. Philadelphia: University of Pennsylvania Press, 1976.

Brown, T. Allston. *History of the American Stage.* Facsimile Edition. New York: Benjamin Blom, 1969 (originally 1870).

Browne, Junius Henri. *The Great Metropolis; A Mirror of New York.* Hartford, Conn./San Francisco: American Publishing, 1869.

Bryan, George B. *American Theatrical Regulation, 1607–1900: Conspectus and Texts.* Metuchen, N.J.: Scarecrow, 1993.

Bryan, Vernanne. *Laura Keene: A British Actress on the American Stage.* Jefferson, N.C.: McFarland, 1997.

Bullough, Vern, and Bonnie Bullough. *Cross Dressing, Sex, and Gender.* Philadelphia: University of Pennsylvania Press, 1993.

Burge, James C. *Lines of Business: Casting Practice and Policy in the American Theatre, 1752–1899.* New York: Peter Lang, 1986.

Burke, Martin J. *The Conundrum of Class.* Chicago: University of Chicago Press, 1995.

Burns, William. *Female Life in New York City.* Philadelphia: T. B. Peterson, 1875. Available online as part of the digital collection Wright American Fiction, 1851–1875, at http://purl.dlib.indiana.edu/iudl/wright2/wright2-0432.

Busby, Roy. *British Music Hall: An Illustrated Who's Who from 1850 to the Present Day.* London/Salem, N.H.: Elek, 1976.

Butch, Richard. *The Making of American Audiences: From Stage to Television, 1750–1990.* Cambridge/New York: Cambridge University Press, 2000.

Butler, Judith. *Bodies That Matter: On the Discursive Limits of "Sex."* New York: Routledge, 1993.

Calkins, Raymond. *Substitutes for the Saloon: An Investigation Originally Made for the Committee of Fifty.* Second revised edition. Boston: Houghton Mifflin, 1919.

Chauncey, George. *Gay New York: Gender, Urban Culture, and the Making of the Gay Male World, 1890–1940.* New York: Basic Books, 1994.

Chicago, City of. *Charter and Ordinances [of the City of Chicago].* Chicago: N.P., 1866.

———. *Laws and Ordinances Governing the City of Chicago.* Edited by Murray Floyd Tuley. Chicago: Bulletin Print Co., 1873.

———. *The Municipal Code of Chicago: Comprising the Laws of Illinois Relating to the City of Chicago and the Ordinances of the City Council.* Edited by Egbert Jamieson and Frances Adams. Chicago: Beach Barnard Printers, 1881.

Cincinnati, Council of. "An Ordinance to Amend and Reduce into One the Ordinances in Relation to Theaters, Shows, Concerts, and Other Exhibitions and Performances, and to Repeal an Ordinance and Parts of Ordinances Therein Named." *Cincinnati Daily Gazette*, December 27, 1879: 8.

———. "Ordinance No. 3,171: An Ordinance Delegating Authority to the Mayor of Cincinnati to Grant and Issue Licenses with Power to Revoke the Same, and to Amend and Reduce into One the Ordinances in Relation to Theaters, Shows, Concerts, and Other Exhibitions and Performances, and to Repeal Certain Ordinances and Parts of Ordinances Named Therein." *Cincinnati Daily Gazette*, February 2, 1881: 10.

Coben, Stanley. "The Assault on Victorianism in the Twentieth Century." Pp. 160–81 in *Victorian America.* Edited by Daniel Walker Howe. Philadelphia: University of Pennsylvania Press, 1976.

Cockrell, Dale. *Demons of Disorder: Early Blackface Minstrels and Their World.* New York: Cambridge University Press, 1997.

Cogan, Frances B. *All-American Girl: The Ideal of Real Womanhood in Mid-Nineteenth-Century America.* Athens: University of Georgia Press, 1989.

Cook, James W. *The Arts of Deception: Playing with Fraud in the Age of Barnum.* Cambridge: Harvard University Press, 2001.

Costonis, Maureen Needham. "The Personification of Desire: Fanny Elssler and American Audiences." *Dance Chronicle* 13.1 (1990): 47–67.

Cumbler, John T. *Working-class Community in Industrial America: Work, Leisure, and Struggle in Two Industrial Cities, 1850–1930.* Westport, Conn.: Greenwood, 1979.

Davis, Hartley. "The Business Side of Vaudeville." *Everybody's* 17 (1907): 527–37.

Davis, Tracy C. *Actresses as Working Women: Their Social Identity in Victorian Culture.* London: Routledge, 1991.

Davison, Peter Hobley. *Contemporary Drama and the Popular Dramatic Tradition in England.* Totowa, N.J.: Barnes & Noble, 1982.

Deland, Margaret. "The Change in the Feminine Ideal." *Atlantic Monthly* 105.3 (March 1910): 289–302.

D'Emilio, John, and Estelle B. Freedman. *Intimate Matters: A History of Sexuality in America.* New York: Harper & Row, 1988.

Dennett, Andrea Stulman. *Weird and Wonderful: The Dime Museum in America.* New York: New York University Press, 1997.

Di Meglio, John E. *Vaudeville U.S.A.* Bowling Green, Ohio: Bowling Green State University Popular Press, 1973.

Dreiser, Theodore. *Sister Carrie: An Authoritative Text, Backgrounds, and Sources Criticism.* Edited by Donald Pizer. New York: Norton, 1970.

Dudden, Faye E. *Women in the American Theatre: Actresses and Audiences, 1790–1870.* New Haven: Yale University Press, 1994.

Dunlap, James Francis. "Queen City Stages: Professional Dramatic Activity in Cincinnati, 1837–1861." PhD dissertation, Ohio State University, 1954.

Edwards, Richard Henry. *Popular Amusements.* Studies in American Social Conditions 8. Reprint New York: Arno, 1976 (originally Association Press, 1915).

Ehrenberg, Lewis A. *Steppin' Out: New York Nightlife and the Transformation of American Culture, 1890–1930.* Westport, Conn.: Greenwood, 1981.

Ellington, George. *The Women of New York, or the Under-World of the Great City.* New York: New York Book Co., 1869.

Engle, Ron, and Tice L. Millier, eds. *The American Stage: Social and Economic Issues from the Colonial Period to the Present.* New York: Cambridge University Press, 1993.

Erdmann, Andrew L. *Blue Vaudeville: Sex, Morals, and the Mass Marketing of Amusement, 1895–1915.* Jefferson, N.C.: McFarland, 2004.

Faderman, Lillian. *To Believe in Women: What Lesbians Have Done for America—A History.* New York: Houghton Mifflin, 1999.

Faulk, Barry J. *Music Hall and Modernity: The Victorian Discovery of Popular Culture.* Athens: University of Ohio Press, 2004.

Feldberg, Michael. *The Turbulent Era: Riot and Disorder in Jacksonian America.* New York: Oxford University Press, 1980.

Finson, Jon. *The Voices That Are Gone: Themes in 19th-Century American Popular Song.* New York: Oxford University Press, 1994.

Fisher, Judith L., and Stephen Watt, eds. *When They Weren't Doing Shakespeare: Essays on Nineteenth-Century British and American Theatre.* Athens: University of Georgia Press, 1989.

Foner, Eric. *A Short History of Reconstruction.* New York: Harper & Row, 1990.

Foster, George G. *New York by Gas-Light and Other Urban Sketches.* Edited by Stuart M. Blumin. Berkeley: University of California Press, 1990.

Franceschina, John Charles. *David Braham: The American Offenbach*. New York: Routledge, 2003.

Gilbert, Douglas. *American Vaudeville, Its Life and Times*. New York: Dover, 1963 (originally 1940).

Glazer, Walter Stix. *Cincinnati in 1840: The Social and Functional Organization of an Urban Community during the Pre–Civil War Period*. Columbus: University of Ohio Press, 1999.

Glenn, Susan A. *Female Spectacle: The Theatrical Roots of Modern Feminism*. Cambridge: Harvard University Press, 2000.

Graham, Franklin T. *Histrionic Montreal: Annals of the Montreal Stage, with Biographical and Critical Notes of the Plays and Players of a Century*. Montreal: Lovell, 1902.

Grand Rapids, Michigan, City of. *Ordinances of the City of Grand Rapids*. Compiled by Wm. Wisner Taylor. Grand Rapids: Daily Democrat Book and Job Printing, 1883.

———. *Ordinances of the City of Grand Rapids*. Compiled by Wm. Wisner Taylor. Grand Rapids: Daily Democrat Printing, 1888.

Grandstaff, Russell James. "A History of the Professional Theatre in Cincinnati, Ohio, 1861–1886." PhD dissertation, University of Michigan, 1963.

Grau, Robert. *Forty Years Observation of Music and the Drama*. New York: Broadway Publishing Co., 1909.

———. "'$2 Vaudeville' Coming? Its Possibility and Scope." *Variety*, December 11, 1909: 36.

Green, Helen. "One Day in Vaudeville." *McClures* 40 (1912): 637–47.

Gross, Stuart D. *Frankie and the Barons*. Fowlerville, Mich.: Wilderness Adventure Books, 1991.

———. *Saginaw: A History of the Land and the City*. Woodland Hills, Calif.: Windsor, 1980.

Hamm, Charles. "'The Old Home Ain't What It Used to Be'; or American Song in the Postwar Years." Pp. 253–83 in *Yesterdays: Popular Song in America*. New York: Norton, 1979.

Hankins, Mary Louise. *Women of New York*. New York: Mary Louise Hankins & Co., 1861. Available online as part of the digital collection Wright American Fiction, 1851–1875, at http://purl.dlib.indiana.edu/iudl/wright2/wright2-1092.

Hanners, John. *"It Was Play or Starve": Acting in the Nineteenth-Century American Popular Theatre*. Bowling Green, Ohio: Bowling Green State University Popular Press, 1993.

Hartnett, Stephen J. *Democratic Dissent and the Cultural Fictions of Antebellum America*. Urbana: University of Illinois Press, 2002.

Hartt, Rollin Lynde. *The People at Play*. The Leisure Class in America. Reprint New York: Arno, 1975 (originally Houghton Mifflin, 1909).

Henderson, Mary C. *The City and the Theatre: New York Playhouses from Bowling Green to Times Square*. Clifton, N.J.: James White, 1973.

Hobson, Barbara Meil. *Uneasy Virtue: The Politics of Prostitution and the American Reform Tradition*. New York: Basic Books, 1987.

Hofstadter, Richard. *Social Darwinism in American Thought*. Boston: Beacon, 1992 (originally University of Pennsylvania Press, 1944).

Höher, Dagmar. "The Composition of Music Hall Audiences, 1850–1900." Pp. 73–92 in *Music Hall: The Business of Pleasure*. Edited by Peter Bailey. Milton Keynes: Open University Press, 1986.

Holt, Michael F. *Political Parties and American Political Development from the Age of Jackson to the Age of Lincoln*. Baton Rouge: Louisiana State University Press, 1992.

Horton, William Ellis. *About Stage Folks*. Cambridge: Harvard University Press, 1902.

Hoster, John. "Vulgar in Vaudeville Sped with Its Sponsor: Passing of Koster & Bial's Begins Era of Cleanliness." *New York Morning Telegraph*, July 23, 1901. Found in Robinson Locke Envelope #1065, Billy Rose Collection, New York Public Library at Lincoln Center.

Howe, Daniel Walker. "Victorian Culture in America." Pp. 3–28 in *Victorian America*. Edited by Daniel Walker Howe. Philadelphia: University of Pennsylvania Press, 1976.

Howe, Daniel Walker, ed. *Victorian America*. Philadelphia: University of Pennsylvania Press, 1976.

Howe, Frankie. "Circuit Court Testimony, Frankie Howe, 31 December, 1895, Saginaw County, Michigan." Held in the Eddy Historical Collection of Saginaw Public Library, Saginaw, Michigan.

Hunt, Alan. *Governing Morals: A Social History of Moral Regulation*. Cambridge/New York: Cambridge University Press, 1999.

Hutton, Laurence. *Curiosities of the American Stage*. New York: Harper, 1891.

Ireland, Joseph Norton. *Records of the New York Stage, from 1750 to 1860*, vol. 2. New York: Morrell, 1867.

Jackson, Richard, ed. *Early Burlesque in America: Evangeline (1877)*. New York: Garland, 1994.

Jenkins, Henry. *What Made Pistachio Nuts: Early Sound Comedy and the Vaudeville Aesthetic*. New York: Columbia University Press, 1992.

Johnson, Claudia D. *American Actress: Perspective on the Nineteenth Century*. Chicago: Nelson-Hall, 1984.

Johnson, Stephen Burge. *The Roof Gardens of Broadway Theatres, 1883–1942*. Theater and Dramatic Studies 31. Ann Arbor, Mich.: UMI, 1985.

Kahn, E. J., Jr. *The Merry Partners: The Age and Stage of Harrigan and Hart*. New York: Random, 1955.

Kift, Dagmar. *The Victorian Music Hall: Culture, Class, and Conflict*. Translated by Roy Kift. Cambridge: Cambridge University Press, 1996.

Kilar, Jeremy. *Michigan's Lumbertowns: Lumbermen and Laborers in Saginaw, Bay City, and Muskegon, 1870–1905*. Detroit: Wayne State University Press, 1990.

Kimmel, Michael. *Manhood in America: A Cultural History*. New York: Free Press, 1996.

Kingsdale, Jon M. "The 'Poor Man's Club': Social Functions of the Urban Working-Class Saloon." Pp. 255–83 in *The American Man.* Edited by Elizabeth H. Pleck and Joseph H. Pleck. Englewood Cliffs, N.J.: Prentice-Hall, 1980.

Lahr, John. *Automatic Vaudeville: Essays on Star Turns.* New York: Knopf, 1984.

Larkin, Jack. *The Reshaping of Everyday Life, 1790–1840.* Everyday Life in America. New York: Harper & Row, 1988.

Laurie, Joe. *Vaudeville: From the Honky-tonks to the Palace.* Port Washington, N.Y.: Kennikat, 1972 (originally 1953).

Lause, Mark A. *Young America: Land, Labor, and the Republican Community.* Urbana: University of Illinois Press, 2005.

Leavitt, Michael Bennett. *Fifty Years in Theatrical Management, 1859–1909.* New York: Broadway Publishing, 1912.

Leinwand, Theodore B. *The City Staged: Jacobean Comedy, 1603–1613.* Madison: University of Wisconsin Press, 1986.

Levine, Lawrence. *Highbrow/Lowbrow: The Emergence of Cultural Hierarchy in America.* Cambridge: Harvard University Press, 1988.

———. *The Unpredictable Past: Explorations in American Cultural History.* New York/ Oxford: Oxford University Press, 1993.

Levy, Lester. *Give Me Yesterday: American History in Song, 1890–1920.* Norman: University of Oklahoma Press, 1975.

———. *Grace Notes in American History: Popular Sheet Music from 1820 to 1900.* Norman: University of Oklahoma Press, 1967.

Lewis, Robert M., ed. *From Traveling Show to Vaudeville: Theatrical Spectacle in America, 1830–1910.* Baltimore: Johns Hopkins University Press, 2003.

Licht, Walter. *Industrializing America: The Nineteenth Century.* Baltimore: Johns Hopkins University Press, 1995.

Livingston, James. *Pragmatism and the Political Economy of Cultural Revolution, 1850–1940.* Chapel Hill: University of North Carolina Press, 1994.

Logan, Olive. *Apropos of Women and Theatres, with a Paper or Two on Parisian Topics.* New York: Carleton, 1869.

Manifold, John S. *The Penguin Australian Songbook.* Melbourne: Penguin, 1964.

Marks, Edward B. *They All Sang: From Tony Pastor to Rudy Vallée.* New York: Viking, 1934.

Martin, Isabelle. "Stage Clothes." *The Theatre* 20.166 (December 1914): 283–84, 296–97.

Matlaw, Myron, ed. *Nineteenth Century American Plays: Seven Plays including the Black Crook.* New York: Applause, 2001.

Matthison, Edith Wynne, and Lillian Russell. "Is the Stage a Perilous Place for the Young Girl?" *The Theatre* 23.179 (January 1916): 22.

Maxwell, Periton. "Stage Beauty in Breeches." *The Theatre* 24.186 (August 1916): 73, 75, 96.

McArthur, Benjamin. *Actors and American Culture, 1880–1920.* Philadelphia: Temple University Press, 1984.

McCabe, James Dabney. *Lights and Shadows of New York Life; or, The Sights and Sensations of the Great City*. New York: Farrar, Straus and Giroux, 1970 (originally Philadelphia: National Publishing Co., 1872).

McConachie, Bruce. *Melodramatic Formations: American Theatre and Society, 1820–1870*. Iowa City: University of Iowa Press, 1992.

246

McCullough, Jack W. *Living Pictures on the New York Stage*. Ann Arbor, Mich.: UMI, 1983.

McLean, Albert. *American Vaudeville as Ritual*. Lexington: University of Kentucky Press, 1965.

McNamara, Brooks. *The New York Concert Saloon: The Devil's Own Nights*. New York: Cambridge University Press, 2002.

McNamara, Brooks, ed. *American Popular Entertainments: Jokes, Monologues, Bits, and Sketches*. New York: Performing Arts Journal Publications, 1983.

Melosh, Barbara, ed. *Gender and American History since 1890*. New York: Routledge, 1993.

Meyerowitz, Joanne. "Sexual Geography and Gender Economy: The Furnished Room Districts of Chicago, 1890–1930." Pp. 43–71 in *Gender and American History since 1890*. Edited by Barbara Melosh. New York: Routledge, 1993.

———. *Women Adrift: Independent Wage Earners in Chicago, 1880–1930*. Chicago: University of Chicago Press, 1988.

Middleton, Richard. *Studying Popular Music*. Milton Keynes/Philadelphia: Open University Press, 1990.

Mihm, Stephen. *A Nation of Counterfeiters: Capitalism, Con Men, and the Making of the United States*. Cambridge: Harvard University Press, 2007.

Milwaukee, Common Council of. *Charter and Ordinances of the City of Milwaukee and Amendatory Acts Together with a List of Officers and Rules and Regulations of the Common Council*. Published by order of the Common Council. Milwaukee: Daily Sentinel Book and Job Office Print, 1852.

———. *The General Ordinances of the City of Milwaukee: With Amendments Thereto and an Appendix*. Published by order of the Common Council. Milwaukee: Burdick, Armitage & Allen, 1888.

Minsky, Morton. *Minsky's Burlesque*. New York: Arbor, 1986.

Montgomery, David. *Citizen Worker: The Experience of Workers in the United States with Democracy and the Free Market during the Nineteenth Century*. Cambridge/New York: Cambridge University Press, 1993.

M.T.M. "Wanted a New Type of Femininity." *The Theatre* 5.47 (January 1905): 23.

Mullenix, Elizabeth Reitz. *Wearing Breeches: Gender on the Antebellum Stage*. New York: St. Martin's, 2000.

Nadis, Fred. *Wonder Shows: Performing Science, Magic, and Religion in America*. New Brunswick, N.J.: Rutgers University Press, 2005.

Nasaw, David. *Going Out: The Rise and Fall of Public Amusements*. New York: Basic Books, 1993.

Needham, Maureen, ed. *I See America Dancing: Selected Readings, 1685–2000.* Urbana: University of Illinois Press, 2002.

New York, State of. *Census for the State of New York, for 1865.* New York: Van Benthuysen, 1867.

———. *Revised Statutes of the State of New York, as Altered by the Legislature; Including the Statutory Provisions of a General Nature, Passed from 1828 to 1835 Inclusive.* 3 vols. Albany: Packard & Van Benthuysen, 1835.

———. *Statutes at Large of the State of New York Comprising the Revised Statutes, As They Existed on the 1st Day of July, 1862, and All the General Public Statutes Then in Force.* Edited by John W. Edmonds. 5 vols. Albany: Weare C. Little, Law Bookseller, 1863.

Odell, George C. D. *Annals of the New York Stage,* vols. 5–15. New York: Columbia University Press, 1931–49.

Ohio, State of. *The Annotated Revised Statutes of the State of Ohio.* Edited by Clement Bates. 3 vols. Cincinnati: W. H. Anderson, 1897.

Peiss, Kathy. "'Charity Girls' and City Pleasures: Historical Notes on Working-Class Sexuality, 1880–1920." Pp. 57–69 in *Passion and Power: Sexuality in History.* Edited by Kathy Peiss and Christine Simmons. Philadelphia: Temple University Press, 1989.

———. *Cheap Amusements: Working Women and Leisure in Turn-of-the-Century New York.* Philadelphia: Temple University Press, 1986.

Peiss, Kathy, and Christine Simmons, eds. *Passion and Power: Sexuality in History.* Philadelphia: Temple University Press, 1989.

Pencak, William, Matthew Dennis, and Simon P. Newman, eds. *Riot and Revelry in Early America.* University Park: Pennsylvania State University Press, 2002.

Pittsburgh, City of. *A Digest of the Acts of Assembly Relating to and the General Ordinances of the City of Pittsburgh from 1804 to Nov. 12, 1908.* Prepared under resolution of the Councils by Robert T. McElroy. Pittsburgh: Market Review Publishing Co., 1908.

Pleck, Elizabeth H., and Joseph H. Pleck, eds. *The American Man.* Englewood Cliffs, N.J.: Prentice-Hall, 1980.

Powers, Madelon. *Faces along the Bar: Lore and Order in the Workingman's Saloon, 1870–1920.* Chicago: University of Chicago Press, 1998.

Preston, Katherine K. *Opera on the Road: Traveling Opera Troupes in the United States, 1825–60.* Urbana: University of Illinois Press, 1993.

Preston, Katherine K., ed. *Irish American Theater: The Mulligan Guard Ball (1879) and Reilly and the 400 (1891), Scripts by Edward Harrigan, Music by David Braham.* New York: Garland, 1994.

Rodger, Gillian. "'He Isn't a Marrying Man': Gender and Sexuality in the Repertoire of Male Impersonators, 1870–1930." Pp. 105–33 in *Queer Episodes in Music and Modern Identity.* Edited by Sophie Fuller and Lloyd Whitesell. Urbana: University of Illinois Press, 2002.

———. "Legislating Amusements: Class Politics and Theater Law in New York City." *American Music* 20.4 (Winter 2002): 381–98.

———. "Male Impersonation on the North American Variety and Vaudeville Stage, 1868–1930." PhD dissertation, University of Pittsburgh, 1998.

Rosenberg, Charles E. "Sexuality, Class, and Role in 19th-Century America." Pp. 219–54 in *The American Man*. Edited by Elizabeth H. Pleck and Joseph H. Pleck. Englewood Cliffs, N.J.: Prentice-Hall, 1980.

Rosenbloom, Joshua L. *Looking for Work, Searching for Workers: American Labor Markets during Industrialization*. Cambridge: Cambridge University Press, 2002.

Rosenzweig, Roy. *Eight Hours for What We Will: Workers and Leisure in an Industrial City, 1870–1920*. New York: Cambridge University Press, 1983.

Rotundo, E. Anthony. *American Manhood: Transformations in Masculinity from the Revolution to the Modern Era*. New York: Basic Books, 1993.

Royle, Edwin Milton. "The Vaudeville Theatre." *Scribners* 26 (1899): 485–95.

Rydahl, Eugene Elvin. "A History of the Legitimate Theatre in East Saginaw, Michigan, from 1860–1884." PhD dissertation, University of Iowa, 1958.

Saginaw, Michigan, City Council. *Proceedings of the Common Council of Saginaw, MI*. Saginaw, Mich.: The Council, 1895–96.

———. *Proceedings of the Common Council of Saginaw, MI*. Saginaw, Mich.: The Council, 1896–97.

———. *Proceedings of the Common Council of Saginaw, MI*. Saginaw, Mich.: The Council, 1898–99.

Samuels, Charles, and Louise Samuels. *Once upon a Stage: The Merry World of Vaudeville*. New York: Dodd, Mead, 1974.

Sanjek, Russell A. *American Popular Music and Its Business: The First Four Hundred Years*, vol. 2: *1790–1909*. New York: Oxford University Press, 1988.

Sante, Luc. *Low Life: Lures and Snares of Old New York*. New York: Farrar, Strauss, Giroux, 1991.

Saxton, Alexander. *The Rise and Fall of the White Republic: Class Politics and Mass Culture in Nineteenth-Century America*. London/New York: Verso, 1990.

Schlereth, Thomas J. *Victorian America: Transformations in Everyday Life, 1876–1915*. Everyday Life in America. New York: Harper Collins, 1991.

Schlesinger, Arthur Meier. *The Rise of the City, 1878–1898*. A History of American Life 10. New York: Macmillan, 1933.

Senelick, Laurence. *The Age and State of George L. Fox, 1825–1877*. Expanded edition. Iowa City: University of Iowa Press, 1999.

———. *The Changing Room: Sex, Drag, and Theatre*. London: Routledge, 2000.

———. "Variety into Vaudeville: The Process Observed in two Manuscript Gagbooks." *Theatre Survey: The American Journal of Theatre History* 19.1 (May 1978): 1–15.

Senelick, Laurence, ed. *Gender in Performance: The Presentation of Difference in the Performing Arts*. Hanover, N.H.: University Press of New England, 1992.

Shapiro, Henry D., and Jonathon D. Sarna. *Ethnic Diversity and Civic Identity: Patterns*

of Conflict and Cohesion in Cincinnati since 1820. Urbana: University of Illinois Press, 1992.

Shaw, Mary. "The Actress on the Road." *McClures* 38 (July 1911): 263–72.

Shifflett, Crandall A. *Victorian America, 1876 to 1913.* New York: Facts on File, 1996.

Short, Ernest. *Fifty Years of Vaudeville.* London: Eyre & Spottiswoode, 1946.

Sikes, Wirt. *One Poor Girl: The Story of Thousands.* Philadelphia: Lippincott, 1869.

Simmons, Christina. "Modern Sexuality and the Myth of Victorian Repression." Pp. 17–42 in *Gender and American History since 1890.* Edited by Barbara Melosh. New York: Routledge, 1993.

Skipworth, Alison. "Backstage Scandal: Are the Morals of the Actress Any Different from Those of the Average Church Member?" *The Theatre* 29.21 (July 1919): 26.

Skirt, The. "Women on 'Small Time' and the 'Chasing' Manager: 'The Skirt' Says Publicity Is the Only Cure, and Offers Aid to Those Annoyed by the Leeches." *Variety,* March 5, 1910: 5.

Slide, Anthony. *Images of America: New York City Vaudeville.* Charleston, S.C.: Arcadia, 2006.

———. *The Vaudevillians: A Dictionary of Vaudeville Performers.* Westport, Conn.: Arlington, 1981.

Slide, Anthony, ed. *The Encyclopedia of Vaudeville.* Westport, Conn.: Greenwood, 1994.

———. *Selected Vaudeville Criticism.* Metuchen, N.J.: Scarecrow, 1988.

Slout, William L. *Olympians of the Sawdust Circle: A Biographical Dictionary of the Nineteenth Century American Circus.* 2005. Available online at www.circushistory.org/history.htm (accessed 4/16/2007 at 2:30 P.M.).

———. *Theatre in a Tent: The Development of a Provincial Entertainment.* Bowling Green, Ohio: Bowling Green University Popular Press, 1972.

Slout, William L., ed. *Life upon the Wicked Stage.* Clipper Studies in the Theatre 14. San Bernardino, Calif.: Borgo, 1996.

———. *Old Gotham Theatricals by Col. Tom Picton.* Clipper Studies in the Theatre 12. San Bernardino, Calif.: Borgo, 1995.

Smith, Bill. *The Vaudevillians.* New York: Macmillan, 1976.

Smith, Matthew Hale. *Sunlight and Shadow in New York.* Hartford, Conn.: J. B. Burr, 1869.

Smith-Rosenberg, Carol. "Discourses of Sexuality and Subjectivity: The New Woman, 1870–1936." Pp. 264–80 in *Hidden from History: Reclaiming the Gay and Lesbian Past.* Edited by Martin Duberman, Martha Vicinus, and George Chauncey. New York: Meridian, 1989.

———. *Disorderly Conduct: Visions of Gender in Victorian America.* New York: Knopf, 1985.

Snyder, Robert W. *The Voice of the City: Vaudeville and Popular Culture in New York.* New York: Oxford University Press, 1989.

Sobel, Bernard. *A Pictorial History of Vaudeville.* New York: Citadel, 1961.

Spaeth, Sigmund. *Read 'Em and Weep: The Songs You Forgot to Remember.* Garden City, N.Y.: Doubleday, 1927.

Spitzer, John. "'Oh Susanna': Oral Transmission and Tune Transformation." *Journal of the American Musicological Society* 47.1 (1994): 90–136.

Stansell, Christine. *City of Women: Sex and Class in New York, 1789–1860.* New York: Knopf, 1986.

Staples, Shirley. *Male-Female Comedy Teams in American Vaudeville, 1865–1932.* Ann Arbor, Mich.: UMI, 1984.

Stein, Charles W. *American Vaudeville as Seen by Its Contemporaries.* New York: Knopf, 1984.

Stoddart, Drayton. *Lord Broadway, Variety's Sime.* New York: Funk, 1941.

Sutherland, Daniel. *The Expansion of Everyday Life, 1860–1876.* Everyday Life in America. New York: Harper Collins, 1989.

Tait, Peta. *Circus Bodies: Cultural Identity in Aerial Performance.* London: Routledge, 2004.

Tchen, John Kuo Wei. *New York before Chinatown: Orientalism and the Shaping of American Culture, 1776–1882.* Baltimore: Johns Hopkins University Pres, 1999.

Toll, Robert C. *Blacking Up: The Minstrel Show in Nineteenth Century America.* New York: Oxford University Press, 1974.

———. *On with the Show! The First Century of Show Business in America.* New York: Oxford University Press, 1976.

Trachtenberg, Alan. *Democratic Vistas, 1860–1880.* New York: Braziller, 1970.

———. *The Incorporation of America: Culture and Society in the Gilded Age.* New York: Hill & Wang, 1882.

Traister, Barbara Howard. *Heavenly Necromancers: The Magician in English Renaissance Drama.* Columbia: University of Missouri Press, 1984.

Vivian, Imogen Holbrook. *A Biographical Sketch of Charles A. S. Vivian, Founder of the Order of Elks.* San Francisco: Whittaker & Ray, 1904.

Voss, Kim. *The Making of American Exceptionalism: The Knights of Labor and Class Formation in the Nineteenth Century.* Ithaca: Cornell University Press, 1993.

Walters, Ronald G. *American Reformers, 1815–1860.* New York: Hill & Wang, 1978.

Wells, Kate Gannett. "The Transitional American woman." *Atlantic Monthly,* December 1880: 817–23.

Wertheim, Arthur Frank. *Vaudeville Wars: How the Keith-Albee and Orpheum Circuits Controlled the Big-Time and Its Performers.* New York: Palgrave Macmillan, 2006.

Wicker, Elmus. *Banking Panics of the Gilded Age.* Cambridge: Cambridge University Press, 2000.

Wilentz, Sean. *Chants Democratic: New York City and the Rise of the American Working Class, 1788–1850.* Twentieth anniversary edition. New York: Oxford University Press, 2004.

Williams, William H. A. *'Twas Only an Irishman's Dream: The Image of Ireland and the Irish in American Popular Song Lyrics, 1800–1920.* Urbana: University of Illinois Press, 1996.

Woods, Leigh. "Two-a-Day Redemptions and Truncated Camilles: The Vaudeville Repertoire of Sarah Bernhardt." *New Theatre Quarterly* 10.37 (February 1994): 11–23.

Young, George M. "'Pop' Vaudeville." *Variety*, December 11, 1909: 22.

Zellers, Parker. "The Cradle of Variety: The Concert Saloon." *Educational Theatre Journal* 20.4 (December 1968): 578–85.

———. *Tony Pastor: Dean of the Vaudeville Stage.* Ypsilanti: Eastern Michigan University Press, 1971.

Ziter, Edward. *The Orient on the Victorian Stage.* Cambridge: Cambridge University Press, 2003.

Index

255

256

259

GILLIAN M. RODGER is an associate professor
of musicology and ethnomusicology at the
University of Wisconsin–Milwaukee.

Music in American Life

Hard Luck Blues: Roots Music Photographs from the Great Depression
  Rich Remsberg
Restless Giant: The Life and Times of Jean Aberbach and Hill and Range Songs
  Bar Biszick-Lockwood
Songs in Black and Lavender: Race, Sexual Politics, and Women's Music
  Eileen M. Hayes
Champagne Charlie and Pretty Jemima: Variety Theater in the Nineteenth Century
  Gillian M. Rodger

The University of Illinois Press
is a founding member of the
Association of American University Presses.

Designed by Dennis Roberts
Composed in 10/13.5 Janson Text LT Std
with Electra LT Std display
by Barbara Evans
at the University of Illinois Press
Manufactured by Sheridan Books, Inc.

University of Illinois Press
1325 South Oak Street
Champaign, IL 61820-6903
www.press.uillinois.edu